Teaching for Understanding

At a time when test results can be everything, high scores may be pursued whatever the cost. Perhaps more than many would admit, the result is a lack of understanding.

Teaching for Understanding describes why understanding is worthwhile and what understanding means, particularly in the subjects commonly taught in schools, colleges and higher education. It draws on recent research to provide a framework of strategies known to support the understanding processes. Learners may fail to understand for a variety of reasons. Why this happens and what can be done is discussed, including inappropriate conceptions of learning amongst teachers and learners, matters to do with motivation, the assessment of understanding, and what learners can do to help themselves.

Unlike many books on learning, *Teaching for Understanding* focuses directly on the problem of understanding and how to support it. It recognizes and illustrates the variation of understanding in different contexts and provides a well-founded framework for thinking about understanding and how it might be fostered. Understanding can be an early casualty in teaching and learning and an aim of *Teaching for Understanding* is to make it a central and enduring concern at all levels of education. This accessible text will prove an invaluable guide for teachers in training and in service as well as lecturers and advisers in education and educational psychologists.

Douglas Newton is Professor of Education at Newcastle University, where his current research centres on the nature of understanding. He has written many books and articles for academics, researchers and teachers, including *Coordinating Science across the primary school* with Lynn Newton (Falmer Press, 1998).

Teaching for Understanding

What It Is and How To Do It

Douglas P. Newton

London and New York

First published 2000
by RoutledgeFalmer
11 New Fetter Lane, London EC4P 4EE

Simultaneously published in the USA and Canada
by RoutledgeFalmer
29 West 35th Street, New York, NY 10001

RoutledgeFalmer is an imprint of the Taylor & Francis Group

© 2000 Douglas P Newton

Typeset in Garamond by Taylor & Francis Books Ltd
Printed and Bound in Great Britain by TJ International Ltd,
Padstow, Cornwall

British Library Cataloging in Publication Data
A catalogue record for this book is available from the British Library

Library of Congress Cataloging in Publication Data
Teaching for understanding : what it is and how to do it / Douglas P. Newton.
Includes bibliographical references and index.
1. Teaching. 2. Effective teaching. 3. Learning. I. Title.
LB1025.3 .N495 2000
371.102–dc21

ISBN 0–415–22790–9 (hbk)
ISBN 0–415–22791–7 (pbk)

Contents

   What is Teaching for Understanding *about? It is a book for any teacher or
   student teacher who wants learners do more than memorize and recall information. It describes the nature of understanding, it provides a framework for
   supporting understanding in the classroom, it offers strategies for fostering
   understanding, and it sets the task in a wider context. It offers something to
   all teachers, whether they work with children or adults. Chapter 1 sets the
   scene and provides an outline of the book.*

   *How can something that is valuable be neglected? Chapter 2 points to ways in
   which understanding is very worthwhile. It also describes how it may not be a
   central concern. Teaching and learning are subject to many pressures. Some act
   against the pursuit of understanding are discussed.*

If understanding is to be supported, it helps to have some idea of what it is. Chapter 3 describes various kinds of understanding and some ways in which they are different. Particular attention is given to understandings in subjects commonly taught in formal education. A clear notion of what will count as understanding in the target topic is a first step.

Understanding cannot be transmitted from teacher to learner. Chapter 4 describes mental processes that the learner uses in constructing an understanding. It is these processes that the teacher (and learner) should try to support. There are limits to what the mind can do and it helps to know what they are.

Chapter 5 brings together the nature of understanding and the processes of understanding and begins to illustrate how understanding can be supported. It emphasizes that many teachers may have or may easily acquire many of the skills. The trick is in using them deliberately, purposefully and systematically in a press for understanding. How strategies, such as those included in the list of subheadings, contribute to this press is described. Some are of relatively wide application while others are fairly specific to particular learning contexts.

> *Analogy may serve as the basis for an understanding. Chapter 6 describes the nature of analogies and how they may provide this basis. There are certain conditions which must be satisfied if an analogy is to be effective. These are discussed and developed into steps for teaching with analogy. Some dangers of using analogies are highlighted.*

> *A live teacher is not essential for learning in all formal education. For instance, textbooks and ICT may have the role of teacher for significant periods of time. Chapter 7 uses these to illustrate what such surrogate teachers might do for understanding and describes ways in which they might be made more effective. Some of their strengths and weaknesses are discussed.*

> *Learners may fail to understand or construct an understanding which is unacceptable. Chapter 8 looks at reasons for understanding failure and what may underpin some understandings that are not acceptable. Some misunderstandings can resist change. Strategies which may help to overcome them are described.*

Contents

There can be a tendency to expect a press for understanding to be sufficient in itself. Many things bear upon teaching and learning. Chapter 9 outlines some of them and looks at students' approaches to learning. It sets the scene for subsequent chapters.

Amongst the things that shape learning in a classroom are conceptions of what counts. The potential impact of teachers' and learners' misconceptions of learning is described in Chapter 10. How to modify such misconceptions is also discussed.

Not all students are interested or even willing learners. Chapter 11 describes the role of motivation in learning and explores the implications of values, expectancy and emotions for support for understanding. Ways of enhancing motivation by attending to these three aspects are described and illustrated.

While a teacher might press for understanding, the learner is not helpless. Chapter 12 describes what underpins self-help and provides examples of strategies that learners can use to help them construct an understanding. Strategies that are easy to recall and apply are recommended. The ability to think about thinking develops with age but, allowing for that, learners can learn how to learn. How this learning can be fostered is described.

Understanding is a private matter and is not directly accessible for scrutiny. Ways of judging its quality have to be devised. Chapter 13 describes and illustrates some of these. The 'what', 'why', 'when', 'how' and 'where' of assessment are discussed, and potential effects of assessment on the quality of students' learning are considered.

Chapter 14 draws together the main points of the other chapters and decribes a way of proceeding in order to ensure that there is a press for understanding, whether the teacher is experienced or new to teaching. Some obstacles that impede those with a concern for understanding are described. The need to spread and maintain such a concern is highlighted.

The glossary lists some words that have a specialized meaning or name key concepts used in Teaching for Understanding. *Its purpose is to allow the book to be read in a variety of ways.*

Illustrations

1 Introduction

Why a Concern for Understanding?

At a time when test results can be everything, high scores may be pursued whatever the cost. Perhaps more often than many would admit, the cost is a lack of understanding. At the same time, some people seem to judge learning only by its quantity: more means better. Today, collecting information is often easy, but understanding it can be what really matters. There are also those who see learning only in terms of its immediate practical utility and how employable it makes the learner. This point of view cannot be dismissed, but learning serves other worthwhile ends as well. It may, for instance, enlighten; but that would only come through understanding. And, as achieving an understanding can sometimes be difficult, it is not surprising that it easily slips into the background.

Many of our daily thoughts and tasks do not call for understanding. For instance, there is no need to understand knots to fasten a shoe lace. Some situations, like fastening shoe laces, repeat themselves and the same response without understanding is effective. But we are often faced with situations that are not like those we have met before. Illness, for instance, varies enormously. How are its symptoms to be interpreted and the illness treated? A kind of knowing that enables a flexible response is what is needed. Knowing what literally under-stands illnesses has the potential to do that. Halford (1993) has put it in broader terms: understanding offers a cognitive autonomy that helps to free its owner from the inflexible act, domination and exploitation. Of course, not all understanding serves a material or immediately practical end. As Luke (1996) has said:

> when we understand we can do useful things, like invent things, develop better strategies for business success, and we even feel better. I am richer not poorer in the face of the rising sun for understanding something about how it may have formed, for how it creates the heat and light that enable life.

An understanding is an economical way of knowing that captures innumerable particulars about the world and reduces them to a coherent, manageable and even satisfying order.

Because of its potential, understanding is an indicator of the quality of learning. We should pursue it with vigour in learning, and be reminded that quality counts. Just as understanding is a significant part of the quality of learning, providing support for understanding is a significant part of the quality of teaching. 'Doesn't everyone teach for understanding?' a colleague once asked. Some do, some think they do, and others frequently do not. This book is about how to support understanding in both children and adults. It is for any teacher, experienced or otherwise, who wants learners do more than reproduce what they have been told.

A Thumbnail Sketch of Some Underlying Ideas

Understanding is a very personal thing. 'Only connect...' is E.M. Forster's epigraph for *Howards End*. The prize is the greater meaning that can flow from the union of isolated thoughts. All it takes is a connection but making it may not be easy. Understanding is not something that can be passed or transmitted from one person to another. No one can make the connection for someone else. Where there are connections to be made, the mental effort has to be supplied by the learner.

Fortunately, the process can be supported, and that is what this book is about. In order to talk of supporting understanding, there needs to be some idea of what understanding means. Unfortunately (or interestingly, according to your point of view) understanding refers to a variety of mental products and processes and can mean different things in different contexts. This book aims to provide a basis for some understanding of understanding and show how understanding might be supported in diverse contexts.

In the past, psychology has revealed little that is not obvious to the teacher. For instance, experience soon shows that repetition increases the likelihood that something will be memorized and what was taught today is more likely to be recalled than what was taught yesterday. Similarly, experiments on the learning of rats seem to say little about helping people grasp the meaning of a work of art, a scientific theory or an historical event.

More recent developments in psychology have more to offer. From one perspective, it seems that the mind is a little like a library. In a sense, it behaves like a huge repository for knowledge just as a library is a huge store for books. In the library, books may be taken from the shelves and sorted on a table. If there is room on the table, recent acquisitions may be added, integrated with other books and taken to appropriate shelves for storage. The mind behaves as though it has a working space that serves as its table. Just like the library table, it has a limited capacity. New information may be routed to the working space. Existing knowledge may already be there, or be taken from the long-term store and added to it. If there is enough mental capacity, the information and knowledge could be organized, related, integrated, used and returned to the store. Not all new information or new organizations are worth keeping, and much may be discarded. Some, however, find their way to the mental shelves and may be taken down and used later. The mind's repository has an enormous capacity but its table, where it does its organizing, relating and integrating, is tiny in comparison. We need to use its space efficiently if we are to relate elements of information and construct understandings of it. It can help if information is presented to us in some organized way, if we have relevant information to hand, and if we have a degree of facility in handling it.

Of course, the mind's activity is not confined to its table top and a lot goes on that we are not aware of. In formal education, we usually want learners to reflect on and verbalize their understandings, but the unconscious activity cannot be ignored as it contributes to the conscious processes and may even produce understandings itself.

Putting together some inkling of the nature of understanding and ideas about how the mind handles it can lead to testable ideas about what might support understanding. As the aim is to provide a practical framework for supporting understanding, I have drawn on a variety of ideas with the potential to foster it in a wide range of learners. Cognition may be modelled in various ways. Just as a house might be described in terms of its rooms and their function, there are macro or molar models of cognition. The library analogy is an example of a macro model. But, at a micro or molecular level, the house may also be described in terms of its bricks and mortar. In the same way, cognition may be modelled by complex networks of interacting units that, some argue, resemble the activity of brain cells (Bechtel and Abrahamsen, 1991; Hill, 1997). For practical purposes, however, macro models of cognition are very useful in that they can be applied more or less immediately to the kinds of mental activities that are relevant to understanding (Baddeley, 1993). They largely underpin the explanations offered in this book. Nevertheless, readers may need to remind themselves that such models are only models; they do not necessarily imply that the brain is physically constructed like the model.

Direct support for making mental connections between ideas is, of course, only a part of the picture. Some learners have to be persuaded that what is expected of them is worthwhile, otherwise they may not engage in learning tasks at all. Others may not know what really counts when they engage in learning. Still others may need to learn how to make the best of their thinking processes so that they can function as independent learners. Even when learning seems to be going well, there is the inescapable fact that no one knows what is in another person's mind. This means that ways of gauging the quality of learning have to be found. Unfortunately, these may interfere with the processes of understanding and impede their progress.

These illustrate that the total learning environment has several components and these components can interact and bear upon the quality of learning. They are not simply additional features that can be ignored in moving from ideas about learning to ideas about instruction (Hargreaves, 1986; Sternberg, 1986).

The Structure of the Book

You will not be surprised to find that I think the best way to approach this book is to read it from the beginning through to the end and in the order presented. Nevertheless, recognizing that readers have different interests and needs, other routes through the book are possible. Figure 1.1 shows the structure. Each column represents a more or less self-consistent group of chapters, and each group might serve as a starting point for a particular interest. The first block is about the value of understanding, what understanding means in different contexts, and understanding as constructing mental relationships. The second block describes mental engagement for understanding and what fosters it, a framework for supporting understanding and the use of analogies, the support provided by surrogate teachers such as textual materials and information technology, and understanding failure. The third block relates to the variety of factors that bear upon a person's learning behaviours, conceptions of understanding, motivation and self-regulated learning. The final chapters deal with evaluating and assessing understanding and with bringing various threads together. Most chapters begin with a brief overview and end with a summary, and there is a short glossary to help those who prefer to dip into the book.

Although not infallible, understanding is a very powerful way of relating to the world. When it slips into the background because external test results matter more or through lack of time, indolence or ignorance, the loss for each learner could be considerable. Understanding can make learning more sure, more durable and more valuable for the learner. It is worth pursuing as a means to an end and as an end in itself.

Figure 1.1   A Schematic Diagram Showing the Structure of the Book

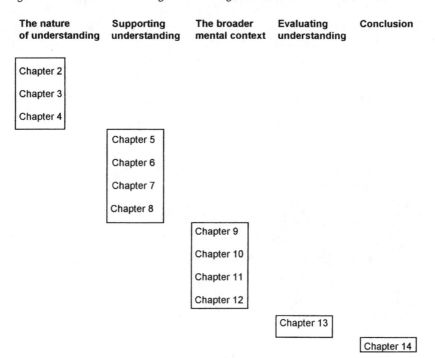

References

Baddeley, A. (1993) *Your Memory*, London: Prion.

Bechtel, W. and Abrahamsen, A. (1991) *Connectionism and the Mind*, Cambridge, MA: Blackwell.

Halford, G.S. (1993) *Children's Understanding: The Development of Mental Models*, Hillsdale, NJ: Lawrence Erlbaum.

Hargreaves, D.J. (1986) *The Developmental Psychology of Music*, Cambridge: Cambridge University Press.

Hill, W.F. (1997) *Learning*, 6th edn, New York: Longman.

Luke, M.O. (1996) 'Some Thoughts About the Relationship Between Information and Understanding', paper presented at the American Society for Information Science Conference, San Diego, May 20–2.

Sternberg, R.J. (1986) 'Cognition and Instruction: Why the Marriage Sometimes Ends in Divorce', in R.F. Dillon and R.J. Sternberg (eds), *Cognition and Instruction*, San Diego: Academic Press, pp. 375–82.

2 Understanding: A Worthwhile Goal

Overview

That understanding is a good thing seems self-evident. Like many things that are self-evident, the reasons are not always apparent so some are mentioned here. Given that understanding can be worthwhile and is a requirement of many programmes of study, why is it sometimes a secondary concern? The teaching and learning situation is complex and answers lie in that complexity.

What Does Understanding Offer?

We want students to learn. At times, it might be sufficient for them to memorize something and recall it on demand, but at other times, they should understand. Understanding is often assumed to be a good thing and potentially worth more than memorization. Yet, as learning things off by heart is often easier and quicker than understanding them, is understanding worth the effort? What does it have to offer?

First, understanding can satisfy a number of personal needs. For instance, we often feel dissatisfied with merely knowing that event B followed event A. What we are curious about is *why* B followed A. The historian Henry Adams said, 'I don't give a damn what happened, what I want to know is why it happened' (Miller, 1996). The questions that arrive on editors' desks of popular journals like the *New Scientist* show a similar inclination (for example, why do boomerangs come back? Why is it more difficult to swim in a pool that is very full?). Ultimately, knowing why things are as they are or happen as they do can help us relate to the world, both natural and physical (Davalos, 1997). Laurie Lee recollected what it was like not to understand when, as a child, he found himself surrounded by nature: 'For the first time in my life I was alone in the world whose behaviour I could neither predict nor fathom. I put back my head and howled' (Lee, 1959). That is not to say that the understanding which helps us relate is always correct, final, absolute or an exact match for someone else's understanding. What it does do, however, is serve the function of giving order to our mental worlds. This, in turn, can be instrumental in helping us cope with the external world.

Second, understanding can facilitate learning. For instance, Hawkins and Pratt (1988), teaching at Christmas in New Zealand, noticed that Christmas cards are potentially meaningless to 9- and 10-year-old New Zealanders. Christmas for them is warm, blue and gold – and without robins! They realized that a teacher cannot assume that the conventional signs and symbols on such cards evoke the same meaning for the child as for the teacher. Adults may take an understanding of them for granted. In the belief that learning is more efficient when reasons are known, they explained this pictorial, cultural shorthand and saw a better grasp of the meanings of Christmas. In the USA, Hiebert and Wearne (1996) carried out a very useful longitudinal study of children learning maths as they moved through grades 1 to 4 (6 to 9 years). They were able to show that understanding of place value and multidigit addition and subtraction facilitated the invention and modification of ways of solving arithmetical problems. The instruction was not concerned with teaching algorithms but focused on, for example, quantifying sets of objects, examining ways of representing quantities (orally, writing numbers, using objects). Children were encouraged to develop their own procedures and explain them to other children. Underpinning the approach was a belief that children are more likely to understand if they have the chance to construct relationships themselves. One assessment task for the youngest children was to deduce how many teams of ten players could be made from sixty-four children. Interviews checked for understanding of the procedures the children used. Hiebert and Wearne found that understanding helped children make sense of instruction about procedures that came later. There was increased retention and progress was generally more rapid for those who had shown understanding, and it also helped the children choose more efficient procedures. When an algorithm was not known, those who understood could often find a solution themselves.

Hiebert and Wearne concluded that understanding has real value in enhancing and facilitating learning. But note that, at least in mathematics, this does not mean that understanders will necessarily obtain more correct answers than non-understanders: non-understanders can be quite proficient in using an algorithm. The facilitation is in the speed of learning new procedures, in the flexible use of knowledge in novel situations and in the retention of the learned material. Further support for this conclusion is in Winkles' (1986) study of the learning of trigonometry amongst 14-year-olds. He compared an 'achievement' group with an 'achievement with understanding' group. Again, there was evidence of an enhanced ability to think flexibly in the understanding group when dealing with novel problems.

In a very different context, Minnaert and Janssen (1992) have also demonstrated the role of understanding in facilitating further learning in their university students of psychology in Belgium.

Third, a capacity to respond flexibly in different situations is a valuable one to have. Diagnosing an illness, finding a fault in an electrical circuit, responding to developments in the marketplace or in the relationships between people, for instance, can all benefit from understanding. It can have the potential to free a learner from the limitations of memorized knowledge. Someone whose responses are tied inflexibly to particular circumstances is at a loss when those circumstances change. As Halford (1993) put it, understanding can confer a certain cognitive autonomy on its owner. It has the potential to enable effective, independent interaction with the world. It can enable people to think for themselves and make reasoned choices (Meijer, 1991). In effect, it frees people from inflexible, non-adaptive behaviours and it includes a capacity to explain, justify, think critically and, in certain circumstances, to predict and control events (Johnson-Laird, 1985; Petroski, 1993). For instance, knowing the causes of condensation can enable us to explain its occurrence and prevent it in a particular room. Understanding enables its owner to evaluate the arguments of others and give them due weight. For example, a politician attempting to persuade us of the merits of a course of action might draw an analogy with an event in the past. Understanding something of such events can help in evaluating the attempted justification.

Fourth, at a time when information is likely to be cheap and prolific, what makes sense of a 'data smog' will be at a premium. The press of a button can bring vast quantities of information to your attention. This glut of information is likely to lack organization, and some of it may be of dubious quality. An understanding may help to sort and order the information and support reasoning and critical capacities (Shenk, 1997). The ability to generate new understandings will also be an asset when faced with the need to extract essentials and construct a coherent structure from such information.

Fifth, Arthur Koestler (1961) once described creativity as 'bisociation', the bringing together of two ideas to produce another. In understanding, the inferring of relationships between mental elements is such a process. Of course, most of the time, the relationship is neither new nor earth-shattering. Often it may not even reach the level of consciousness or may be forgotten as quickly as the connection is made. When it does produce a novel connection or a new structure with some import, then we tend to see it as a significant, creative event. From this perspective, the creative event is a brightly coloured drop in the larger ocean of understandings. If we value creativity and wish to foster it, understanding and its processes are important.

Given what understanding has to offer, the answer has to be, yes, it can be worth the effort. Understanding usually offers more than memorization.

David Perkins asked, 'What can you do with knowledge you don't understand?' (Perkins, 1992). Put like that, memorization looks rather bleak. But, both memorization and understanding can be legitimate learning ends, and Biggs and Moore (1993: 21) have pointed out that the two are not antagonistic: 'You can't form a view of something unless you know the facts. The problem occurs when you stop at the facts.' If you were to sit in on a lesson, lecture, seminar or tutorial, you must expect to hear 'facts'. In history, there must be talk of people, places and times; in science, there is talk of voltages, chemical reactions and the occurrence of species in an environment. This is necessary if there is also to be talk of connections, patterns and structures. Relationships cannot exist without something to relate.

Understanding as a Common Educational Goal

In Britain, as elsewhere, school programmes often have understanding as a goal. For example, children have been expected to:

- understand and respond to the texts they read and, develop their understanding of Standard English in English lessons, and develop explicit understanding of how language and text work, (and, in Wales, understand and respond to a variety of materials in Welsh);
- develop their understanding of place value, relationships between numbers, operations, patterns and properties of shape, properties of position and movement, measures, and probability in mathematics lessons;
- develop an understanding of aspects of life processes, materials and physical processes in science lessons; in Scotland, the guidelines for environmental studies mention 'understanding living things and the processes of life', while in Northern Ireland, the requirements for science and technology require pupils to 'understand that humans have skeletons and muscles to support their bodies and help them move';
- develop an understanding of mechanisms, and the form and function of products in design and technology lessons;
- understand how information technology (IT) devices can be used in information technology lessons;
- understand aspects of the past and chronology in history lessons;
- develop an understanding of a range of places and themes in geography lessons;
- develop understanding of the work of artists in art lessons;
- develop understanding of music from different times and places in music lessons;
- understand small-sided games in physical education lessons;
- understand different kinds of behaviour using moral categories (DFE, 1995; SCAA, 1996; SOED, 1993; DENI, 1996; QCA, 1998).

In higher education, Stewart Sutherland (1994) sees understanding as the feature that distinguishes education from training. 'In a particular field of study, be it chemistry or history', he writes, 'understanding implies the ability to recognize faulty reasoning, to construct hypotheses which go beyond the evidence available and to identify the kinds of evidence which will verify or falsify the hypotheses. Training and the imparting of skills can legitimately fall well short of that.' If an employer needs someone to do an unchanging task, then rote learning is likely to suffice. Barnett (1994) believes that, 'for higher education, understanding is a central and irreducible concept'. Understanding, he argues, is a mental state fulfilling certain demanding criteria that do not apply to the possession of knowledge. These centre on what makes understanding worthwhile: its flexibility in application, its durability, the way it facilitates further learning, and the way it enables critical abilities. Nevertheless, when a new graduate was interviewed about learning in his subject, he said he felt that understanding was 'a luxury' (Newton, Newton and Obserski, 1998). Why should this be?

A Worthwhile Goal but a Secondary Concern

In spite of good reasons to value understanding, it is not a central concern in every classroom. In England and Wales, there has been a tendency to favour a reproduction of information (Ofsted, 1993a, 1993b, 1993c). For instance, in primary science lessons, 'why' questions can be fairly rare events (Newton, 1999). At the same time, there is evidence that children may not always see understanding as the point of the exercise (Newton and Newton, 1998). Further, an anxiety about learning in a subject can lead to a reliance on memorization when it is not appropriate. Students about to begin higher education also tend to favour the acquisition of factual information (Hardman, 1997). They have diverse conceptions of the kind of learning that is appropriate or adequate. In history, for instance, such students may see events as well-determined, essentially predictable with reasoning leading to the truth (Newton and Newton, 1998).

Understanding avoidance is not unique to Britain. In the USA, there is also evidence of a lack of concern for understanding in a variety of educational contexts (for example, Dahlgren, 1984; Hounsell, 1984; Hallden, 1986; Prawat, 1989; McLaughlin and Talbert; 1993; Bruer, 1994). It is almost as if there is a silent conspiracy: 'I won't ask a hard question if you don't' (Gardner and Boix-Mansilla, 1994: 210). In Canada, Sierpinska (1994: 1) writes that 'very often [students' work] is a strategic activity aiming at going through the school and graduating with as little intellectual investment as possible'. In Australia, Wildy and Wallace (1992) similarly note that understanding is not always a high priority.

Why does understanding have such a low priority? Sandberg and Barnard (1997) argue that understanding is often difficult and students do not spontaneously engage in cognitive activity that fosters it. But a cognitive economy of effort – including mental laziness – is not all of it. Would-be learners arrive with an assortment of conceptions, abilities, skills, knowledge, interests, attitudes, beliefs, aspirations, expectations, habits of mind and preferences. Gibbs (1992) describes a variety of factors which bear upon a student's learning behaviour. For example, some students attend a course because regulations oblige them to do so, while others do so out of interest. Some may be more inclined to seek understanding while others simply want to pass the examination.

At the same time, teachers teach in different ways and their conceptions of worthwhile learning can be different. Some might emphasize the acquisition of facts and procedures while others stress causes and reasons (Newton and Newton, 1997). A teacher's own subject knowledge and understanding is likely to be important here. For instance, it is not uncommon for teachers to have to teach outside their own area of subject specialism. When understanding is unsure, it is more likely to be avoided in teaching (Newton, 1999). Teaching and learning are also embedded in particular contexts. The availability of expertise, specialist rooms and time will shape what is on offer. If there are examinations, something will have to be taught that can be examined. Altogether, this makes for an untidy, dynamic interaction that determines what students do about their learning. This issue is returned to in Chapter 9.

Success in a subject may be a means to an end but success may not need understanding. Students can describe strategies for persuading an examiner that they understand. For example, they list the ploy of stating statistics and quotations in history and writing everything they know about a topic. In science, this becomes the stating of definitions (Newton and Newton, 1998). These strategies point to examination success as the primary goal: understanding is less fortunate. Some examinations may place little emphasis on understanding. When they do, understanding may be one path to success but a mix of limited understandings and memorization may achieve the same goal, perhaps more readily.

Marton and Saljo (1976) found that some learners adopt a surface approach to learning in which information is treated as unconnected facts. They are able to write a description of an event or describe how to carry out some procedure. They may even be able to state reasons but these float free in the students' mind. What is often needed is a deep approach which establishes relationships that the student grasps and relates to existing knowledge. In practice, a student's approach is unlikely to be at one extreme or the other but will lie somewhere between the two (Volet and Chalmers, 1992). The approach may even vary from subject to subject and situation to situation. A desire to achieve also figures in it. Those motivated in this way may seek to achieve through a deep approach while others do so through a shallow approach (Biggs, 1987; Andrews et al., 1994). The intensity of this motivational element varies from person to person and context to context. I doubt if any student could or even needs to enter an examination understanding everything but, when examination success is paramount, as that student said, understanding can be a luxury.

Gaining an understanding can be very worthwhile, satisfying and fulfilling, but may be difficult to achieve and not a prime concern. When understanding is desirable, it would help to have some idea of its nature. Nickerson (1985) writes, 'What it means to understand is a disarmingly simple question to ask but one that is likely to be anything but simple to answer'. He goes on, 'if understanding is a primary goal of education, an effort to understand understanding would seem to be an obligation'. Knowing what understanding means in a particular context can clarify goals for the teacher and the learner. This is the subject of the next chapter.

Summary

Understanding can satisfy personal needs, facilitate learning, enable flexible learning and enhance retention of knowledge. Although it may be acknowledged to be a worthwhile goal, it can be obscured by circumstances. Both teachers and students may have other priorities, students may perceive it to be a luxury that they cannot afford, and in some circumstances, a teacher may not be predisposed to teach for understanding.

References

Andrews, J., Violata, C., Rabb, K. and Hollingsworth, M. (1994) 'A Validity Study of Bigg's Three-Factor Model of Learning Approaches', *British Journal of Educational Psychology* 64: 167–85.

Barnett, R. (1994)*The Limits of Competence*, London: Open University Press.

Bartlett, F.C. (1932) *Remembering: A Study in Experimental and Social Psychology*, Cambridge: Cambridge University Press.

Biggs, J.B. (1987) *Learning Process Questionnaire Manual*, Melbourne: Australian Council for Educational Research.

Biggs, J.B. and Moore, P.J. (1993) *Process of Learning*, 3rd edn, New York: Prentice Hall.

Bruer, J.T. (1994) *Schools for Thought*, Cambridge, MA: MIT Press.

Dahlgren, L.O. (1984) 'Outcomes of Learning', in F. Marton, D. Hounsell and N.J. Entwistle (eds), *The Experience of Learning*, Edinburgh: Scottish Academic Press, 19–35.

Davalos, S. (1997) 'Using Hypertext Functionality to Provide Understanding Support', *Journal of Educational Multimedia and Hypermedia* 6: 231–48

Dehaene, S. (1997) *The Number Sense*, London: Allen Lane.

DENI (Department of Education for Northern Ireland) (1996) *The Northern Ireland Curriculum, Key Stages 1 & 2, Programmes of Study and Attainment Targets*, Bangor: HMSO.

DFE (Department for Education) (1995) *The National Curriculum Orders*, London: DFE.

Eklund-Myrskog, G. (1997) 'The Influence of the Educational Context on Student Nurses' Conceptions of Learning and Approaches to Learning', *British Journal of Educational Psychology* 67: 371–81.

Gardner, H. and Boix-Mansilla, V. (1994) 'Teaching for Understanding in the Disciplines and Beyond', *Teachers College Record* 96: 198–218.

Gibbs, G. (1992) 'Improving the Quality of Student Learning Through Course Design', in R. Barnett (ed.), *Learning to Effect*, Buckingham: Soc. Res. in Higher Education/Open University.

Haberlandt, K. (1997) *Cognitive Psychology*, Boston: Allyn & Bacon.

Halford, G.S. (1993) *Children's Understanding: The Development of Mental Models*, Hillsdale: Lawrence Erlbaum.

Hallden, O. (1986) 'Learning History', *Oxford Review of Education* 12: 53–66.

Hardman, F. (1997) 'A-level English Language and English Literature: Contrasts in Teaching and Learning', in A.E. Edwards, C. Fitzgibbon, F. Hardman, R. Haywood and N. Meagher (eds), *Separate but Equal? A Levels and the GNVQ*, London: Routledge.

Hawkins, J.P. and Pratt, D.L. (1988) 'And Robins I Have Never Seen...', *Educational Studies* 14: 97–103.

Hayden, T., Arthur, J. and Hunt, M. (1997) *Learning to Teach History in the Secondary School*, London: Routledge.

Hiebert, J. and Wearne, D. (1996) 'Instruction, Understanding and Skill in Multidigit Addition and Subtraction', *Cognition and Instruction* 14: 251–83.

Hounsell, D. (1984) 'Learning and Essay-Writing', in F. Marton (ed.), *The Experience of Learning*, Edinburgh: Scottish Academy Press.

Johnson-Laird, P.N. (1985) 'Mental Models', in A.M. Aitkenhead and J.S. Slack (eds), *Issues in Cognitive Modelling*, Hove: Lawrence Erlbaum.

Koestler, A. (1961) *The Watershed*, London: Heinemann.

Lee, L. (1959) *Cider with Rosie*, London: Hogarth Press.

Marton, F. and Saljo, R. (1976) 'On Qualitative Differences in Learning', *British Journal of Educational Psychology* 46: 4–11.

McLaughlin, M.W. and Talbert, J.E. (1993) 'Introduction: New Views of Teaching', in D.K. Cohen, M.W. McLaughlin and J.E. Talbert, *Teaching for Understanding: Challenges for Policy and Practice*, San Fransisco, Jossey-Bass, 1–10.

Meijer, W.A.J. (1991) 'Factual Knowledge and Understanding: What Teachers May Learn From Stage Actors', *Religious Education* 86: 74–82.

Miller, A.I. (1996) *Insight of Genius*, New York: Springer-Verlag.

Minnaert, A. and Janssen, P.J. (1992) 'Success and Progress in Higher Education', *British Journal of Educational Psychology* 62: 184–92.

Newton, D.P. and Newton, L.D. (1997) 'Teachers' Conceptions of Understanding Historical and Scientific Events', *British Journal of Educational Psychology* 67: 513–27.

—— (1998) 'Enculturation and Understanding: Some Differences Between Sixth Formers' and Graduates' Conceptions of Understanding', *Teaching in Higher Education* 3: 339–63.

—— (1999) 'Knowing What Counts as Understanding in Different Disciplines', *Educational Studies* 25: 35–54.

Newton, D.P., Newton, L.D. and Oberski, I. (1998) 'Learning and Conceptions of Understanding in History and Science: Lecturers and New Graduates Compared', *Studies in Higher Education* 23: 43–58.

Newton, L.D. (1999) 'Teaching for Understanding in Primary Science', paper presented at the Fourth Summer Conference for Teacher Education in Primary Science, University of Durham, 7–9 July.

Nickerson, R.S. (1985) 'Understanding Understanding', *American Journal of Education* 93: 201–39.

Ofsted (1992) *English Key Stages 1, 2 and 3, Third Year, 1991–92*, London: HMSO.

—— (1993a) *Science Key Stages 1, 2, 3 and 4, Fourth Year, 1992–93*, London: HMSO.

—— (1993b) *Geography Key Stages 1, 2 and 3, Second Year, 1992–93*, London: HMSO.

—— (1993c) *History Key Stages 1, 2 and 3, Second Year, 1992–93*, London: HMSO.

Perkins, D. (1992) *Smart Schools: From Training Memories to Educating Minds*, New York: Free Press.

Petroski, H. (1993) *The Evolution of Useful Things*, London: Pavilion, 245.

Prawat, R.S. (1989) 'Teaching for Understanding', *Teaching and Teacher Education* 5: 315–28.

QCA (Qualifications and Curriculum Authority) (1998) *Understanding in Education for Citizenship and the Teaching of Democracy in Schools*, London: DfEE.

Sanberg, J. and Barnard, Y. (1997) 'Deep learning is difficult', *Instructional Science* 25: 15–36.

SCAA (School Curriculum and Assessment Authority) (1996) *A Guide to the National Curriculum*, London: Teacher Training Agency.

Sierpinska, A. (1994) *Understanding in Mathematics*, London: Falmer.

Shenk, D. (1997) *Data Smog*, London: Abacus.

SOED (Scottish Office for Education), (1993) *Curriculum and Assessment in Scotland: National Guidelines: Environmental Studies, 5–14*, Edinburgh: SOED.

Sutherland, S. (1994) *Universities in the Twenty-First Century*, London: Paul Hamlyn, 1–20.

Volet, S.E. and Chalmers, D. (1992) 'Investigation of Qualitative Differences in University Students' Learning Goals', *British Journal of Educational Psychology* 62: 17–34.

Wildy, H. and Wallace, J. (1992) 'Understanding Teaching or Teaching for Understanding', *American Educational Research Journal* 29: 143–56.

Winkles, J. (1986) 'Achievement, Understanding, and Transfer in a Learning Hierarchy', *American Educational Research Journal* 23: 275–88.

3   The Nature of Understanding

Overview

The word 'understanding' commonly denotes a variety of mental processes, states and structures. Some features of understanding are described and the variety of understandings is illustrated through classroom subjects. Some variables of understanding are listed and the public and personal nature of understanding outlined. Features that can be particularly relevant in formal instruction are highlighted.

Different Kinds of Understanding

We might say we understand a road sign, a joke, a word, a sentence, a book, a picture, a person, an action, an intention, a product of an action, a procedure, a game, an event, a description, an explanation, an argument, a proof, art, music, physics – there seems no end to it (Rosenberg, 1981). But what we mean by understanding in the context of a road sign is not quite the same as in the context of a book or a person. Nevertheless, we feel that understanding is the right word to use in these contexts. How can that be? While they may be different, they share a family resemblance (Wittgenstein, 1958; Hofstadter, 1985). Near relatives, like understandings in organic and inorganic chemistry, have many features in common. Distant relatives, like understandings in chemistry and in art, have less in common.

Mental Connections and Structures

Bartlett (1932) described understanding as a mental attempt to connect something that is given with something other than itself. For Paul (1944), it was when the mind 'selects, pieces and patterns the relevant observed facts together, rejecting the irrelevant, until it has sewn together a logical and rational quilt of knowledge'. Similarly. Nickerson (1985) sees understanding as, 'the connecting of facts, the relating of newly acquired information to

15

what is already known, the weaving of bits of knowledge into an integrated and cohesive whole.' This relating or linking of thoughts, ideas and information to form a coherent whole is an important feature of understanding, particularly evident in formal education (Hounsell, 1984). If it was knitting, the pattern would say *K2tog* (knit two stitches together to make one). The act of knitting parallels a process of understanding and the garment is like the mental product that results.

There is, however, more to it that that: we can knit garments for different purposes. Suppose we might hear an account of the sinking of the *Titanic*. Understanding might enable us to describe the event. We might notice that the ship's passengers fell into certain groups when it came to their behaviour. McKenzie (1985) describes classification as 'a fundamental intellectual process by which ideas and phenomena are sorted, compared, analysed, and integrated into a coherent whole.' This might simplify and make sense of an otherwise incomprehensible chaos. We might also connect the actions of the crew with the collision with the iceberg. This constitutes a causal understanding. Someone else might connect the structure of the ship with its response to being holed. The second causal understanding is more likely to suit an engineer's purpose if the aim is to build a ship to withstand such collisions. Perkins (1986) has drawn useful parallels between technology and understanding. In both, something is created to serve a purpose. Accordingly, he described academic understanding as knowing the structure of the topic, the structure's purpose and why it serves that purpose.

At the same time, conscious reflection may not always be essential for an understanding. The understanding that a carpenter could have of wood, a sculptor of clay and a mother of her baby may not have been achieved by conscious reflection. In unconscious or implicit learning, the learner is not usually aware of the detection of contingencies and covariations and the making of connections. For instance, in what is commonly referred to as intuition, a complex situation may be processed unconsciously but the nature of the processing often remains inaccessible to conscious thought (Berry and Dienes, 1993). Claxton (1997) argues that Western education has long neglected unconscious mental processes. For instance, the 'undermind', as he calls it, is often able to deal with intricate, ill-defined situations but needs time to do so before it offers its products to the conscious mind. We are all familiar with those occasions when an obstinate problem has been put aside and a way into it emerges later. At the same time, when we refer to conscious reflection, unconscious operations, such as pattern analysis, underpin it (Nelson, 1986).

Sierpinska (1994: 33) surmises that, 'finding a unifying principle, does not apply, perhaps, to all acts of understanding'; or at least, to all uses of the word. She describes mental 'order and harmony' as the central criterion, and this might be achieved in a 'holistic, non-conceptualized grasp of the situation'. This may also be found in Dilthey's view of understanding as an empathetic response to a situation. He contended that you cannot understand what you have not experienced (Plantinga, 1980). Again, existentialists argue that understanding is not exclusively an intellectual effort (Kerdeman, 1998) or, as Reid has pointed out, not always one that deals in sentence-like truths (Reid, 1986).

As the term *'understanding'* is commonly used, some mental garments merit it more than others. The one or two idle stitches that connect the shape of a cloud on a sunny day with a remembered animal do not usually qualify. On the other hand, grasping a description or the cause of an event mentally usually does. Indeed, Piaget (1978) felt that only mental structures that answer the question 'why' deserve to be called understanding. Johnson-Laird's view is that:

> The psychological core of understanding, I shall assume, consists of having a 'working model' of the phenomenon in your mind. If you understand inflation, a mathematical proof, the way a computer works, DNA or a divorce, then you have a mental representation that serves as a model of an entity in much the same way as, say, a clock functions as a model of the earth's rotation.
>
> (Johnson-Laird, 1985)

This also allows understandings that are like descriptions. Similarly, descriptive and causal understandings are included by Halford (1993: 1) who writes: 'understanding means having an internal mental representation or mental model that corresponds to the concept, task, or phenomenon'. The more complex the mental structure, the more likely it is to be described as an understanding.

As well as the complexity of the garments, there is also their variety. Reid (1986) complains of an assumed dualism in understanding in which cognition counts and feelings do not. He argues that feeling and thinking are inseparable in understanding in the arts so cognition alone is not sufficient for understanding in this domain. Although there are parallels between the arts and the sciences (for example, a mental state or structure may enable anticipation in the arts just as they enable prediction in the sciences), what are called understandings in the two domains are not identical. It could be argued that the word *'understanding'* should be confined to states and structures that are essentially cognitive and another term should be used for those involving feeling. Whether this makes a sharp distinction is debatable and, since common practice is to use understanding without distinction in very different areas of the curriculum it is, for practical purposes, largely academic. For this reason, a broad view of what understanding encompasses has to be taken.

So far, understanding has been largely discussed as a mental particular. Another way is to see it in terms of what it lets you do (Fodor, 1998).

Perkins (1994) has described understanding in this way. Instead of asking about what is represented in the mind, he has described understanding as 'the ability to think and act flexibly with what one knows'. You will recall that one of the things that makes understanding worthwhile is that it can enable flexible behaviour. Perkins's description makes a mental flexibility the criterion for what counts as understanding. A practical advantage of this perspective is that it directs attention to observable behaviours. It may, however, draw attention away from the diversity of mental representations that we might call understanding and the varied nature of the understanding processes in different domains. Some knowledge of that diversity seems potentially worthwhile when it comes to supporting understanding in different contexts.

Understandings in Various Academic Subjects

Some similarities and differences between understandings in various subjects will now be illustrated. To begin with, I compare the understanding of events in history and in science. The intention is to show that, even though the aim is to gain a 'causal' understanding of events, the nature of that understanding is likely to be different in different subjects.

History and Science Compared

Understanding a historical event in the world of human affairs can amount to constructing a plausible account of it (Emmet, 1985; Humphreys, 1989; Becher, 1994). Historical events do not exist in isolation: they are shaped by those around them and the people in them. This makes the events unique, and the historian's interest is often in understanding their particular courses. Social patterns and trends and the players' motives and frailties figure in that understanding. Historians like Oakeshott (1983) have emphasized the uniqueness of the event and believe it can offer few generalizations of relevance to other events. In short, history has no lessons for the present. Others, like Carr (1987), have emphasized patterns and trends as potentially transferable generalizations. The connections between episodes in an event may also be viewed differently. On the other hand, Armytage (1965: i) referred to the way 'Historians undertake to arrange sequences...assuming in silence a relation of cause and effect'. Oakeshott, for instance, was unhappy with 'cause' and preferred 'antecedent condition'. Nevertheless, Haydn et al. (1997) use 'cause' but prefer 'consequence' to 'effect'. Evans (1997), reviewing recent tendencies in historiography, also uses 'causation' in connection with constructing an evidence-based explanation of an event, and the term is common in professional literature (for example, Howells, 1998).

Events, however, are different in science. Understanding a scientific event amounts to constructing an account of an occurrence in the physical or natural world. This account includes causal mechanisms drawn from 'universals of fact' (Emmet, 1985; Kitcher and Salmon, 1989). While a particular event may be unique in its detail, the scientist is frequently interested in its essence. Instances of the same causal mechanism may be seen or arranged. Since they draw on universals of fact, their course can be predicted and theories may be testable.

Oakeshott, emphasizing the uniqueness of the historical event, saw great distinctions between history and science. Carr, on the other hand, emphasized patterns and trends and saw some parallels with scientific events. Both, however, agreed that there are fundamental differences in, for instance, the nature of causation in and available information about historical and scientific events. Where history and science differ is in the kinds of relationships that might legitimately be inferred in a situation. Although the relationships a student constructs may be genuine, what counts depends on the context (Hewstone, 1989).

Understanding in history and science comprises more than the understanding of events. There is, for instance, the understanding of concepts and situations; terms like 'democracy' and 'energy' have to be understood. There is the understanding of procedures for producing a desired end. This might amount to no more than knowing what to do next, or it could include knowing the reasons for the actions of a procedure. The reasons for each action are also likely to require a conceptual understanding of evidence (and of variables and a fair test in science (Gott and Duggan, 1996)). Mathematics is now used to illustrate the variety of understandings within one subject.

Mathematics

In mathematics, understanding is applied to a wide range of very different mental acts. Concerning number and space, learners can be expected to:

> understand patterns, concepts, notations and procedures, equivalences, relations among numbers and quantities, how mathematics is related to situations involving physical objects, quantities of money and other concrete things, problems and situations, language, language of mathematics, instructions, the linear structure of positive integers, reasonings, the sequence of numerals.
>
> (Sierpinska, 1994: 2)

However, there is evidence that we are born with or soon develop a sense of number or, strictly speaking, 'numerosity' (Dehaene, 1997). Wynn (1992) showed that children under five months of age expect one and one to make two. She held a toy so that an infant could see it then hid it behind a screen. She then showed the child another, identical toy and placed that behind the screen. However, a toy could be removed without the child seeing it. When the screen was lowered, the child would see one or two toys. The 'impossible' event of only one toy attracted a longer period of attention than the 'correct' event of two toys. This is taken to indicate that the infant has expectations that $1+1=2$. Beyond the smallest numbers, this numerosity is progressively less precise and generally operates at the unconscious level. Symbols, however, make precision possible.

In the classroom, there can be a concern for conceptual and procedural understanding. The first refers to an understanding of mathematical concepts like equality, operations, limit, and why, for instance, $-1-1$ is -2, -1×-1 is $+1$, and the sum of the series $-1+1-1+1...$ is not $1/2$, as Liebniz believed, or why a proof is sufficient for its purpose (Sierpinska, 1994). The second concern refers to knowing how to carry out mathematical operations, as in the instrumental understanding of algorithms, often taken further to include why they work (VanLehn, 1990; Davis, 1994; Newton, 1994). Such matters are potentially open to classroom discussion, reflection and conscious understanding. They are those which might figure in teachers' and learners' verbal interaction.

While mathematics is a vehicle for communicating about number and space, it is also a hybrid language which also uses words (which Shuard and Rothery (1984) called Mathematical English). English, of course, is a vehicle in its own right and, at the same time, makes literature possible. Both the vehicle and the literature may be the subject of formal study.

Language and Literature

The understanding of a narrative could amount to comprehending the words and sentences and mentally representing their meaning. The original words may be forgotten as the representation, often functioning as a mental model, captures the essence of the situation. As the narrative progresses, the model is updated and the course of events is stored in long-term memory (Johnson-Laird, 1983; Van Dijk and Kintsch, 1983; Bower and Morrow, 1990). Much of this can occur at an automatic, unconscious level of thought.

In the study of language or literature, however, we may be required to reflect on such things. Relationships between characters and the elements of the plot may be explored and made explicit. A narrative may be deconstructed and related to others. Historical context and biography may be introduced to explain the content and structure of the material. The vehicle has become an object of study in its own right. Understanding resulting from reflection has a significant part in such study.

An actor might take the narrative, perhaps in the form of a play, and construct a character for one of the players. The components of this character must relate to one another in a way that is plausible in the play's context. If successful, the actor would be said to understand the part. Other actors are likely to construct different plausible versions of this character. In this instance, the construction process is unlikely to be altogether conscious and reflective but is often enhanced by conscious reflection (Ustinov, 1977).

There has been a tendency to focus on understanding constructed from verbal symbols (Clancey, 1997). Art, dance, mime and music are essentially non-verbal.

Music

Music has been described as a metaphorical description of a situation but, as Serafine (1986) has pointed out, 'it is not clear what people are knowing or mentally doing when they engage in the business of music'. She describes understanding music as the product of a search for relationships between tonal-rhythmic events and the identification of melodic, harmonic and rhythmic patterns. However, formal knowledge is neither necessary nor sufficient for that understanding (Serafine, 1988). The relationships inferred in listening to music about a situation and in reading about the same situation could be different in kind. Gardner (1983) and Reid (1986) argue that making sense of experiences like music cannot be achieved by explanation alone because they involve feelings, some of which are without names. As in comprehending words and sentences, much of the processing may be rapid, automatic and unconscious (Fiske, 1992). Nevertheless, reflection, analysis, deliberation and the conscious seeking of relationships is not absent from understanding in music. Richardson (1996) offers a model of 'musical thinking' in which understanding stems from knowing the reasons for the effect of a piece of music and perceiving relationships between its components that have value for the listener. At an elementary level, for instance, this may be instigated by questions such as: 'What would be the effect if we played a cymbal here instead of a triangle?' and, 'What makes the passage sound so brilliant?' (Stanwick, 1988, 1992).

For the performer, the musical score is a procedural map (Davidson and Scripp, 1992). As with words, a lot may be left unsaid in the map and the performer constructs a particular understanding of the piece. Practice is likely to have made the process of playing the notes automatic, so cognitive resources are available for regulating the actions and shaping the form of the music in accordance with that understanding; what Stanwick (1992) has called 'thoughtfulness in kinaesthetic activity'. While enactive understanding probably enables a rapid realization of a piece of music in accordance with the map, this may be shaped by reflective understanding constructed and developed before and during the act. There are some parallels between music and art.

Art

Art is also largely non-verbal in nature. It has been described as 'a language

– a form of cognitive expression which communicates ideas, feeling and emotions' (Seefeldt, 1995). Colour–form patterns may be constructed and integrated into meaningful parts and a whole. The process may be unconscious and automatic, but it can also involve conscious deliberation. Styles of art change with time. What one artist attempts may be different to another. For instance, modernist theories of aesthetic experience focus on the emotional impact and the immediate felt relations of order and fulfilment. Post-modernist art, on the other hand, tends to deals with content, such as psychological or philosophical concepts, rather than form. They produce 'documents' which have to be 'read' for meaning 'rather than merely contemplating aesthetic qualities in an art object' (Wolcott, 1996).

For Thomas (1991), works of art such as paintings or music have significance rather than meaning: 'both pictures and music seem to be able to refer without attaching any connotation to the reference'. For Hirsch (1967), the significance of a work of art is a kind of 'response' to it. Some call this response understanding, others prefer 'insight'. Insight and reflective understanding can be distant relatives as far as family resemblance is concerned, but insight is often informed by conscious reflection. In the classroom, a teacher is likely to expect and encourage conscious reflection and, as Reimer (1970) puts it, 'To the degree that an art educator is clear about the kind of meaning present in his subject he can be effective in sharing the meaning and value of his subject with students'.

Games

Understanding how to play a game, such as football or hockey, involves knowing the situation as a coherent whole and acting in a way intended to produce a particular effect. The particular state of the game, the location of players, their relation to one another and their attributes have to be known, something like understanding the current state of a narrative. In addition, a preferred state has to be mentally constructed. To bring about a change from current to preferred state, an appropriate course of action needs to be recalled and adapted or constructed. Various motor and kinaesthetic skills are then used to realize the desired effect (see, for instance, Turner and Martinek, 1995).

In practice, this all has to happen very quickly. There is not a lot of time to stand, reason and plan. Much of the processing may be unconscious, the current state of the game being continually updated. Preferred states may be constructed and abandoned in rapid succession as the game progresses. Experience probably supports the process of game understanding and a rapid, appropriate response to a situation. Nevertheless, at least some of the mental processes can be consciously attended to. Turner and Martinek's (1995) model for understanding in game play aims to make players reflect on the situation and consciously consider decisions. Turner (1996) has demonstrated that raising the players' awareness of tactics and decision making in games can improve their play.

This complex assemblage of both strongly and loosely related understandings illustrates their nature in domains that are commonly the subject of instruction. Understandings can differ in a number of ways and in more than one way at once. Particularly relevant to the content of understanding in many school subjects are its *relational components*, the *nature of the relationships* constructed amongst those components, and the *level of understanding*.

Some Understanding Variables

Relational Components

Understanding is impossible without content: there must be something to connect and relate. The relational components are what are related. These could be facts, patterns, complex structures, tonal–rhythmic events or combinations of these. In general, components are promiscuous. Relationships may be inferred between any elements but, in practice, formal education often confines itself to the content of relatively self-contained domains. One difference between understandings in such subjects is usually in the relational components. Those in physics, for instance, are to do with inanimate entities while those in history often relate to people and their motives. Within either of these areas, further differences between components exist. Inanimate entities may be stars, planets, hand-sized objects, atoms or subatomic particles. People and their motives are just as varied.

The Nature of the Relationships

There are various kinds of relationship. A relationship may, for example, capture the spatial dispositions of things or the effect of one variable on another. The nature of the relationship may, in some situations, also indicate the goal of the understanding. Spatial relationships, for example, may enable someone to construct a mental representation of the route to a particular shop. In other situations, a variety of relationships may be needed to satisfy the goal. Consider understanding the action of a simple camera. It is possible to know the spatial arrangement of its parts, what to do with those parts and why this produces an image. The first may satisfy the goal of descriptive understanding, the second a procedural understanding and the third causal understanding (Newton, 1996). Understanding, though, is not just about making mental connections. Mental connections may already exist and a new understanding may revise them or embed the earlier understanding in a wider one (Byers and Erlwanger, 1985).

Levels of Understanding

Whatever is to be understood, relationships between its components must be constructed. However, each component is not a free entity. It relates to others outside the immediate object of understanding. These in turn relate to others. Three centuries ago, Locke (1690) pointed out that, ultimately, everything is related to everything else. Each nest of relationships is embedded in a larger nest. This makes it impossible to delineate what constitutes a complete understanding of something. Few could claim an *absolute* understanding of anything but they might legitimately claim *an* understanding. Nickerson (1985) writes that 'we may be willing to stop short of defining understanding as knowing *all* there is to know about something...' For practical purposes, we *must* stop short of expecting an absolute understanding. Locke made the point that it is possible to understand a relationship between ideas even when the ideas themselves are not fully understood.

The point is that there are levels or degrees of understanding. What one student constructs (consciously or unconsciously) may have few connections and relate poorly to existing experience or knowledge. Another student may construct detailed, numerous and complex connections, integrated extensively with prior knowledge and encompassing other levels of understanding. Over time, a student may move to a different level of understanding as knowledge develops and the initial structure is revised, enriched and more widely integrated. As Zazkis (1998) has put it, 'to understand something better means to assimilate it in a richer and more abstract schema'. Understanding may develop by degrees through the acquisition of a sequence of progressively more complex and encompassing concepts (Miyake, 1981). Typically, this movement towards higher levels of understanding takes time and may not be smooth. It may be spontaneous or it could arise from responses to tasks or questions provided by a teacher; or it may not occur at all.

Authorized and Personal Mental Structures

All understandings are more or less idiosyncratic. This is in part due to differences in prior knowledge which learners bring to the situation. Nevertheless, in some subjects there are patterns and relationships that are generally accepted by a professional community, sometimes referred to as authorized or public understandings. (In this sense, understanding is only partly in the head; it may also exist 'independently' in a community (Davis, 1997)). Reasonably, these understandings are targets that teachers want learners to construct. In science and engineering, for instance, generalizations about the behaviour of materials would be amongst these. Similarly, various accounts of events in history may be considered particularly plausible and so are considered worth teaching. The emphasis is on the construction of a mental representation that reflects the structure of the target. However, there are occasions when target structures are relatively few. Understanding can amount to making connections of a personal and unique significance. This is well-illustrated in understanding some oriental poetry, such as the couplet: 'Swiftly the years, beyond recall. Solemn the stillness of this spring morning' (Johnson-Laird, 1990). You must make what personal understanding of it you will.

Students may also construct understandings that others see as highly implausible or otherwise inadmissible. The students' experience may be such that the relationships they construct seem well-founded to them. Vosniadou has described children's conceptions of the shape of the world. At first, they believe it to be flat. Later, they compromise with a disc, a hollow sphere, a flattened sphere and, finally, a full sphere. Each one is, presumably, quite reasonable to the child (Vosniadou, 1992). Misconceptions of this nature can, at times, be difficult to change. They can also develop in the normal course of formal learning. In a sequence of learning experiences, sometimes extending over relatively long periods of time, earlier experiences may give rise to learning that is adequate at the time but proves to be an obstacle later.

Providing Support for Understanding

Although an understanding might arise through unconscious processes, a teacher is usually concerned to make it the subject of conscious thought. This enables an interaction between teacher and learner and often facilitates a verbal demonstration of the state or development of understanding. That is, the understanding can be discussed or described. Indeed, Brown (1987: 66) sees 'the most stringent [criterion] of understanding [as involving] the availability of knowledge to consciousness and reflection'. In the chapters that follow there is an emphasis on what Perkins (1994) has called conscious, reflective understanding. This is what the teacher of academic subjects can interact with most readily. Nevertheless, the unconscious development of understanding cannot be ignored. Indeed, providing opportunities for this to occur could be a strategy for supporting understanding. Sooner or later, however, the teacher is likely to want this understanding to be conscious and open to reflection.

Summary

Searching for patterns, connections, correlations and relationships is thought to be an innate tendency (Caine and Caine, 1994). From a biological point of view, this can have an evolutionary advantage as it orders the world and can make events more predictable. Nevertheless, the process is not infallible and relationships can be imposed that are not there. The astronomer Percival Lowell (1855–1916) believed he could see evidence of canals on Mars, an unfortunate making of connections between marks which, in reality, do not form continuous lines.

Some understandings may have been achieved through conscious reflection and some by unconscious processes. They have a variety of forms in which the relational components, the nature of the relationships and the level of understanding are all different. A particular subset could be chosen as being worthy of the term understanding but, popularly, the word refers to a variety of mental structures or states. Since it tends to have this wider meaning in teaching and learning, it is practical to consider it from that point of view. Like a family, the members resemble one another to varying degrees, but differences have to be acknowledged, small in some instances and considerable in others. Some understandings are authorized or public and are targets of instruction. Others are less constrained and more personal.

References

Armytage, W.H.G. (1965) *Four Hundred Years of English Education*, Cambridge, Cambridge University Press.

Bartlett, F.C. (1932) *Remembering: A Study in Experimental and Social Psychology*, Cambridge: Cambridge University Press.

Becher, T. (1994) 'The Significance of Disciplinary Differences', *Studies in Higher Education* 19: 151–61.

Berry, D.C. and Dienes, Z. (1993) *Implicit Learning*, Hove: Lawrence Erlbaum.

Bower, G.H. and Morrow, G. (1990) 'Mental Models in Narrative Comprehension', *Science* 247: 44–8.

Brown, A.L. (1987) 'Metacognition, Executive Control, Self-Regulation, and Other Mysterious Mechanisms', in F.E. Weinert and R.H. Kluwe (eds), *Metacognition, Motivation and Understanding*, Hillsdale, NJ: Lawrence Erlbaum, 65–116.

Byers, V. and Erlwanger, S. (1985) 'Memory in Mathematical Understanding', *Educational Studies in Mathematics* 16: 259–81.

Caine, R. and Caine, G. (1994) *Making Connections: Teaching and the Human Brain*, Alexandria, VA: Association for Supervision and Curriculum Development.

Carr, E.H. (1987) *What is History?* London: Penguin.

Clancey, W.J. (1997) 'Conceptual Coordination: Abstraction Without Description', *International Journal of Educational Research* 27: 5–19.

Claxton, G. (1997) *Hare Brain Tortoise Mind*, London: Fourth Estate.

Davis, A. (1994) 'Constructivism', in A. Davis and D. Pettitt (eds), *Developing Understanding in Primary Mathematics*, London: Falmer: 11–13.

—— (1997) 'Understanding Mathematics', *Journal of Philosophy of Education* 31: 355–64.

Davidson, L. and Scripp, L. (1992) 'Surveying the Coordinates of Cognitive Skills in Music', in R. Colwell (ed.), *Handbook of Research on Music Teaching and Learning*, New York: Schirmer, 392–413.

Dehaene, S. (1997) *The Number Sense*, London: Allen Lane.

Emmet, D. (1985) *The Effectiveness of Causes*, Albany, NY: State University of New York Press.

Evans, R.J. (1997) *In Defence of History*, London: Granta.

Fiske, H. (1992) 'Structure of Cognition and Music Decision-Making', in R. Colwell (ed.), *Handbook of Research on Music Teaching and Learning*, New York: Schirmer, 360–76.

Fodor, J.A. (1998) *Concepts*, Oxford: Clarendon.

Gardner, H. (1983) *Frames of Mind*, New York: Basic Books.

Gott, R. and Duggan, S. (1996) 'Practical Work: Its Role in the Understanding of Evidence in Science', *International Journal of Science Education* 18: 791–806.

Halford, G.S. (1993) *Children's Understanding: The Development of Mental Models*, Hillsdale, NJ: Lawrence Erlbaum.

Haydn, T., Arthur, J. and Hunt, M. (1997) *Learning to Teach History in the Secondary School*, London: Routledge.

Hewstone, M. (1989) *Causal Attribution*, Blackwell: Oxford.

Hirsch, E.D. (1967) *Validity in Interpretation*, New Haven, CN: Yale University Press.

Hofstadter, D.R.H. (1985) *Metamagical Themas: Questing for the Essence of Mind and Pattern*, New York: Bantam.

Hounsell, D. (1984) 'Understanding Teaching and Teaching for Understanding', in F. Marton, D. Hounsell and N.J. Entwistle (eds), *The Experience of Learning*, Edinburgh: Scottish Academic Press, 19–35.

Howells, G. (1998) 'Being Ambitious with the Causes of the First World War: Interrogating Inevitability', *Teaching History* 92: 16–19.

Humphreys, P. (1989) *The Chances of Explanation*, Princeton, NJ: Princeton University Press.

Johnson-Laird, P.N. (1983) *Mental Models*, Cambridge: Cambridge University Press.

—— (1985) 'Mental models', in A.M. Aitkenhead and J.M. Slack (eds), *Issues in Cognitive Modeling*, Hove: Lawrence Erlbaum.

—— (1990) 'What is Communication?', in D.H. Mellor (ed.), *Ways of Communicating*, Cambridge: Cambridge University Press, 1–13.

Kerdeman, D. (1998) 'Hermeneutics and Education: Understanding, Control, and Agency', *Educational Theory* 48: 241–66.

Kitcher, P. and Salmon, W.C. (1989) *Scientific Explanations*, Minnesota Studies in the Philosophy of Science XIII, Minneapolis, MN: University of Minneapolis.

Locke, J. (1690) *An Essay Concerning Human Understanding*, abridged and edited by J.W. Yolton, London: Dent, 1993.

McKenzie, L. (1985) 'Philosophical Orientations of Adult Education', in S. Brookfield (ed.) (1988), *Training Educators of Adults*, New York: Routledge, 211–16.

Miyake, N. (1981) 'The Effect of Conceptual Point of View on Understanding', *Quarterly Newsletter of the Laboratory of Comparative Human Cognition* 3: 54–6.

Nelson, K. (1986) *Event Knowledge*, Hillsdale, NJ: Lawrence Erlbaum.

Newton, D.P. (1994) 'Teaching Mathematics for Understanding: Support for the Novice Teacher from the Textbook', *Curriculum* 15: 33–41.

—— (1996) 'Causal Situations in Science: A Model for Supporting Understanding', *Learning and Instruction* 6: 201–17.

Nickerson, R.S. (1985) 'Understanding Understanding', *American Journal of Education* 93: 201–39.

Oakeshott, M. (1983) *On History*, Oxford: Basil Blackwell.

Paul, L. (1944) *The Annihilation of Man*, London: Methuen.

Perkins, D.N. (1986) *Knowledge Design*, Hillsdale, NJ: Lawrence Erlbaum.

—— (1994) *The Intelligent Eye*, Santa Monica, CA: The Getty Center for Education in the Arts.

Piaget, J. (1978) *Success and Understanding*, London: Routledge & Kegan Paul.

Plantinga, T. (1980) *Historical Understanding in the Thought of Wilhelm Dilthey*, Toronto: University of Toronto Press.

Reid, L.A. (1986) *Ways of Understanding and Education*, London: Heinemann.

Reimer, B. (1970) *A Philosophy of Music Education*, Englewood Cliffs, NJ: Prentice-Hall.

Richardson, C.P. (1996) 'Understanding the Critical Process', *The Journal of Aesthetic Education* 30: 51–61.

Rosenberg, J.R. (1981) 'On Understanding the Difficulty of Understanding Understanding', in H. Parret and J. Bouveresse (eds), *Meaning and Understanding*, Berlin: de Gruyter.

Seefeldt, C. (1995) 'Art – A Serious Work', *Young Children* 50: 39–42.

Serafine, M.L. (1986) *Music as Cognition*, New York: Columbia University Press.

Shuard, H. and Rothery, A. (1984) *Children Reading Mathematics*, London: John Murray.

Sierpinska, A. (1994) *Understanding in Mathematics*, London: Falmer.

Stanwick, K. (1988) *Music, Mind and Education*, London: Routledge.

—— (1992) *Musical Education and the National Curriculum*, London: Tufnell.

Thomas, R.S.D. (1991) 'Meanings in Ordinary Language and in Mathematics', *Philosophia Mathematica* 13: 37–50.

Turner, A. (1996) 'Teaching for Understanding: Myth or Reality?' *Journal of P.E., Recreation, and Dance* 67: 46–8.

Turner, A. and Martinek, J.J. (1995) 'Teaching for Understanding: A Model for Improving Decision Making During Game Play', *Quest* 47: 44–63.

Ustinov, P. (1977) *Dear Me*, London: Heinemann.

Van Dijk, T.A. and Kintsch, W. (1983) *Strategies for Discourse Comprehension*, New York: Academic Press.

VanLehn, K. (1990) *Mind Bugs: The Origins of Procedural Misconceptions*, Cambridge, MA: Massachusetts Institute of Technology.

Vosniadou, S. (1992) 'Knowledge Acquisition and Conceptual Change', *Applied Psychology: An International Review* 41: 347–57.

Wittgenstein, L. (1958) *Philosophical Investigations*, Oxford: Basil Blackwell.

Wolcott, A. (1996) 'Is What You See, What You Get? A Post Modern Approach to Understanding Works of Art', *Studies in Art Education* 37: 69–79.

Wynn, K. (1992) 'Addition and Subtraction by Human Infants', *Nature* 358: 749–50.

Zazkis, R. (1998) 'Odds and Ends of Odds and Evens: An Enquiry into Students' Understanding of Even and Odd Numbers', *Educational Studies in Mathematics* 36: 73–89.

4   Making Connections

Overview

Understanding cannot be transmitted; the connections have to be made by the learner. Some ways of doing this are outlined and illustrated. Their limitations and their consequences are described.

Constructing a Mental Representation

Analogies can be useful when it comes to thinking about how the mind works. At one time, it was common to draw parallels with a telephone exchange. More recently, the computer has provided a popular analogy and a source of terminology. For instance, the organization of the mind is often referred to as its architecture (Figure 4.1). Paralleling the RAM (Random Access Memory) of a computer is the concept of working memory, where processing can take place. Information can be stored for long periods on the computer's hard disk, and this is paralleled by the long-term store. Neither the computer nor the mind can process incoming information unless it is in a form which suits its way of working. The encoder 'translates' information into a form the mind can operate on (Bruer, 1994; Cohn et al., 1995).

The analogy has proved useful, but it nevertheless has its limitations. The brain is not a digital device. For instance, instead of using number to represent magnitudes, it generally uses magnitudes to represent number. A consequence is that we can only be approximate in our feel for large numbers (Dehaene, 1997). People are also subject to emotions, feelings, motives and moods, and these figure in our thinking. Different ways of modelling the mind's processes are possible. For example, patterns of electrical excitation in certain networks of connections between nodes have been shown to simulate the mind's ability to acquire aspects of language, concepts, sequences and patterns to some extent. These gain their plausibility from parallels with brain cells and their connections (Billman, 1998; Elman, 1998). However, when we talk of making a connection in understanding, we mean a connection

Figure 4.1   A Cognitive Architecture

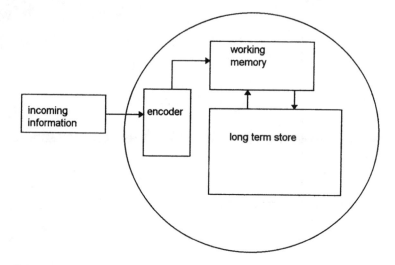

between thoughts and ideas, not a connection between brain cells, and it is often of more practical value to think at a less microscopic level.

Working Memory

Working memory is where information can be held, worked on, related to other mental elements, organized and shaped (Ribaupierre and Hitch, 1994). Working memory is of limited capacity. We seem unable to hold and process more than a few different items of information at once, at least consciously. For instance, Johnstone (1984) has shown how university students' success in problem solving plummets as the number of pieces of information they have to process increases (Figure 4.2).

Baddeley's (1990) model of working memory has proved particularly useful in explaining a variety of thinking phenomena (Niaz and Logie, 1993). It behaves as though it has a central executive, an articulatory loop, a primary acoustic store and a visio-spatial sketch pad. The central executive coordinates the other components. Spoken words automatically enter the articulatory loop, where they can be maintained for short intervals as though they were an inner 'voice', controlled by the articulatory muscles. It has limited size, so fewer long words can be maintained in it than short words. The primary acoustic store is like an inner 'ear', which can store sound-based representations temporarily. The visio-spatial sketchpad is the equivalent of an inner 'eye'. It can retain and manipulate representations of visual images and attends to visio-spatial relations. Deficiencies in one subsystem may, at least in part, be compensated for by others (see Chalifoux, 1991, for a useful summary).

Figure 4.2   The Relationship Between Correct Responses and Amount of Information

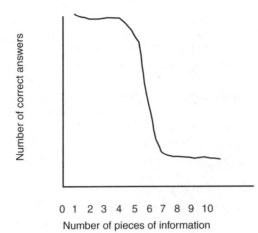

0 1 2 3 4 5 6 7 8 9 10
Number of pieces of information

(y-axis: Number of correct answers)

However, working memory does not operate in isolation. Incoming information has to be interpreted and possibly supplemented. This needs access to and draws on prior knowledge in the long-term store. Suppose, for instance, you were to be faced with the archetype of classroom problems: it takes four people two days to dig a hole, how long will it take if there are three people? First, you need to know (prior knowledge) what the words mean, individually and collectively. This enables you to construct a mental representation of the hole-digging problem. You may already know (prior knowledge) a relevant algorithm or procedure, and you draw that into working memory. In articulating it, however, you soon find that fractions of a day are involved. You need to know how many hours there are in a day (prior knowledge), and so on. The point is that, during these processes, relevant information is also brought into working memory from the long-term store.

Prior knowledge does not have to be fragmented facts, such as the number of hours in a day. It can be theories of the world in the broadest sense. Suppose someone is faced with the question: Will this sink in a bucket of water? They may hold the object, examine it and feel its weight, but they must call upon prior knowledge and relate this object to those things they know to sink and those they know will float. Experience may have generalized this knowledge into a predictive theory: for example, *all things that are light for their size float*. Prior knowledge is related to the new information to build a coherent mental structure that represents the situation. If a coherent structure results from the mental processing, this reduces some aspect of the situation from many random, unconnected elements to possibly one interrelated unit. If this representation is likely to be useful, it may end up in the long-term store for later recall, but often such structures are temporary and are soon abandoned.

In short, 'working memory is the hub of cognition. Its functions include both the storage and the manipulation of information'. Working memory 'is where the cognitive action is', but there can be no cognition without mental representation (Haberlandt, 1997: 212; Billman, 1998). Encoding puts information in a form that the mind can deal with. Most think of this as being diagram-like or sentence-like (Rips, 1998).

Mental models are of the first kind. They capture the parts and relations in what is to be understand, behave in much the same way as it would do and are often easy to process (Johnson-Laird, 1983; Holland at al., 1986; Payne, 1988). For instance, if a book A is on a table and B is on top of A, then a mental model of this situation immediately shows the relation of A to the table and to B.

Sentence-like representations are of the second kind. Reasoning proceeds by processing sentence-like assertions or propositions. This is probably better illustrated by propositions that cannot be visualized easily. Suppose *A is a dilp* and *A is on the gub*. Adding the assertions, *B is a dilp* and *B is on A*, and if *clat* means nothing stands on the item concerned, then we can infer that *A is not clat*. In practice, situations to be understood are often complex. Not everything is easy to represent as a mental model (hence the choice of nonsense words for the example). Alternatives, options, constraints and uncertainty, for example, can be more readily represented as propositions. Sentence-like representations have a wide scope but can be difficult to process. An annotated mental model is a compromise in that it includes propositions for those things that are difficult to model. In the case a hungry cat sitting on a mat, a mental model of a cat on a mat might include a propositional memo or tag to remind us that the cat is hungry. In practice, as the scope of propositional tags increases in these hybrids, the representations become more propositional in nature. In effect, there is no clear dividing line between propositional representations and mental models (Newell, 1990). To illustrate, some examples follow.

The Number Line

Dehaene (1997) has described an automatic association between numbers and space. There is a tendency to associate small numbers with the left and large numbers with the right. This is not related to left or right-handedness, but is associated with the direction of writing. In cultures where writing is left to right, the association is reversed. The number line is a refinement of this automatic association. Bruer (1994: 85) describes it as 'a central conceptual structure of early number skills'. Over time, the child builds a representation of the connections between the number names, their order and the process of moving up or down the line by adding or subtracting 1.

By building into it a number problem and manipulating or articulating this mental representation, a child can find a meaningful solution. At its simplest, this could amount to a fairly pure mental model that represents numbers in order along the mental equivalent of a line.

A Scene in a Story

Comprehending a narrative amounts to translating the words and sentences into their underlying conceptual propositions. Words cannot describe everything in a scene so this produces something rather like a mental play script. We depend on prior knowledge to make good the shortfall and draw on it to construct a mental model of the scene (Bower and Morrow, 1990). If the book says, 'The cat sat on the mat', we represent a cat sitting on a mat. Its particular posture and the texture of the mat are supplied by prior knowledge. We may even add some detail of the room in which the cat sits. If the story goes on, 'The cat licked a paw, stood, flicked its tail and walked across the room', we update the mental model and it moves on to include these actions. The precise way that cat licked, flicked and walked, however, is provided by prior knowledge of such behaviour. Since this is often different in different people, their mental representations are unlikely to be identical.

We also use our knowledge of the world to knit together causal relationships amongst the actions, rather like a director makes a full stage production from the script. Readers keep a mental list of each character's goals and track how the events relate to these goals. In other words, the mental model is likely to be an annotated one. As the number of goals increases, the time taken to understand an action increases. While the scenes may change, the characters and their goals form a thread through them. Readers tend to track the character's thread rather than objects (Bower and Morrow, 1990).

Munte at al. (1998) showed that mental processing is easier for chronologically ordered sentences than for those where chronology is disrupted. For example, 'Before she read the book, she went to the library', takes more mental resource than, 'After she read the book, she went to the library'. The latter calls for a straightforward update of the mental representation: first she read the book, then she went to the library. This sequence is what we experience in the world. The former is not in the normal order of events; an updating of a mental representation would need a mental reversal.

Solving Syllogisms

Some syllogisms can be mentally manipulated fairly readily. For instance.

More than half the musicians were classically trained.
More than half the musicians were in rock groups.

Therefore, some musicians were both classically trained and in rock groups.

But these are difficult to prove by standard methods. How does the mind deal with them? Johnson-Laird (1983) has argued that it constructs a mental model to represent the situation. On paper, it might be represented by:

$m = c$
$m = c$
$m = c = r$
$m = r$
$m = r$

(m: a musician, c: classically trained, r: a rock group, = means a connection)

Such a model allows the overlap to be detected. These studies also strongly suggest that we are not equipped with a set of reasoning rules like those of formal logic. We tend to make mistakes because we are content to represent only some of the possibilities. Limitations of working memory space also make it difficult for us to handle some problems.

Causal Reasoning in Science

When a scientific event is to be understood in terms of known laws of nature, the situation has to be represented. Often it must be simplified to its essentials (and that calls on prior knowledge about what is likely to be a useful simplification). This more or less simplified mental representation then has to be articulated according to particular rules (for example, the laws of nature) until some match with the event is obtained (Newton, 1996) (Figure 4.3).

Figure 4.3   Understanding a Scientific Event

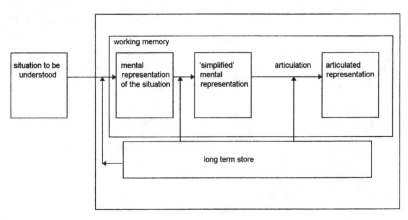

As an example, consider understanding why the image in a simple, pinhole camera is upside down. The learner sees the physical situation and represents it. This representation, however, includes a lot that is not directly relevant to this particular understanding. The colour of the box does not matter, for instance. The learner needs to focus only on those aspects which are relevant and what is relevant is often more apparent to an expert than a learner. In effect, this amounts to a simplification of the representation. The learner must also know the way in which such situations are typically represented. Instead of representing all light from the source, only extreme rays are usually included (Figure 4.4a). The learner needs to know that light travels in straight lines and manipulate the mental representation accordingly (Figure 4.4b). However, the crossing of the rays at the pinhole has also to be noticed and its significance inferred (briefly, the light which came from the top is now at the bottom on the film, that which came from the bottom is now at the top on the film, so this will produce an image that is upside down).

Reasoning About Time Zones

Schnotz and Preuss (1995) have tested the way people calculate the time at different places. For example, they asked, 'What time is it in Rio, when it is 14h in Mexico?' They again found evidence that at least some people based their reasoning on a mental model of the situation. Something which behaves like a world time line is constructed. Mexico is located on it and the

Figure 4.4a   Pinhole Camera

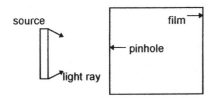

Figure 4.4b   The Production of an Inverted Image

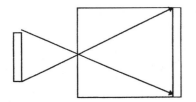

place of Rio located relative to Mexico (Figure 4.5). Rio is east of Mexico by three time zones. This makes Rio time 17hr. Others might have reasoned on a sentence-like basis and some could have applied an algorithm, but this does not necessarily require an understanding of time zones.

The Undermind

Understanding may occur unconsciously in what Claxton (1997) has called the 'undermind'. This does not seem to function like deliberate, conscious thought. Deliberate thought often focuses on a limited range of mental entities. In a sense, it closes off paths and devotes resources to ones that seem potentially productive. If they are unproductive, it can be difficult to establish new directions. Putting the topic from your mind may allow associated mental activity to die away so that when it is taken up again, new starting points and new routes are easier to take. Putting a topic out of the conscious mind, however, does not always eliminate it at the unconscious level. At the unconscious level, activity seems less focused than that at the conscious level. Thoughts, perhaps stimulated by current events, may develop and interact with existing activity to produce new, unexpected connections. These may rise into consciousness as, at least, a partly fashioned understanding sometimes referred to as an intuition or insight.

Unconscious processes require no attention: they can deal with complex situations, they seem to be relatively independent of conscious processing abilities as measured by intelligence tests, and what they produce is durable and robust. It is probable that these aspects of the undermind evolved before those of conscious processing (Berry and Dienes, 1993).

Constraints on Constructing Understanding

Conscious Processes

Working memory provides mental resources for inferencing and reflection but has limited capacity. Capacity is the maximum mental resource that someone can make available. As the storage demand increases, there is less resource for processing. Capacity varies from one person to another. In practice, the maximum resource is unlikely to be available all the time (Halford, 1993). Capacity may be less when someone is tired, distracted or trying to do something else at the same time.

Figure 4.5   Time at Rio: Three Times Zone East

Mexico			Rio			
14	15	16	17	18	19	20

The demand or intrinsic load is a property of the task, not the person. It represents the mental effort required to perform the task (Halford, 1993). When we ask someone to concentrate on a task, we often mean that they should devote as much of their processing resources to it as they can and exclude other tasks. Difficulty is experienced if the task demand is at or beyond the limits of someone's available processing capacity at a given time. Difficulty may also be experienced when a task of low demand is presented in such a way that someone has to devote considerable mental resources to understanding the presentation, expectations, requirements and outcome – the extrinsic load of the instructional format. Similarly, the need for many processing steps, each of relatively low demand, may overload working memory so that the task becomes difficult. Of particular interest in understanding is what Sweller (1994) has called element 'interactivity'. Where many elements must be interrelated, possibly in complex ways, this places a high demand or load on working memory. In other words, the intrinsic load of the task is high.

Sweller also distinguishes between controlled processing and automatic processing. Controlled processing is when information is consciously attended to, as when a new reader must laboriously process each written word. Automatic processing is when much less of the task needs to be processed consciously, as when an experienced reader is not aware of the processing of words and the construction of meaning. Automatic processing frees cognitive resources so that more complex tasks are manageable. This explains the effect of chunking in facilitating mental manipulation. For instance, an experienced chess player knows clusters of moves at the automatic level and can manipulate these clusters with relative ease. A novice tends to have to allocate resources to the moves within each chunk. This increases the load and limits reasoning facility.

Chunking also operates at the level of individual words like 'tree'. If we were unfamiliar with the concept of 'tree' and had to process 'tall planty thing with hard, thick, relatively rough stem which separates into thinner structures repeatedly and bears green flattish structures above ground and is anchored into place with branchy things below ground (that are not quite like those above ground)' while reasoning about the effects of deforestation, overload would never be far away. Sweller and Chandler (1994) prefer to use the term schema for organized information of this kind. A schema is defined as 'a cognitive construct that permits one to treat multiple elements of information as a single element' (Marcus et al., 1996): 'Learning through schema acquisition reduces cognitive load by reducing the number of interacting elements with which working memory must deal.'

Mayer and Moreno (1998) offer evidence that working memory includes an auditory working memory and a visual working memory. An explanation using words and pictures may exceed visual working memory capacity and so be difficult to understand. This may be avoided, however, by presenting the explanation as pictures accompanied by an oral narrative, thereby using the capacities of both working memory systems, rather than just one.

Deficiencies in particular components of working memory can result in specific difficulties. For instance, when that part which deals with visio-spatial information is weak, children are poor at scanning, rotating and generating object images. Consequently, they are likely to be weak at tasks involving these, such as matching shapes that are presented in different orientations (Cornoldi et al., 1995). Similarly, measures of working memory capacity can predict reading comprehension and a low capacity tends to be associated with reading difficulties. Working memory deficiencies also relate to lower achievement in mathematics (Swanson, 1994) and academic perfor-mance in general (Swanson et al., 1990). However, it must not be assumed that the converse is true. Deficiencies in performance may have other causes, such as inadequate attention (Hulme and Roodenrys, 1995).

Unconscious Processes

In many educational contexts, making knowledge available to conscious reflection is an important aim. Unconscious learning is generally inacces-sible to conscious reflection. Inaccessibility also makes such learning relatively difficult to modify. Verbal instruction may have little effect, so inappropriate learning may develop and be persistent. Unconscious learning also tends to be tied to the situation in which it is acquired and may not transfer readily to new situations. The process itself is easily disrupted by pressure, anxiety and demands for action. It may also proceed at a leisurely pace (Berry and Dienes, 1993; Allen and Reber, 1998). The need for an immediate response seems to switch it to the conscious, focused mode of thinking.

Developing Processes of Understanding

Using working memory effectively may be skills that can be developed (Sigel, in Ellsworth and Sindt, 1994). The relationships that are to be inferred must be known or capable of construction. The learner must be able to discriminate the relevant from the irrelevant (being able to see the wood in the trees). In conscious understanding, there must be a recognition of the need for an inference (Yekovich et al., 1991) and a willingness to make that inference. Carefully constructed questions are effective in helping children focus attention and construct relevant relationships (Newton, 1997). Processing autonomy could be developed by using questions to scaffold chil-dren's thinking and then by progressively withholding the scaffold. This may also be used to ensure that learners know what counts as understanding in a given context. Nevertheless, we must not assume that demand must be routinely taken out of everything. Learning to cope with higher (but manageable) demand is potentially useful as it prepares the learner for real world situations and events (McNamara et al., 1996).

Knowing What Counts as Understanding

Understanding cannot be transmitted but has to be constructed by the learner. For conscious understanding, this means the learner must know what counts as understanding in a given context. While we are generally born with the ability to infer relationships, the kind of relationship and the structure that is admissible in a given context must be known. Knowing what counts in a particular subject is learned through a process of enculturation. Enculturation is a cognitive socialization in which individuals learn what is an acceptable epistemic form in a subject (Gellatly, 1997; Collins and Ferguson, 1993). Perkins et al. (1993) describe four dimensions of enculturation: learning from exemplars, by transmission, through activities and during interaction. A learner acquires ways of thinking about a subject from experience of the beliefs, practices and structures that prevail in that body of knowledge (Bishop, 1988). Becher (1989) has described the importance of the cultural frame of a discipline in establishing its intellectual values and defining its domain for a student.

Enculturation is provided by, for instance, experience, a teacher's example, questions and evaluations of a learner's performance. Lave (1997) argues that a powerful source of enculturation is the learner's actions that bring success or, at least, avoid criticism. Actions may be taken to produce the expected answer, not to generate understanding.

Volet and Lawrence (1988) traced the origin of some students' inappropriate learning goals to their misconceptions of academic requirements. It would be wrong to assume that students' conceptions of understanding are either absent, incorrect, ill-formed, naive or alike. Students are likely to arrive with conceptions that may be coherent and tenaciously held but seem to them to be adequate (Newton and Newton, 1998). Students' conceptions of learning are highly correlated with their approaches to studying. Those who think of learning in quantitative terms tend to find it difficult to adopt a deep approach to learning. But, in Finland, Eklund-Myrskog (1997) has demonstrated a relationship between student nurses' conceptions of learning and their approaches to learning. Usefully, those who saw the value of understanding attempted to understand more.

There are also teachers' conceptions to consider. They may have inadequate conceptions of the nature of a subject such as history, so that some teachers lack an awareness of the nature of historical learning and fail to develop a distinctively historical element in their teaching (OFSTED, 1993a, 1993b). Design and Technology teachers have also been found to be uncertain about the nature of the subject and what makes it different to other subjects (DES, 1992; OFSTED, 1993c; Newton and Hurn, 1996).

Strauss (1993), in studying teachers' mental models of children's learning in elementary arithmetic, concluded that instruction in part, 'reflects what the teacher believes about how knowledge in his or her discipline is organized'. Crossover teaching, when teachers teach outside their areas of specialism, is one situation where inappropriate beliefs could make themselves felt.

Maturation, Development and Understanding

Understanding is also bound by a child's development. If a child is unable to relate more than two items of information, this limits the complexity of the understanding that can be achieved. By about one year old, a child can process one item; by two years old, this has increased to two; by five years old, it has increased to three; by eleven years old it may have increased to four, the average level for adults (Halford, 1993). Processing speed also increases with age. This does not necessarily mean that there is a growth in capacity. It could be that what is there is being used more efficiently (Engle et al., 1991). Case (1985) is of the view that the total processing space is constant and equal to the sum of the space needed for processing and the short term storage space. With age, less processing space is needed to do a given task (due to, for instance, the effect of chunking and automaticity) so more is available for temporary storage.

Culture, Practices and Understanding

Children acquire a culture that shapes how they view the world. If, for instance, there is a tendency to view the world in mechanistic terms, concepts will be available to support understanding in those terms. On the other hand, if the prevailing view is animistic, understandings are likely to be constructed that are in accordance with that. Even the medium used to represent what is to be learned can shape the understanding that results. For example, in a study of flowers, if the learner is to draw them, the emphasis will be on visual characteristics. A video, on the other hand, could highlight their movement. For this reason, the introduction of a phenomenon through several media – or the one which focuses clearly on the desired kind of understanding – is advisable (Forman, 1996).

There are constraints on our ability to understand. The limitations of working memory make tasks of high interactivity potentially difficult to understand. The mental act of processing itself may be inefficient, undeveloped or unpractised. Even if practised, there is the need to know what counts as understanding in a given situation. This amounts to having a clear view of the purpose of understanding and what content will satisfy that purpose. This, in turn, will tend to be shaped by a culture and limited by a learner's stage of development.

Understanding and Multiple Intelligences

Gardner (1993) put forward the idea of multiple intelligences. In it, he describes a linguistic intelligence, a musical intelligence, logical-mathematical intelligence, a spatial intelligence, a bodily-kinaesthetic intelligence and a personal intelligence. It is unlikely that anyone will be graced with or develop an equal and substantial measure of all of these. However, a greater endowment of, say musical intelligence, could mean that it is easier for that person to develop understandings in music. On the other hand, what is called a greater intelligence in music may be a greater facility in developing understandings in music. Some factors which affect such facilities will be discussed in the next chapter.

Reconstructed Knowledge

Memorization implies that a copy of what was to be learned can be reproduced. To achieve this, someone might recite the words over and over again until the pattern of sounds can be reproduced at will. Arranging the words into rhythmic verses can help, presumably because this constrains the possibilities and offers cues for what comes next. Understanding, on the other hand, tends to preserve relationships and structures. An account of what has been understood is usually stated in the learner's own words, perhaps using some of the original words. In this sense, it is a reconstruction of what was to be learned.

We sometimes read of bards and storytellers who tell stories and sing songs of several hours' duration, supposedly word for word each time. Demos Zogic, a Yugoslavian tavern keeper some fifty years ago, was one such. He had an enormous repertoire of narrative songs and chants, one of which lasts seventeen hours. He claimed that each performance was word for word the same. In practice, recordings show they were not. The gist was the same each time, but the words varied. His skill was in producing each version in a metrical format to accompany the music he played. Not being literate, he does not use the expression 'word for word' in the same sense as a literate person would. What he means is that he is repeating the song faithfully according to the story (Ellis and Beattie, 1986). This matches the experience of understanding. Zogic understood the story and reconstructed it in his own words. A reconstruction was never exactly like an earlier one because the words were not memorized. If he had not understood the story to begin with, he would have had no choice but to memorize the words and recite them.

While understanding cannot be transmitted, the processes can be supported. This involves engaging the learner with the topic in ways that are likely to produce appropriate inferences, order and harmony amongst the mental elements. This is the subject of the next chapter.

Summary

'Working memory is where the action is' (Haberlandt, 1997). It can hold and process information, but has a limited capacity. The amount and nature of prior knowledge is important as this is drawn on in the processing. The limited capacity can make heavily interrelated content difficult to understand. At the same time, content which might be within someone's capacity can be made too complex by the way it is presented. Automatic processing frees resources for controlled processing. Similarly, chunking of information can make processing possible. Processing skills may be developed and can be supported. Other factors which may limit success in understanding are: knowing what counts as understanding in a given context, the stage of maturation, and the level of development, experience and prior knowledge (where that includes both memorization and understanding). Conscious processes can channel thoughts along particular paths which turn out to be unproductive. Unconscious and less focused processes may allow new paths to be found and different connections to be made so that an understanding may emerge from the undermind. Understanding does not, of course, come with a warrant of validity. Recall of knowledge following understanding can involve a large element of reconstruction.

References

Allen, R. and Reber, A.S. (1998) 'Unconscious Intelligence', in W. Bechtel and G. Graham (eds), *A Companion Guide to Cognitive Science*, Malden, MA: Blackwell, 314–23.

Baddeley, A. (1990) *Human Memory: Theory and Practice*, Boston: Allyn & Bacon.

Becher, T. (1989) *Academic Tribes and Territories*, Milton Keynes: Open University Press.

Berry, D.C. and Dienes, Z. (1993) *Implicit Learning*, Hove: Lawrence Erlbaum.

Billman, D. (1998) 'Representations', in W. Bechtel and G. Graham (eds), *A Companion Guide to Cognitive Science*, Malden, MA: Blackwell, 649–59.

Bishop, A.J. (1988) *Mathematical Enculturation*, Dordrecht: Kluwer.

Bower, G.H. and Morrow, G. (1990) 'Mental Models in Narrative Comprehension', *Science* 247: 44–8.

Bruer, J.T. (1994) *Schools for Thought*, Cambridge, MA: MIT Press.

Case, R. (1985) *Intellectual Development: Birth to Childhood*, New York: Academic Press.

Chalifoux, L.M. (1991) 'The Implications of Congenital Deafness for Working Memory', *American Annals of the Deaf* 136: 292–99.

Claxton, G. (1997) *Hare Brain, Tortoise Mind*, London: Fourth Estate.

Cohn, E., Cohn, S. and Bradley, J. (1995) 'Notetaking, Working Memory, and Learning in Principles of Economics', *Journal of Economic Education* 20: 291–307.

Collins, A. and Ferguson, W. (1993) 'Epistemic Forms and Epistemic Games: Structures and Strategies to Guide Enquiry', *Educational Psychologist* 28: 25–42.

Cornoldi, C., Vecchia, R.D. and Tressoldi, P.E. (1995) 'Visio-Spatial Working Memory Limitations in Low Visio-Spatial, High Verbal Intelligence Children', *Journal of Child Psychiatry* 36: 1053–64.

Dehaene, S. (1997) *The Number Sense*, London: Allen Lane.

DES (Department of Education and Science) (1992) *Technology, Key Stages 1, 2 and 3*, London: HMSO.

Eklund-Myrskog, G. (1997) 'The Influence of the Educational Context on Student Nurses' Conceptions of Learning and Approaches to Learning', *British Journal of Educational Psychology* 67: 371–81.

Ellis, A. and Beattie, G. (1986) *The Psychology of Language and Communication*, London: Weidenfeld and Nicolson.

Ellsworth, P.C. and Sindt, V.G. (1994) 'Helping the "Aha" to Happen: The Contributions of Irving Sigel', *Educational Leadership* 51: 40–4.

Elman, J.L. (1998) 'Connectionism, Artificial Life and Dynamical Systems', in W. Bechtel and G. Graham (eds), *A Companion to Cognitive Science*, Malden, MA: Blackwell, 488–505.

Engle, R.W., Carullo, J.J. and Collins, K.W. (1991) 'Individual Differences in Working Memory for Comprehension and Following Directions', *Journal of Educational Research* 84: 253–62.

Forman, G. (1996) 'A Child Constructs an Understanding of a Water Wheel in Five Media', *Childhood Education* 72: 269–73.

Gardner, H. (1993) *Frames of Mind*, 2nd edn, London: Fontana.

Gellatly, A. (1997) 'Why the Young Child has Neither a Theory of Mind nor a Theory of Anything Else', *Human Development* 40: 32–50.

Haberlandt, K. (1997) *Cognitive Psychology*, Boston: Allyn & Bacon.

Halford, G.S. (1993) *Children's Understanding: The Development of Mental Models*, Hillsdale: Lawrence Erlbaum.

Holland, J.H., Holyoak, K.J., Nisbett, R.E. and Thagard, P.R. (1986) *Induction: Processes of Inference, Learning and Discovery*, Cambridge, MA: MIT Press.

Hulme, C. and Roodenrys, S. (1995) 'Practitioner Review: Verbal Working Memory and Its Disorders', *Journal of Child Psychiatry* 36: 373–98.

Johnson-Laird, P.N. (1983) *Mental Models*, Cambridge: Cambridge University Press.

Johnstone, A.H. (1984) 'New Stars for the Teacher to Steer By?' *Journal of Chemical Education* 61: 847–9.

Lave, J. (1997) 'The Culture of Acquisition and the Practice of Understanding', in D. Kirshner and J.A. Whitton (eds) *Situated Cognition*, Mahwah, NJ: Lawrence Erlbaum.

McNamara, D.S., Kintsch, E., Sanger, N.B. and Kintsch, W. (1996) 'Are good texts always better?', *Cognition and Instruction* 14: 1–43.

Marcus, N., Cooper, M. and Sweller, J. (1996) 'Understanding Instructions', *Journal of Educational Psychology* 88: 49–63.

Mayer, R.E. and Moreno, R. (1998) 'A Split-Attention Effect in Multimedia Learning: Evidence for Dual Processing Systems in Working Memory', *Journal of Educational Psychology* 90: 312–20.

Munte, T.F., Schiltz, K. and Kutas, M. (1998) 'When Temporal Terms Belie Conceptual Order', *Nature* 395, 3 September: 71–3.

Newell, A. (1990) *Unified Theories of Cognition*, Cambridge, MA: Harvard University Press.

Newton, D.P. (1996) 'A Model for Supporting the Understanding of Causal Situations in Science', *Learning and Instruction* 6: 201–17.

Newton, D.P. and Hurn, N. (1996) 'Teachers Assessing Design and Technology: An Effect of Curriculum Organisation', *International Journal of Technology and Design* 6: 137–49.

Newton, D.P. and Newton, L.D. (1997) 'Teachers' Conceptions of Understanding Historical and Scientific Events', *British Journal of Educational Psychology* 67: 513–27.

—— (1998) 'Enculturation and Understanding: Some Differences Between Sixth Formers' and Graduates' Conceptions of Understanding', *Teaching in Higher Education* 3: 339–63.

Newton, L.D. (1997) 'Teachers' Questioning for Understanding in Science', *British Journal of Curriculum and Assessment* 13: 109–22.

Niaz, M. and Logie, R.H. (1993) 'Working Memory, Mental Capacity and Science Education, Towards an Understanding of the "Working Memory Overload Hypothesis"', *Oxford Review of Education* 19: 511–25.

OFSTED (1993a) *Geography Key Stages 1, 2 and 3, Second Year, 1992–93*, London: HMSO.

OFSTED (1993b) *History Key Stages 1, 2 and 3, Second Year, 1992–93*, London: HMSO.

OFSTED (1993c) *Technology Key Stages 1, 2 and 3, Second Year, 1991–9*, HMSO: London.

Payne, S.J. (1988) 'Methods and Mental Models in Theories of Cognitive Skill', in J. Self, *Artificial Intelligence and Human Learning*, London: Chapman and Hall.

Perkins, D., Jay, E. and Tishman, S. (1993) 'New Conceptions of Thinking: From Ontology to Education', *Educational Psychologist* 28: 67–85.

Ribeaupierre, A. and Hitch, G.J. (1994) *The Development of Working Memory*, Hove: LEA.

Rips, L.J. (1998) 'Reasoning', in W. Bechtel and G. Graham (eds), *A Companion Guide to Cognitive Science*, Malden, MA: Blackwell, 299–305.

Schnotz, W. and Preuss, A. (1995) 'Task Dependent Construction of Mental Models as a Basis for Conceptual Change', *Research Report No. 6*, University of Jena.

Strauss, S. (1993) 'Teachers' Pedagogical Content Knowledge about Children's Minds and Learning: Implications for Teacher Education', *Educational Psychologist* 28: 279–90.

Sweller, J. (1994) 'Cognitive Load Theory, Learning Difficulty, and Instructional Design', *Learning and Instruction* 4: 295–312.

Sweller, J. and Chandler, P. (1994) 'Why Some Material is Difficult to Learn', *Cognition and Instruction* 12: 185–233.

Swanson, H.L. (1994) 'Short Term Memory and Working Memory: Do Both Contribute to Our Understanding of Academic Achievement in Children and Adults With Learning Disabilities?' *Journal of Learning Disabilities* 27: 34–50.

Swanson, H.L., Cochran, K.F. and Ewers, C.A. (1990) 'Can Learning Disabilities be Determined by Working Memory Performance?' *Journal of Learning Disabilities* 23: 59–67.

Volet, S.E. and Lawrence, J.A. (1988) 'University Students' Representations of Study', *Australian Journal of Education* 32: 139–55.

Yekovich, F.R., Thompson, M.A. and Walker, C.H. (1991) 'Generation and Verification of Inferences by Experts and Trained Nonexperts', *American Educational Research Journal* 28: 189–209.

5 Mental Engagement

Overview

This chapter begins to illustrate the application of the content of the preceding chapters to support for understanding. Teaching orientations and a press for understanding are described and various ways of fostering understanding are illustrated. Throughout, the need for an active, mental engagement with what is to be understood is emphasized. It is suggested that many teachers may not need to change their strategies but may need to use them more strategically.

A Teaching Orientation

Teaching for understanding is not a way of teaching, it is an overall orientation which allows any reasonable strategy that supports understanding (Putnam et al., 1992). The process of understanding may be supported in a variety of ways and by teachers who may use very different approaches. For example, Garnett and Tobin (1988) studied two Australian teachers with very different styles and approaches. They successfully supported understanding in their classrooms but gave very different kinds of lessons. They did, of course, have some things in common. Both has strong subject knowledge and were interested in it. Both were experienced teachers and had routines for managing behaviour, often anticipating problems and deflecting learners into more productive activity. In both classrooms, on-task engagement was high.

Teacher D tended to use whole class interaction. He identified prerequisite knowledge and skills, provided logical frameworks and clear explanations, and linked new knowledge to old knowledge. The relevance of the work was made explicit and his questions were often demanding and expected more than recall. He was also aware of common misconceptions and had strategies in mind for dealing with them.

Teacher G, on the other hand, used a lot of independent and group work.

The learners were given a significant amount of responsibility for their own progress while he had the role of facilitator. Students tended to support one another, and G interacted with individuals in the class to ensure that learning was appropriate. He also tended to expect the students to think about potential applications of what they had learned.

These teachers had very different ways of teaching but both, to use Kazemi's term, 'pressed' for higher level thinking (Kazemi, 1998). Kazemi contrasted two teachers, one who showed a high 'press' and another with a low 'press'. In a mathematics lesson, both classes were in groups attempting to solve a problem. They showed signs of being engaged in and enjoying the task. Both Teacher C and Teacher A moved from group to group monitoring the children's work. Eventually, the work was stopped and the children were asked to explain how they had solved the problem. The lessons sound very similar, but there were important differences. In Teacher C's class, 'explanations were not limited to descriptions of steps taken to solve the problem'. The children were expected to supply mathematical reasons and to explain why they chose particular strategies. In Teacher A's class, on the other hand, the children simply gave procedural accounts of their solutions. Justification of the procedures was not required. Consequently, there was a higher press for conceptual understanding in Teacher C's lesson than in Teacher A's lesson.

Sternberg captures something of the press for understanding in his insistence on the analytical, creative and practical aspects of thinking. The first involves analysing, judging, evaluating, comparing, contrasting and critiquing. Creating involves inventing, discovering, imagining and supposing. The practical aspect relates to implementing, using, applying and the seeking of relevance (Sternberg, 1985; Sternberg et al., 1998). Lessons with activities of this kind are likely to require the learner to attend to, identify and relate elements of knowledge, create integrated structures, and develop these in applying them in particular contexts and in identifying their relevance. For example, in learning about public services, a primary school child might acquire the concept, design a public service, describe its purpose and why it will achieve its purpose, and relate it to other public services. This contributes to a press for understanding because the child is expected to engage in the task in ways which establish relationships and reasons and to develop them by using them.

Mental Engagement

In the final analysis, learners must make mental connections themselves. This requires a mental effort on their part, sometimes referred to as an active engagement with what is to be understood. Active mental engagement improves academic performance (Ablard and Lipschultz, 1998). Unfortunately, active is sometimes taken to mean physically active. It is true that a practical, hands-on engagement with the world is valuable in that it often supports understanding (Nelson, 1986). But physical activity alone does not guarantee mental effort. Active hands do not necessarily indicate active minds or, at least, active in making appropriate connections. It does not follow that engaging in practical work must lead to an understanding or to an understanding that is acceptable. It needs a teacher to monitor and shape mental activity. In some circumstances, practical activity can even hinder understanding (Sweller and Chandler, 1994; Asoko 1996; Cavalcante et al., 1997). By focusing on *mental* engagement, practical engagement becomes one strategy among several. A single strategy may not be the most effective way of teaching since people also learn in different ways (Riding and Rayner, 1998). What benefits one may not be the best strategy for another. In practice, several, mutually supporting strategies may be needed to maximize support for understanding.

Explanation

It is sometimes said that merely telling learners is a waste of time. This is an overstatement. We often tell people things with great effect, and it is not surprising to find teachers telling learners of all ages. Experience has taught teachers it can work, particularly when it has the form of an explanation which takes into account the nature of understanding and the attributes of our mental resources. Experience has often shown teachers that reminding the learner of related matters, ordering the elements of information, not introducing too much new information at once and avoiding irrelevance is helpful. Again based on experience, teachers may also acquire a stock of topic-specific explanations which they have found to be effective. Much of this, however, tends to be largely atheoretical. Making the construction of an explanation a more systematic and more conscious process which draws on theoretical and empirical study is likely to improve existing practice and develop it with new ideas.

Brown and Atkin's (1988) produced a simple typology of explanations. They describe three main types: interpretative, descriptive and reason-giving, approximating to responses to the questions of what, how and why. Interpretative explanations relate to the meaning of a term or statement. (Examples they give are, 'What is a biome?' and 'What is a novel?') Descriptive explanations describe processes, structures and procedures. (Examples are 'How is sulphuric acid made?' and 'How is a sentence used in logic?') Reason-giving explanations supply reasons based on generalizations about the world, motives, obligations or values. These include causal explanations of events.

Parallels can be drawn between these types of explanation and various forms of understanding that often need to be constructed. For instance, if someone understands what a biome is, they have constructed relationships which link elements of the subject together in a coherent way. If someone understands the making of sulphuric acid, they have constructed a coherent arrangement of the events which result in sulphuric acid. If this is also a reason-giving explanation, he or she knows the reasons for those events and their arrangement. These events will be subject to scientific causality in this instance, but reason-giving explanations vary in form across disciplines, according to 'the rules of evidence and testimony which are extant in the subject area' (Becher, 1994).

It is not surprising that explanation supports understanding. Explanations attempt to provide conceptual structures that more or less parallel the mental structure we want to support. When explanations provide structures that relate directly to the domain to be understood, they are *homologous*. When they provide a structure that relates to that domain indirectly, they are *analogous*. Attention in this chapter is on homologous explanations; analogies are described in the next chapter. In practice, a complex explanation may be a composition of both homologous and analogous explanation.

Pre-requisites and Explaining

Since the aim is to help someone make mental connections, they must have the prior knowledge which helps them do that. Before explaining, it is wise to check that this is so. Whatever kind of explanation, a grasp of the meaning of words and concepts and the presence of particular factual knowledge may need to be checked. For instance, if children are to understand that doubling the pull on an elastic band more or less doubles its length, they must know what an elastic band is, what a pull is and what doubling means. Such pre-requisites should be present, readily accessible or relatively easy to acquire during the explanation. If they are not, understanding may not even have a starting point.

Often, an adequate mental representation of a situation is needed at the start because, without it, little of value may develop. A mental representation depends crucially on the interaction between pre-requisite knowledge and the description. The latter should provide clear, concise information in comprehensible language (Brown, 1998). There should be sufficient detail to prevent the misinterpretation of crucial relationships, locations, characters and actions. Even given these, an unskilled or inattentive listener or reader may fail to make the expected mental representation. Responses of young children to the Rosie Rabbit story is an instance.

Children aged 4, 5 and 6 heard a story about *How Rosie Rabbit Almost Looked Over the Hedge*. This was a tale about a rabbit whose field was being cluttered by the farmer's rubbish. The initial arrangement of the objects and the subsequent action involved their re-arrangement were described. If the child did not adequately represent the initial situation in working memory, a relevant updating of it would be unlikely as the action progressed. In short, such children would not understand the subsequent action of the story. This was found to be the case for the overwhelming majority of those tested. However, when another group was shown a picture of the initial situation briefly at the beginning of the story, the overwhelming majority of these children were able to demonstrate an understanding of the subsequent action through to the end of the story. Possessing an adequate mental representation of the situation at the outset is a powerful advantage. Experience suggests that this effect is not confined to children or to following stories. Having a clear, well-founded mental representation of the starting point of an event is likely to support appropriate updating or manipulation of that representation subsequently (Newton, 1994a).

Often, explanations are reason-giving. Many learners have developed their own ideas and theories of the way the world works and they bring them with them. These theories are often derived from a limited experience of the world. Some will be quite adequate, and a teacher could draw them into consciousness and encourage their use and extension. Others will be satisfactory as far as they go but need further extension and development before they can be used in certain contexts. Some will be profoundly flawed and may resist revision and impede further learning. For example, when giving an in-service course, I found a teacher who believed that it was the depth of the water that determined whether something would float. According to this theory, an object which sinks in a dish of water, may float in a bucket of water. If this proves not to be deep enough then a bath, a river or the sea might do the trick. Dealing with ideas of this kind is discussed in Chapter 7, and it has been the focus of a lot of research. Nevertheless, it is important to note that not all prior knowledge, theories and ideas are disabling or inappropriate or need to be radically revised.

Conceptual Structures in Explanations

Mayer (1989: 43) showed that conceptual models help understanding. He defined a conceptual model as, 'words and/or diagrams that are intended to help learners build mental models of the system being studied; a conceptual model highlights the major objects and actions in a system as well as the causal relations among them.' For instance, in describing how brakes work, he supplemented the account with diagrams showing the brakes in the on and off position. Another example was a block diagram showing the way that atmospheric nitrogen is fixed in ammonia which produces nitrates and eventually releases nitrogen back into the atmosphere. In some cases, the effect of such models was to improve conceptual recall by as much as 144 per cent. Creative problem solving, an application of the understanding, was improved by as much as 460 per cent.

Mayer felt that good models guided attention to what mattered most, helped the making of internal connections amongst the information and also helped the learner construct external connections with existing knowledge. He concluded that a 'good model' should be:

- *complete* in that it contains 'all the essential parts, states, or actions of the system as well as the essential relationships among them';
- *concise* in that it is provides information at a level of detail that suits the learner and summarizes and epitomizes what is to be understood;
- *coherent* in that it hangs together in a transparent and meaningful way for the learner;
- *concrete* in that it is 'at a level of familiarity that is appropriate for the learner';
- *conceptual* in that it based on potentially meaningful 'material that explains how some systems operate';
- *correct* in that it corresponds to the actual situation to be understood;
- *considerate* in that it is presented in a manner that uses vocabulary and organizations appropriate to the learner.

The success of Mayer's models can be understood in terms of working memory action. For instance, a complete, concise, coherent, concrete and considerate model reduces processing demands. A conceptual and correct model provide the basis for something that is adequate to think with. Guiding attention to what is relevant reduces the need to maintain every detail in working memory pending decisions about what is important. Highlighting where internal and external connections are to be constructed also saves time and mental effort in what might be a fruitless search for them.

Bridging Gaps in Explanations

Explanations commonly describe an argument, a proof or a sequence of events with the expectation that the links in the chain will be apparent. Looking at textbook explanations, I felt that they sometimes took very large steps, leaving significant gaps that the reader would have to cross alone. Revising such texts to fill the gaps greatly enhanced understanding. For example, in an explanation of the image in a simple camera, one text offered a diagram and the general explanation that, 'The picture was made by some of these rays which pass through the pinhole and strike the screen'. This vague description leaves it to the reader to infer the reason for the inversion of the image. Another text bridged the gap by providing the reason: 'the rays of light cross over as they travel in straight lines through the pinhole'. This text was far more effective in supporting understanding than the first, producing roughly twice as many correct answers on tests of understanding (Newton, 1995). The instructional load had been reduced and the readers could maintain and update a mental representation of the developing situation.

Fewer of them lost the thread of the argument. Bridging in this way tends to make explanations longer so the time taken to read them is greater, but the gain is usually worth it.

In Mayer's terms, incomplete explanations give rise to problematic gaps. When a learner cannot cope with such gaps understanding becomes, at best, fragmented. Parts of the explanation may be understood, but they are not integrated into a coherent whole. When the understanding of one stage is crucial to the understanding of the next, insurmountable gaps can be disastrous. Problematic gaps are an example of what Sweller called imposed instructional load; that is, the load created by the instructor in addition to that supplied by the topic. Filling the gaps solves the problem, but the gaps are not always apparent to those who already understand the topic. An expert's knowledge may be such that reasoning is automatic and hardly reaches consciousness. Consequently, it is easy to leave much unsaid.

The work of Beck et al. (1991: 257) illustrates the improvement in understanding that can result from taking into account pre-requisites, gap bridging and some other aspects of explaining. They list a number of reasons why a reader may fail to make connections amongst the elements of information:

- inadequate background knowledge
- the use of references that are ambiguous, distant or indirect
- the lack of information to activate an appropriate context
- the lack of clear connections between events
- the inclusion of irrelevant events and ideas
- a high density of concepts

They tested their ideas by revising a history text for 10-year-olds. They clarified, elaborated, provided missing information and made connections explicit in the text. The effect was to make the text much longer but the gains were significant. For example, the original text began:

> In 1763 Britain and the colonies ended a 7-year war with the French and Indians.

This was replaced by:

> About 250 years ago, Britain and France both claimed to own some of the same land, here, in North America. The land was just west of where the 13 colonies were. In 1756, Britain and France went to war to see who would get control of this land. Because the 13 American colonies belonged to Britain, the colonists fought on the same side as Britain. Many Indians fought on the same side as France. Because we were fighting against the French and Indians, the war has come to be known as the French and Indian War. The war ended in 1763.

Not all revisions will need such extensive supplementation, but this illustrates well how much knowledge is often assumed in discourse. The quality of the learning can be greatly enhanced. In this instance, recall showed more elaboration and more appropriate reason-giving for the revised explanation. While this relates to textual explanations, its lessons for verbal explanations are apparent. Prior knowledge is crucially important, and excessive processing demands cause difficulties.

There is a natural tendency to assume that we should always aim to minimize instructional load. Should we always do so? There is evidence that children of 10 years and more with some knowledge of a topic benefit from the presence of some gaps (McNamara et al., 1996). Schnotz (1993) tested 'discontinuous' text on university students and, as expected, found that it proved to be more difficult to understand. Those with prior knowledge, however, processed the text more intensively. It appears that two distinct strategies are used. In 'continuous' text with fewer gaps, effort is directed towards constructing a mental model. In 'discontinuous' text, mental model construction is postponed pending the collection of further information. Those with greater prior knowledge are better equipped to bridge gaps and construct tentative and final models. Perhaps those with the requisite background should be encouraged to use it, but care will still be needed if the gaps are not to be so large that the learner will be defeated or demoralized. Whether or not the gaps should be bridged depends on the prior knowledge of the students and their ability and willingness to use it. Someone who does not know the state of a student's prior knowledge cannot afford to leave large gaps in explanations. When you are teaching your grandmother to suck eggs, this is soon apparent in face-to-face teaching and explanations can be tuned accordingly. The text writer, however, has more difficulty. This issue is returned to in Chapter 7.

While explaining can be effective, it can also benefit from support just as other strategies can benefit from explaining. For example, telling learners what doubling the pull on an elastic band does to its length and why this happens is likely to be made more effective if the explanation is supported by a visual demonstration. It may be made more effective still by letting learners try it for themselves, thereby associating the feeling of the pull with the visible effect on the length of the elastic band. It is also likely that this experience would precede the explanation, ensuring that the requisite knowledge is present. Equally, the children are likely to be called on to attempt an explanation for themselves. In practice, explaining can be made very effective if it is supplemented by other strategies. One of these is questioning.

Focused Questioning

Questioning is considered to be a useful strategy (see for example Kamchak and Eggen, 1993) and teachers often ask lots of questions. The problem is that there is a tendency to ask questions as though they are rice thrown at a wedding. Throwing out lots of questions makes the teacher feel good. They often do little to support understanding but the answers that come back make it feel productive. Carefully focused questions, on the other hand, make all the difference. Focused questions are those aimed at a particular target. The target is determined by the stage of the instruction and the nature of the understanding to be supported. Yekovich et al. (1991) state conditions necessary for inferencing. There must be relevant, accessible prior knowledge or it must be provided or constructed; the relationships must be known or capable of construction; the relevant and irrelevant must be discriminated; and a need for inferencing has to be recognized.

To start with, the target is likely to be pre-requisite knowledge. Questions, therefore, are aimed at stimulating recall of pre-requisites and, perhaps, practising it. They also serve to indicate where prior knowledge is deficient and needs to be made good. Later, the focus will have moved to constructing a relationship so the questions will be about that relationship. In other words, the nature of the question matches the immediate aim of the stage of instruction. Teachers and textbooks often ask mainly factual questions, regardless of the stage (Newton, 1997).

Here are some examples of focused questions in the context of teaching about elementary electricity. They might, for instance, be used to:

1 Set the scene and establish relevance *(Did you see the news about the power cut? Is it important? Why?)*.
2 Elicit relevant prior knowledge, to bring it into conscious thought *(Who can tell me how a torch works?)*.
3 Process this knowledge or develop new knowledge that will be needed in the understanding *(Suppose the torch is switched off, how does this stop the light from coming on?)*.
4 Focus attention on relevant parts of a situation to ensure that they are encoded in the situation model *(Why won't this torch work? Do you think the bulb might be faulty? How could we check it? Would a magnifying glass help?)*.
5 Deflect attention away from irrelevant aspects of a situation so that they do not figure largely in the processing of the mental representation of the situation *(Watch, I'll take it apart so we can see what's inside. What's this mess on the battery?)*.
6 Require predictions about the development of a situation and ensure that the basis of these predictions (articulation of the mental representation) is appropriate *(What would happen if I fastened this wire between there and there?)*.
7 Compare the final state of the event with the predicted state *(Is that what you expected to happen?)*.

8   Rehearse and integrate the process *(So, when we have a break in a circuit, what does it mean? How could be find out where the break is?).*

Not all of these stages are always needed, but it is likely that more than one question in any stage will be necessary to explore fully the various aspects of understanding to be fostered.

Forced Prediction

A particular kind of the focused question is worth special mention. Some learners may construct a mental representation of an initial situation and one of its final state but not link the two together in a causal way. They may not, for instance, know that they are expected to do so (see Yekovich et al.'s (1991) preconditions) or some may choose not to do so in an avoidance of mental effort. If the learners could be put in a position where they were obliged to link the two in a particular way, there is the possibility of understanding.

Newton (1994b) tested forced prediction as a means of doing this. Learners were required to predict step-wise from the initial state to the final state. For example, suppose that the temperature of a material was taken every two minutes and found to be 15, 21, 27, 33, 33, 33, 45, 57 and 69°C. Many glance at this and characterize it as representing an increase in temperature. But the reality is more complex. There is a steady, slow increase, followed by a steady state, followed by a rapid increase at twice the rate of the slow increase. Presenting these figures piecemeal to Year 6, 7 and 8 students (10–13 years) and asking for a prediction about the next temperature was found to be a very effective support strategy for developing a mental representation of the pattern in the data. For example, at the start, the temperature is 15°C, and after two minutes it is 21°C; what will it be after four minutes? This forced prediction gave rise to a richer mental representation of the situation described by the data. This is not to say that the students were more likely to recall the exact figures but more of them did recall the patterns in the data, namely, a slow rise, a steady state, followed by a rapid rise.

'What do you think will happen next?' is the kind of question which might be asked in many situations and events. Children's ability to predict increases steadily with age. By about 9 years of age, many can make a rational prediction but much younger children can often make a prediction, given appropriate conditions such as a story-like context (McNay, 1993; Harlen, 1985). Prediction obliges the learner to attend to the information, to process it and notice patterns and relationships which enable a prediction to be made. Understanding becomes a pre-condition of responding to the question. Having established an understanding which captures the patterns, the details may be lost but the details are often not what is important.

Usually, it is the patterns, connections and relationships that are important. In the example, there was evidence of this when those who had captured the patterns attempted to reconstruct the data. Patterns were preserved in the figures they supplied, but these figures were not always those of the original data.

Scaffolds

Cognitive scaffolds are structures which guide mental processing. They focus attention on the task and area that is immediately relevant then shift it to the next task and area. Focused questioning does this. The question aims to stimulate thought about what is relevant at the time it is asked. Later questions refocus attention and require mental processing about the new cognitive task in hand. There are some related examples, such as *Critical Squares: Games of Critical Thinking and Understanding*, devised in Project Zero at the Harvard Graduate School of Education (Tishman and Andrade, 1997).

Critical Squares comprises a collection of games which, for instance, help the learner make connections with prior knowledge, identify what is relevant, understand a situation, identify reasons, find causes, extend and apply understanding, and reflect on the thinking processes. Groups of learners throw dice and play versions of tic-tac-toe, which determines who answers the preset questions. For example, if you cast the die in the 'Whyzit' game (the Whyzit being an object of study, such as civilization), it might come up with the question: 'What is an unusual purpose of the Whyzit?, or, 'All players: brainstorm at least four ways to change the Whyzit to make it better...'

We might expect such games to support understanding because they mobilize relevant prior knowledge and reduce instructional demand by directing attention to what matters and by sequencing the mental processing. *Think Trix* achieves this using cue cards (Adger et al., 1995). The teacher has cards with symbols which indicate to the student that they should attempt recall, look for cause/effect, go from the example to an idea, go from an idea to an example, look for a similarity, or look for a difference. Learners are first trained in the meaning of the cues and practise responding to them. Later, the teacher holds up the card as a cue when the stage of a discussion is reached where one of these is appropriate. The long-term aim is to develop a degree of autonomy in the learners so that they become able to use the symbols themselves to stimulate their responses.

Another strategy that the authors recommend is the graphic organizer. This is a scaffold in the form of a picture, diagram or chart which guides the learner's thought. It need not be a comprehensive guide, and is often focused on a particular cognitive task. A cue card which asks for a comparison to be made, for instance, does not provide guidance at a finer level. The graphic organizer is often used for that purpose. For example, Bulgren and Scanlon

(1998) describe a 'concept diagram' for Settlers. There is a space for the learner to list key words, a space for the central concept (Settlers) and for the subsuming concept (People), lines for the attributes shared by all settlers, lines for those shared by some, and lines for those never present. Areas are set aside for the listing of specific examples, tied to the attributes, and for a definition of the term Settler. The student's task is to supply the information. Other charts facilitate the differentiation of concepts. Figure 5.1 illustrates a concept diagram relating to an aspect of understanding.

Roth (1990) reminds us of the use of flowcharts, rather like cartoon strips, to sequence procedures and concept maps for showing relationships. Boyle and Yeager's study guides for whole topics provide a more extensive framework to support learning. They comprise the objectives, the reading that has to be done, key words, a list of activities and some guidance on self-assessment. Story maps, on the other hand, are rather like concept maps which connect the setting (characters, time and place), problem, goal, action and resolution. Such maps could be applied in other areas to connect important events, main ideas, other significant ideas and the outcome (Boyle and Yeager, 1997). The long-term aim is for students to adapt and use them themselves. Some scaffolds can be so cumbersome and specific that it is unlikely

Figure 5.1   A concept diagram for comparing maths understanding and science understanding. Those aspects of understanding that they share are entered in the central column; those aspects which are unique to each are entered on either side.

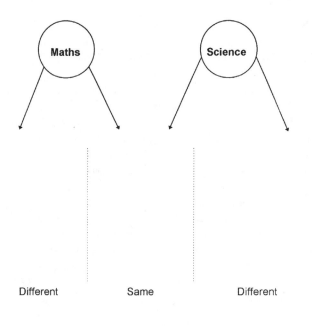

that students will use them unprompted and may be unable to adapt them for other uses.

Scaffolds have often been developed outside the framework described here, but the support they offer is readily explained by it. They provide structure and organize the process of understanding a body of knowledge. In doing so, they reduce processing load and focus attention on what is relevant.

Reducing Processing Load

The ability to solve problems is considered to be valuable. It seems reasonable to expect that giving novices problems to solve will help them to develop that ability. This assumption is not necessarily true. Novices in a particular problem area tend to use a means-end analysis to solve a problem. Means–end analysis is when someone works backwards from the goal to the given. It is an effective strategy in that it solves the problem, but it is often very demanding and imposes large processing loads. The result is that insufficient mental capacity is left for acquiring strategies (schemas and scripts) for working forwards, in the way that an expert in the field would do. In other words, problem solving can actually hinder the acquisition of expert-like behaviour, contrary to expectations.

Sweller (1994) compared the effects of examples as models for problem solving with problem solving *per se*. He also tested the effect of deflecting learners from using a means–end approach in the early stage of solving a particular problem. This he did by making the activity more open in outcomes. For example, one which stimulates a means–end analysis would be: $(a+b)/c=d$, find a.

One strategy to avoid a means–end approach would be to present the equation and invite the students to find out what they can do with it. In effect, this makes the task goal-free. Conventionally, the learner's goal is stated. This often requires a number of steps or stages to achieve. The learner has not yet acquired chunks of strategies which help in the recognition and solution of a problem. Instead, they must hold all details in working memory and process them until some solution emerges. Removing the goal can reduce the instructional demand placed on the learner. Sweller illustrates this, as shown in Figure 5.2.

Sweller concluded that practice in attempting to solve lots of problems is an inefficient strategy for bringing about the learning of moves and transformations. More open activities are needed to begin with. When moves and transformations become more or less automatic, that is the time to practise problem solving: 'Well learned material can be processed automatically without conscious effort allowing attention to be directed elsewhere.' Sweller does, however, point out that the effect is usually only important when the task is demanding. An easy task places a low burden on the

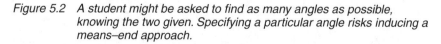

Figure 5.2 A student might be asked to find as many angles as possible, knowing the two given. Specifying a particular angle risks inducing a means–end approach.

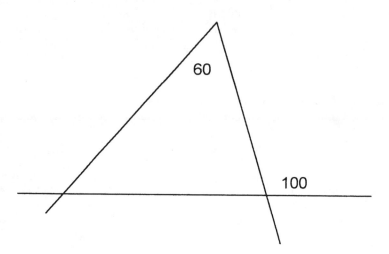

learner, so a further reduction of processing load will have no noticeable effect. (This is important when testing strategies. The task has to be demanding enough for a strategy to show its potential. Care has to be taken not to conclude that strategies are ineffective when they are tested on lightweight tasks.)

Sweller and his co-workers have also found that worked examples are more effective than problem solving in supporting schema acquisition and rule automation (Owen and Sweller, 1985; Cooper and Sweller, 1987; Tarmizi and Sweller, 1988; Sweller, 1989). If examples are all of the same kind, learners may be unable to solve problems that are different to the examples. Increasing the variety of examples, on the other hand, may increase the cognitive load. Paas and Merrienboer (1994) showed this is true but the gains outweigh the cost. If the variety in the examples is carefully managed and structured, the load need not be excessive. Improved schemas are formed and later problem solving is enhanced. Of course, worked examples may not actively engage the student to any great extent. Active engagement can be enhanced by a transition to partially completed examples which the student must complete.

While the nature of what is to be learned is fixed by the interactivity of its elements, we may present a task in different ways. To facilitate understanding, we might aim to reduce this instructional demand. Examples and partially completed solutions to problems which the learner must complete are instances.

Supporting Mental Processes

The impact of note-taking on learning is positive, at least amongst older students. Lecturers who discourage note-taking generally reduce learning. Cohn et al. (1995) have found that note-takers have a better quality of learning. Why might this be? First, note-takers have to select what is significant and summarize it. Done properly, this requires some active processing, that is, mental engagement. Second, the paper can act as an extension to working memory and allow many more things to be stored than could be held at once in the head. Nevertheless, I do not think that this would apply to all note-taking. Some students have the habit of attempting to catch every word. At times, their mental processes must be hard-pressed dividing attention between the written record which, by its nature, must be behind the verbal discourse, and the current state of the discourse. They probably need to be taught how to take notes selectively, and lecturers may help them with advice and timely pauses.

'The palest ink is worth more than the most retentive memory', and so, since working memory has a limited capacity, it makes sense to encourage students to think on paper when the load is well beyond their capacity (Ellis and Beattie, 1986). In a study of the support which pencil and paper can offer, I asked adults to solve some problems of the kind commonly found in 'intelligence' tests. For example, 'Imagine a line of six trees, J, K, L, M, N and O. J is taller than K, L is taller than M, L is smaller than K, N is taller than O, N is smaller than M. Which is the smallest?' This kind of problem is reminiscent of Johnson-Laird's syllogistic reasoning tasks outlined in Chapter 3. Mental representations of each relationship can be constructed, compared and synthesized to produce a solution but the demand for capacity is significant. If, however, each relationship is depicted on paper it becomes relatively simple. 'Taller' readily translates into a longer line or larger figure and the smallest is more or less immediately visible.

Even relationships that are non-spatial can be translated into a spatial equivalent. Possession, for instance, may be translated into a spatial relationship. 'John has a red sweater and a blue sweater', is often shown by writing 'John' with two lines connected to words or signs representing the sweaters. When a relationship can be depicted spatially, pencil and paper can be a useful extension to working memory. It could be useful to have learners practise using them and supplementing their repertoire of strategies with Venn diagrams, tables and graphs, provided that these are meaningful and not mechanical exercises (Newton and Merrell, 1994b). Student-generated diagrams can be more effective than verbal summaries for supporting the learning of relationships (Cheng, 1999; Gobert and Clement, 1999)

Supporting Unconscious Processes

Given a problem to solve or situation to be understood and faced with an initial failure on the part of the learner, unconscious processes might be enlisted. Here, a well-prepared mind often helps. A period of time is now allowed to lapse, allowing time for old tracks to fade and connections to be made. So that the initial information is not eliminated from the undermind, it might be reviewed occasionally then allowed to lapse again. Finally, it is brought back into consciousness and discussed again, perhaps from a new perspective.

A complex situation could also be addressed initially by the unconscious mind. Experience of the situation in which the learner must respond but does not have to reflect upon allows an opportunity for patterns in the situation to be assimilated. Having had the learners respond to the situation directly, approaches that emphasize conscious reflection would now be used to build up a structure which the learner also feels to be intuitively sound. As unconscious learning can be difficult to change, the experience must not risk developing inappropriate learning (Finke and Bettle, 1996). For instance, the kind of general experience someone has of objects floating and sinking can develop an understanding which is limited or unsound. Providing experience as a precursor to a conscious understanding of flotation means that the objects have to be carefully selected to demonstrate clearly the relationship targeted, in this instance perhaps *light for its size*.

Supporting Particular Kinds of Understanding

Much of what has been said so far could apply to several learning contexts. The nature of understanding, however, also varies from subject to subject. This gives rise to strategies that apply in a relatively limited number of contexts. Although perhaps seen as subject-specific strategies, some can be adapted for wider application.

Literature

In studying literature, an aim is for students to understand its form and function, the characters and their actions and the relationships between them. There are various strategies for achieving the aim. For example, 12-year-olds may list questions they would like to ask the characters, write a character journal, take the part of a character and respond to the questions of others (Van Horn, 1997). These are intended to oblige the student to engage mentally with the situation and draw on their own experience. A strategy with older students is to allocate them a different chapter of a book to read. Each presents their interpretation of that chapter to the class to form a 'jigsaw overview of the whole book' (Kohleffel, 1996). As each chapter is presented, those waiting their turn will, presumably, reconsider their interpretations until they have a coherent and consistent account. Once again, active engagement in looking for connections and links is essential.

Marshall (1987) has described how writing about literature helped 16-year-olds form 'relationships amongst ideas that may not have existed before'. He tested the effect of restricted writing, personal analytic writing and formal analytic writing. The restricted writing assignment comprised short-answer questions requiring description, interpretation and generalization (What does John look like? Why is John aggressive with Peter? Was Peter right to treat Jill the way he did?). The personal analytic writing required the students to 'explain and elaborate' their responses to the story. An event is drawn from the story and the student must write an essay explaining their own feelings about a particular aspect of the event. The formal writing assignment was similar, but students had to confine their inferences and conclusions to the textual evidence.

The extended writing opportunities of the personal analytic and formal writing tasks were both superior to the restricted task in enhancing students' reasoned interpretation of the literature. The formal writing task, however, tended to encourage students to look for an authoritative response and closed down other possibilities. The personal analytic task allowed the students to draw on their personal knowledge, values and experience of the world.

This is an interesting study in that it illustrates that understanding is likely to develop during writing about the subject. Composing a written response is not just a process of reporting what is in the mind; the task calls for an organization of ideas and a noticing and seeking of relationships which might not have occurred otherwise. Being a slower and potentially more deliberate process than verbal reporting, rather in tune with the pace of reflection and mental processing, the opportunity is there for the writer to continue the mental engagement with the task. It also allows time for unconscious processing to take place. The nature of these tasks, unlike the restricted writing task, provided the opportunity for a more integrated understanding to be established and longer range connections to be made. The potential value of extended writing in other curriculum areas should not be ignored.

Mathematics

In mathematics, there is an interesting difficulty which often arises when children progress from multiplying by whole numbers greater than one to multiplying by numbers between one and zero. The children can often describe how to solve such a multiplication problem when numbers are absent, but fail to do it when numbers less than one are inserted. It seems that they do not give their general procedure the priority it should have. The change in the problem seems to make children believe that some other procedure is needed. Hardiman and Mestre (1989) suggest that a solution is to have children practise with number-free problems, discussing how they will solve them. Presumably, there is also a need for the children to know the range of problems that a procedure will solve and that, although they will begin with a particular subset, they will go on to others.

The value of discussion in general in mathematics was suggested in the Cockcroft Report (1982) and has been justified in longitudinal studies such as that of Brenner et al. (1997). The point is that it is important to get underneath the surface of a subject and understand why things work and why they are as they are. In mathematics, it might mean why a particular algorithm is successful and why it has a certain range of application. This is, after all, the meaning of 'I under-stand': it is knowing what underpins the surface features that we see, live with and use.

An additional difficulty with mathematics is that the language is already a précis (Byers and Erlwanger, 1985). At school, I was always impressed by the way Latin collapses a piece of English into a small space. Maths does it with a vengeance. Many will benefit from practice in interpreting it. Nevertheless, even when mathematics is presented largely in words, as in a word problem, there is often difficulty in grasping its meaning, that is, in mentally representing it. Strategies which help are translating the problem into a diagram, picture or verbal summary. Brenner et al. (1997) showed the value of having learners represent a problem in several different ways (words, tables, graphs and symbols) before attempting its solution. The act of translating involves a mental engagement with the problem; more than one form of translation opens the possibility of noticing and inferring connections and links that might otherwise be missed. Equally, some students may perform better with one representation rather than another, and introducing several representations gives them that opportunity.

Something which cannot be ignored in any subject is mental development and experience. Dehaene (1997) has pointed out that we are born with a numerosity that allows us to know what one and two mean and, with progressively less precision, larger numbers. For this reason, he advises that mathematical instruction should begin with integers and should be concrete rather than be concerned with, for instance, number bases. In short, he says there should be a 'primacy of intuition over formal axioms'. Correa et al. (1998) describe how young children's addition and subtraction is based on their pre-school modeling with objects and their division is based on the sharing of such objects. This means that an understanding of the operation of division is incomplete since it encompasses more than sharing.

Multiplication is similarly limited. Between about 5 and 12 years, children develop various understandings of 'multiplication'. It can mean, for instance, three lots of four, 3 times 4, 3×4, 3 fours, $4+4+4$, or 1, 2, 3, 4, 5, 6, 7, **8**, 9, 10, 11, **12**. Their unification produces a less fragmented understanding. When a child knows that all these mean the same thing, the number fact 3(4) amounts to 12, a general solution that is economical and that places less demand on mental capacity is possible (Anghileri, 1989). This is not to say that the earlier understandings are not important or should not be developed; they are what give meaning to the number fact. Pirie and Kieren (1994) have described growth in mathematical understanding as having levels. They call the first 'primitive knowing', the initial or starting point knowledge. The second, they call 'image making'. This represents an ability to 'use a mental construct without having to do the particular activities which brought it about'. It means there is a freedom from the physical actions used to learn an operation when solving a problem. At a higher level is 'property noticing', which, as the name suggests, implies that properties of operations are noted and used. Beyond this is a 'formalizing' level in which methods work independent of the specific kinds of number they apply to. Presumably, children who can 'solve' numberless multiplication but fail when numbers between zero and one are not at the formalizing level. This emphasizes that development, experience and prior knowledge cannot be ignored and that understanding is not fixed but, we hope, develops with time.

Science

The opportunity for misconstruing active participation and the personal nature of understanding is evident in science teaching. Practical work can be a powerful tool for supporting understanding but, in practice, things are not quite as simple as giving learners an 'experiment' and leaving them to it.

If the intention is to develop an understanding of scientific investigation, the nature of scientific evidence or of some procedure then a learner might investigate scientifically or carry out a procedure. This direct experience might develop understanding, perhaps even unconsciously. However, this experience is really the raw material to work with and a teacher needs to draw out from it what is relevant, ask questions to help the learner make links and make their understanding open to reflection. Merely performing a task may be insufficient to develop a particular kind of understanding fully. It cannot be left entirely to chance as misconceptions could be as likely to arise as satisfactory conceptions. Explanations, discussions, questions and scaffolds can be relevant in practical work.

If attention is on supporting the understanding of a concept, phenomenon or event, then again direct experience of these is likely to be helpful. But again, this experience is the raw material to work with. Further, this experience may form a basis for an investigation and this, in turn, may strengthen the relationships, patterns and connections noticed before. But, once again, misconceptions can develop unless thinking is monitored and supported (Cavalcante et al., 1997).

Active participation in learning means active mental participation. This can be achieved in a number of ways. One of these is to use a practical activity, particularly where experience of concepts, phenomena, events, and procedures is limited. But, this does not mean it is the only way. For instance, case studies outlining an investigation can also be useful. Conant (1957) was aware of this when he wrote his book *On Understanding Science*, and Sutton (1996) argues that 'the scientist's story is what is important'. The point is that a narrow view of active engagement can deny the learner the range of support that they might find useful. This support could be both hands-on and hands-off. What the hands do may count for little if the mind is not active and engaged.

History

It might seem that a subject like history would present few problems when it came to supporting understanding. Knight (1990), for instance, describes the value of asking the question 'why?' in history at Key Stage 2 (7 to 11 years), and Brophy (1990) writes of the importance of aiming for a coherent and global understanding rather than a fragmented one based on knowledge of isolated scraps of history. Gibson and McLelland (1998) describe what amounts to a scaffolding game requiring the identification and linking of various kinds of historical cause to tell a sequential story. All are concerned with support like that which could be found elsewhere, allowing for differences in the nature of the subject. Nevertheless, it has its unique problems.

Young children can, for instance, distinguish pictures of places and people according to the period but have difficulty with the significance of dates, historical periods or epochs (Barton and Levstik, 1996). On the other hand, some are aware of the ambiguity of the word 'history' and its several meanings. One boy, for instance, illustrated this through his mother's warning: 'Touch the china and you're history' (Levstik and Pappas, 1987). Nevertheless, there are differences between 7 and 11-year-olds that cannot be ignored, and many of these are differences of degree. The linking of history to chronology, an understanding of 'history as the significant past' and of conflict, for instance, develops steadily between these ages. Similarly, older children may move from believing the past is a given, to the past as being reported in a more or less biased way, to the past as a rational reconstruction in response to a question (Lee, 1998). Levstik and Pappas (1987) recommend that younger children be exposed to history through historical fiction. They see this as worthwhile as it is likely to support the development of ideas about the nature of history. But note that it also draws on our ready ability to process and grasp narrative presented in a chronological manner.

Art

As Erickson (1995) points out, there is a tendency for children to use pictures as windows rather than as objects of art. This is often reinforced by the use of pictures in other subjects as windows on the world. Erickson set out to overcome this with children of about 7 years of age and develop in them an understanding of art. According to Parsons (1987), there are stages of aesthetic understanding which, notwithstanding various criticisms (Di Blasio, 1988), have been fairly well confirmed. These stages generally progress from an intuitive delight with colour and associations, through a valuing of realism and skill, an awareness of the artist, an appreciation of a painting tradition, to evaluating art within a tradition. We might expect young children to be in the earliest stages. Over a year, Erickson had such children select pictures. Each was accompanied by information about the picture and its context, written in a way which acknowledged the children's age and experience. There were also questions for them to answer, such as, 'Why do you think the artist made the artwork look the way it does?' By the end of the year, she found that many children could take the artist's perspective and they showed they could view it with an awareness that it was painted when things and attitudes were different. She concludes that this kind of understanding of art, not generally found among primary school children, may be developed by this kind of instruction. Indeed, Schiller (1995) claims some progress in this direction, with pre-school children using pictures and discussion. Using active engagement in the sense of doing, de Prenger (1985) also claims progress in art appreciation by having primary children paint a picture in the style of an artist.

Traditionally, teachers have children paint pictures. The experience probably supports an unconscious understanding of the medium and its purpose. These examples illustrate that other kinds of understanding in a subject exist and ways may be found to support them. I will conclude with one example to illustrate the roles of the teacher and the student in developing understanding.

Games

Playing a game can be learned largely unconsciously through practice. Tactics and responses to particular kinds of situations develop with experience – or may not. To support the process of understanding tactics and applying that understanding, Turner and Martinek (1995) and Werner et al. (1996) suggest one kind of approach. The teacher sets up the game form, usually with small teams. He or she observes the play, and the teacher and students investigate tactical problems and potential solutions. The teacher observes the game again and the process repeats. Turner (1996) and Curtner-Smith (1996) confirm that such an approach can be effective. Note throughout the roles of the teacher and students. The play is monitored and evaluated and students are actively supported in solving problems. Neither the giver nor the receiver of support is passive. This press is a characteristic of providing support for understanding, whatever the subject.

Practice and Theory

Over the years, teachers develop strategies for achieving particular ends. Amongst these are strategies which, in certain circumstances, support understanding. These need not be abandoned (Cavalcante et al., 1997). What is needed is a structure to refine these strategies to maximize their effect and something to underpin new ideas for supporting understanding. At the same time, being aware that a strategy provides a particular kind of support enables a teacher to use it selectively and in a more focused and thoughtful way. It can also sensitize them to any imbalance in their teaching which may occur from time to time.

Taking all this together, support for understanding should target:

- ways of checking, supplementing and activating relevant prior knowledge (e.g., Yekovich et al.'s pre-conditions);
- ways of helping the construction of an initial representation of a situation (e.g., the Rosie Rabbit experiment);
- where appropriate, ways of directing attention to what is relevant and on the simplification and idealization of the initial representation in order to simplify processing and reduce load (e.g., focused questioning);
- ways of requiring the learner to alter, update or articulate the representation (e.g., forced prediction);
- ways of reducing the processing load during articulation (e.g., scaffolding, making connections explicit);
- ways of checking the basis of the articulation (e.g., focused questioning), and ways of checking the outcome of articulation (e.g., focused questioning);
- ways of reducing working memory load (e.g., with pencil and paper);
- ways of engaging unconscious processes in the endeavour (e.g., through direct experience).

This chapter has illustrated the nature of support for understanding and has questioned some assumptions and tendencies. This does not exhaust the kinds of support that might be provided. The next chapter considers the support offered by analogies.

Summary

Failure to understand may stem from a variety of sources. For instance, the learner may fail to construct a mental representation, to simplify, idealize or attend to what is relevant in the representation, to update, manipulate or articulate the representation, to recognize that the manipulation of the representation is required, and to cope with the mental load. In addition, the learner may construct a representation that is irrelevant, manipulate a representation by reference to some misconception, or construct a representation but omit a causal mechanism when it is expected.

Reducing the likelihood of failure is less a particular style of teaching than an orientation. Teachers may foster understanding through very different kinds of lessons. Teaching for understanding need not mean that a teacher must abandon a particular approach that they feel is appropriate for themselves and their students. There should, however, be a press for understanding and this means that both the teacher and the students will be actively engaged in it. The press for understanding can be supported with conceptual structures, by bridging inferential gaps, by supplementing explanations, using focused questioning, forced prediction, scaffolds, by reducing the processing load with pencil and paper and by engaging unconscious processes. While these may be used in a wide variety of situations, subject-specific constraints cannot be ignored. At the same time, there are subject-specific strategies which will supplement the general strategies. Some of these may lend themselves to adaptation for use in other areas.

References

Ablard, K.E. and Lipschultz, R.E. (1998) 'Self-Regulated Learning in High-Achieving Students', *Journal of Educational Psychology* 90: 94–101.

Adger, C.T., Kalynapur, M., Blount Peterson, D. and Bridger, T. L. (1995) *Engaging Students: Thinking, Talking, Cooperating*, Los Angeles, CA and London: Corwin/Sage.

Anghileri, J. (1989) 'An Investigation of Young Children's Understanding of Multiplication', *Educational Studies in Mathematics* 20: 367–85.

Asoko, H. (1996) 'Developing Scientific Concepts in the Primary Classroom: Teaching About Electric Circuits', in G. Welford, J. Osborne and P. Scott, *Research in Science Education in Europe*, London: Falmer, 36–49.

Barton, K.C. and Levstik, L.S. (1996) 'Back when God was Around and Everything', *American Educational Research Journal* 33: 419–54.

Becher, T. (1994) 'The Significance of Disciplinary Differences', *Studies in Higher Education* 19: 151–61.

Beck, I.L., McKeown, M.G., Sinatra, G.M. and Loxterman, J.A. (1991) 'Revising Social Studies Text from a Text Processing Perspective: Evidence of Improved Comprehensibility', *Reading Research Quarterly* 26: 251–76.

Boyle, J.R. and Yeager, N. (1997) 'Blueprints for Learning', *Teaching Exceptional Children* 29: 26–31.

Brenner, M.E. et al. (1997) 'Learning by Understanding: The Role of Multiple Representations in Learning Algebra', *American Educational Research Journal* 34: 663–89.

Brown, B. (1998) 'Language, Lectures and Learning: A Language-Based Approach to Increasing Understanding', *Education* 118: 384–93.

Brown, G.A. and Atkins, M.J. (1988) 'Explaining in Professional Contexts', *Research Papers in Education* 1: 60–86.

Brophy, J. (1990) 'Teaching Social Studies for Understanding and Higher-Order Applications', *The Elementary School Journal* 90: 351–417.

Bulgren, J. and Scanlon, D. (1998) 'Instructional Routines and Learning Strategies that Promote Understanding of Content Area Concepts', *Journal of Adolescent and Adult Literacy* 41: 292–302.

Byers, V. and Erlwanger, S. (1985) 'Memory in Mathematical Understanding', *Educational Studies in Mathematics* 16: 259–81.

Cavalcante, P.S., Newton, D.P. and Newton, L.D. (1997) 'The Effect of Various Kinds of Lesson on Conceptual Understanding in Science', *Research in Science and Technological Education* 15: 185–93.

Cheng, P.C.-H. (1999) 'Interactive Law Encoding Diagrams for Learning and Instruction', *Learning and Instruction* 9: 309–25.

Cohn, E., Cohn, S. and Bradley, J. (1995) 'Notetaking, Working Memory, and Learning in Principles of Economics', *Journal of Economic Education* 20: 291–307.

Conant, J.B. (1957) *On Understanding Science*, New York: New American Library of World Literature.

Cooper, G. and Sweller, J. (1987) 'Effects of Schema Acquisition on Rule Automation and Mathematical Problem-Solving Transfer', *Journal of Educational Psychology* 79: 347–62.

Correa, J., Nunes, T. and Bryant, P. (1998) 'Young Children's Understanding of Division', *Journal of Educational Psychology* 90: 321–29.

Curtner-Smith, M.D. (1996) 'Teaching for Understanding: Using Games Invention with Elementary Children', *Journal of P.E., Recreation and Dance* 67: 33–37.

Dehaene, S. (1997) *The Number Sense*, London: Allen Lane.

Department of Education and Science (DES) (1982) *Mathematics Counts* (The Cockcroft Report), London: HMSO.

DiBlasio, M. (1988) 'Educational Implications of How We Understand Art: An Analysis', *Journal of Aesthetic Education* 22: 103–7.

Ellis, A. and Beattie, G. (1986) *The Psychology of Language and Communication*, London: Weidenfeld and Nicolson.

Erickson, M. (1995) 'Second Grade Students' Developing Art Historical Understanding', *Visual Arts Research* 21: 15–24.

Finke, R.A. and Bettle, J. (1996) *Chaotic Cognition*, Mahwah, NJ: Lawrence Erlbaum.

Garnett, P.J. and Tobin, K. (1988) 'Teaching for Understanding: Exemplary Practice in High School Chemistry', *Journal of Research in Science Teaching* 26: 1–14.

Gibson, I. and McLelland, S. (1998) 'Minimalist Cause Boxes for Maximal Learning', *Teaching History* 92: 26–8.

Gobert, J.D. and Clement, J.J. (1999) 'Effect of Student-Generated Diagrams versus Student-Generated Summaries on Conceptual Understanding of Causal and Dynamic Knowledge in Plate Tectonics', *Journal of Research in Science Teaching* 36: 39–53.

Harlen, W. (1985) *Teaching and Learning Primary Science*, London: Harper & Row.

Hardiman, P.T. and Mestre, J. P. (1989) 'Understanding Multiplicative Contexts Involving Fractions', *Journal of Educational Psychology* 81: 547–57.

Kamchak, D.P. and Eggen, P.D. (1993) *Learning and Teaching: Research Based Methods*, Boston: Allyn & Bacon, 2nd edn.

Kazemi, E. (1998) 'Discourse That Promotes Conceptual Understanding', *Teaching Children Mathematics* 4: 410–14.

Knight, P. (1990) 'A Study of Teaching and Children's Understanding of People in the Past', *Research in Education* 44: 39–53.

Kohleffel, R. (1996) 'Docendo Discimus', *Journal of Adolescent and Adult Literacy* 39: 650–53.

Lee, P. (1998) 'A Lot of Guess Work Goes On', *Teaching History* 92: 29–36.

Levstik, L.S. and Pappas, C.C. (1987) 'Exploring the Development of Historical Understanding', *Journal of Research and Development in Education* 21: 1–15.

Marshall, J.D. (1987) 'The Effects of Writing on Students Understanding of Literary Texts', *Research in the Teaching of English* 21: 30–63.

McNamara, D.S., Kintsch, E., Sanger, N.B. and Kintsch, W. (1996) 'Are Good Texts Always Better?' *Cognition and Instruction* 14: 1–43.

McNay, M. (1993) 'Children's Skills in Making Predictions and Their Understanding of What Predicting Means: A Developmental Study', *Journal of Research in Science Teaching* 30: 561–77.

Mayer, R.E. (1989) 'Systematic Thinking Fostered by Illustrations in Scientific Text', *Journal of Educational Psychology* 81: 240–6.

Nelson, K. (1986) *Event Knowledge*, Hillsdale, NJ: Lawrence Erlbaum.

Newton, D.P. (1994a) 'Pictorial Support for Discourse Comprehension', *British Journal of Educational Psychology* 64: 221–9.

—— (1994b) 'Supporting the Comprehension of Tabulated Data', *British Educational Research Journal* 20: 455–63.

—— (1995) 'Support for Understanding: Discourse Which Aids the Construction of a Functional Mental Model of Causal Situations', *Research in Science and Technological Education* 13: 109–22.

Newton, D.P. and Merrell, C. (1994a) 'Pictorial Support for Discourse Comprehension', *British Journal of Educational Psychology* 64: 221–9.

—— (1994b) 'Helping Children Notice Co-Variation in Tables: The Effect of Some Forms of Graphing', *Research in Education* 51: 41–50.

Newton, D.P. and Newton, L.D. (1994) 'Supporting the Comprehension of Tabulated Data', *British Educational Research Journal* 20: 455–63.

Newton, L.D. (1997) 'Teachers' Questioning for Understanding in Science', *British Journal of Curriculum and Assessment* 8: 28–32.

Owen, E. and Sweller, J. (1985) 'What do Students Learn While Solving Mathematics Problems?' *Journal of Educational Psychology* 77: 272–84.

Paas, F.G.W.C. and Merrienboer, J.J.G. (1994) 'Variability of Worked Examples and transfer of Geometrical Problem-Solving Skills: A Cognitive Load Approach', *Journal of Educational Psychology* 86: 122–33.

Parsons, M.J. (1987) *How We Understand Art: A Cognitive Account of the Development of Aesthetic Experience*, New York: Cambridge University Press.

Pirie, S. and Kieren, T. (1994) 'Growth in Mathematical Understanding: How Can We Characterise It and How Can We Represent It?', *Educational Studies in Mathematics* 26: 165–90.

Premack, D. and Premack, J. (1995) 'Levels of Causal Understanding in Chimpanzees and Children', in J. Mehler and S. Franck (eds), *Cognition on Cognition*, Bradford: MIT.

Prenger, K. de (1985) 'On Understanding: The Artist as a Model', *School Arts* 85: 14–15.

Putnam, R.T., Heaton, R.M., Prawat, R.S. and Remillard, J. (1992) 'Teaching Mathematics for Understanding: Discussing Case Studies of Fifth Grade Teachers', *The Elementary School Journal* 93: 213–28.

Riding, R. and Rayner, S. (1998) *Cognitive Styles and Learning Strategies*, London: Fulton.

Roth, W.M. (1990) 'Map Your Way to a Better Lab', *The Science Teacher* 57: 30–4.

Schiller, M. (1995) 'An Emergent Art Curriculum that Fosters Understanding', *Young Children* 50: 39–42.

Schnotz, W. (1993) 'Adaptive Construction of Mental Representations in Understanding Expository Texts', *Contemporary Educational Psychology* 18: 114–20.

Sternberg, R.J. (1985) *Intelligence Applied: Understanding and Increasing Your Intellectual Skills*, San Diego, CA: Harcourt Brace Jovanovich.

Sternberg, R.J., Torff, B. and Grigorenko, E.L. (1998) 'Teaching Triarchically Improves School Achievement', *Journal of Educational Psychology* 90: 374–84.

Sutton, C. (1996) 'The Scientific Model as a Form of Speech', in G. Welford, J. Osborne and P. Scott, *Research in Science Education in Europe*, London: Falmer, 143–52.

Sweller, H.L. and P. Chandler (1994) 'Why Some Material is Difficult to Learn', *Cognition and Instruction* 12: 185–233.

Sweller, J. (1989) 'Cognitive Technology, Some Procedures for Facilitating Learning and Problem Solving in Mathematics and Science', *Journal of Educational Psychology* 81: 457–66.

—— (1994) 'Cognitive Load Theory, Learning Difficulty, and Instructional Practice', *Learning and Instruction* 4: 285–312.

Tarmizi, R. and Sweller, J. (1988) 'Guidance During Mathematical Problem Solving', *Journal of Educational Psychology* 80: 424–36.

Tishman, S. and Andrade, A. (1997) *Critical Squares: Games of Critical Thinking and Understanding*, Englewood Cliffs, NJ: Teacher Ideas Press.

Turner, A. (1996) 'Teaching for Understanding: Myth or Reality?' *Journal of PE, Recreation and Dance* 67: 46–48.

Turner, A. and Martinek, J.J. (1995) 'Teaching for Understanding: A Model for Improving Decision Making During Game Play', *Quest*: 47–63.

Van Horn, L. (1997) 'The Characters Within Us: Readers Connect with Characters to Create Meaning and Understanding', *Journal of Adolescent and Adult Literacy* 40: 342–7.

Werner, P., Thorpe, R. and Bunker, D. (1996) 'Teaching Games for Understanding: Evolution of a Model', *Journal of P.E, Recreation and Dance* 67: 28–33.

Yekovich, F.R., Thompson, M.A. and Walker, C.H. (1991) 'Generation and Verification of Inferences by Experts and Trained Nonexperts', *American Educational Research Journal* 28: 189–209.

6 Supporting Understanding with Analogies

Overview

The nature of analogies is described and exemplified. Thinking with the help of analogies is a natural process that even young children seem able to handle, given certain conditions. This is illustrated. Various kinds of analogy are mentioned and how they can support understanding is discussed. Analogies may also help learners change their perspective or the way they look at the world. Nevertheless, they have limitations and how these might be dealt with is outlined. Steps for using analogies to support understanding are provided.

Analogies

The previous section focused attention on ways of supporting understanding from within a domain. Examples are drawn from the subject itself and are of the same kind as the situation we want students to think about. In mathematics, for instance, a teacher might illustrate how to solve a particular kind of problem with one of the same kind. This is sometimes referred to as literal, direct, same domain or homologous support for what is to be understood.

Understanding may also be supported using situations drawn from outside the domain. For example, in electronics, certain components behave like gates that open according to particular rules. Real gates are what we find in gardens and fields, not computers. They come from a different domain to the world of electronics but, nevertheless, the parallels can help us understand the function of certain electronic components. The gate is an analogous structure or an analogy for the component. Similarly, a narrow beam of light reflects off a mirror something like the way a ball bounces off a wall. Ball-bouncing belongs to a different domain to light-reflecting, but its action parallels that of light enough to make it useful in explaining reflection from a mirror.

An analogy is intended to support the process of reasoning by using a parallel situation. It is 'midway between the unintelligible and the commonplace' (Halpern et al., 1990). An analogy 'captures parallels across different situations...and can serve as a mental model for understanding a new domain' (Gentner, 1998). It allows knowledge in one domain to be used in another. For instance:

- in psychology the telephone exchange was once a common analogy used to explain the functions of the brain (today, it is not uncommon for the computer to have that role);
- in biology, the baking of a cake has been an analogy for photosynthesis;
- in archaeology, the process of excavation has been likened to the eating a trifle – it is destructive;
- in literature, Tolstoy's *War and Peace* compared the French Army to a herd of cattle trampling the fodder that might have saved it from starvation;
- in language, the pronunciation and inflexion of parts of speech may take the form of similar, known words, particularly when people encounter new words in print;
- in environmental studies, the Earth may be compared to Easter Island where overpopulation and exploitation led to societal collapse;
- analogies themselves have been described as families of resemblances.

Thinking and communicating through parallels is a natural process of human thought (Goswami, 1992). Metaphors serve a similar purpose in enabling us to think of one thing in terms of something else. For instance, we might describe the skeleton of a building, feet like lead, or feeling woolly-headed. Literary devices like these catch attention and make a point. As Samuel Johnson (1709–84) put it, metaphor and simile give you two ideas for one and convey meaning with a perception of delight.

At the same time, analogies are not always appropriate. For example, Campbell (1990) has questioned the use of oral language as an analogy for the acquisition of written language skills. Similarly, Thomas (1991) urges caution in drawing analogies between art in different domains, as between a play and a painting.

The Effect of Analogies

Analogies work because they facilitate the transfer of relationships from the known to the unknown, as in Figure 6.1 (Halpern et al., 1990). This looks like a mentally demanding task and Piagetian psychologists considered reasoning by analogy to develop after about 11 or 12 years of age, when there was some facility with formal operations and correlational reasoning (Zeitoun, 1984). Consequently, analogies have tended to be ignored as support for younger children's thinking. Goswami (1992), however, demonstrated that younger children are capable of analogical reasoning. For instance, children were shown pictures of a ball of Playdoh before and after it was cut. Another picture showed an apple. Children readily reasoned analogically and, from pictures of a cut cake, a bruised apple, a ball, a banana and a cut apple, chose the cut apple as the matching one for the Playdoh.

Goswami found that primary school children could cope with such tasks provided that they know what is expected of them and they understand the basis of the analogy. Problems can stem from a lack of knowledge of the analogical base and relationships with the target. Bearing in mind that analogical reasoning is bridging between known and unknown, this is not unreasonable. There can be no analogical reasoning if the analogical model is not known.

Hatano and Inagaki (1994) observed 5-year-olds using the needs of people as an analogy for the needs of plants. The reasoning went something like this. Plants have to be watered. Why? People need water; plants need water; they have to have a regular drink just as people do. Why do plants die if you give them too much water? If people were to drink too much, they would be ill, fall down and die. It is the same with plants. Similarly, they found 6-year-olds were able to explain a squirrel's sickness, weakness and the effects of old age by analogy with people. Gelman and Markman (1987) noted simple analogical reasoning as early as 3 and 4 years of age. Young children can also generate their own parallels. For example, one 6-year-old was able to depict the tune of 'Row, Row, Row Your Boat' using spaced lines of different lengths to represent phrase structure, rhythm and pitch (Davidson and Scripp, 1992).

The key to success is that what will serve as the analogical model is well-known to the learner. The limited experience of young children means that there may be only a small pot of knowledge to draw on. However, the

Figure 6.1   Analogical Reasoning

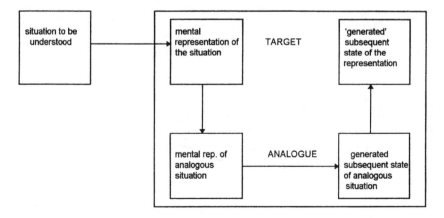

difficulty may be overcome by ensuring that the requisite knowledge is present. Newton and Newton (1995: 387) showed that spending a few minutes raising 6-year-olds' awareness of the flow of water when pumped through a tube by a soap dispenser makes it possible to use this as an effective analogy for teaching about simple electrical circuits (Figure 6.2).

Subsequent tests showed that the children could use this analogy to explain what happened in other electrical circuits. One child described the parallels in the following terms:

Child:	It's [electricity's] just…kind of…a bit like water. It's just going round and into the bulb.
Investigator:	What? The electricity's like water?
Child:	Yes.
Investigator:	How's the electricity like water?
Child:	Because, with the pump, you press that and the water goes round but that goes back to the bottle…Like, say that was the light bulb and this was the battery. Press that…Right? And it would go all into the battery.

Figure 6.2   *A Soap Dispenser and Tube Used to Model a Simple Electrical Circuit*

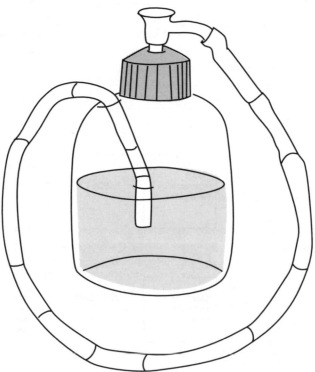

When faced with a circuit which had two opposing batteries and a bulb that did not come on, he was spontaneously able to explain it in terms of two soap dispensers and the opposing flows they were trying to induce.

Analogies have also been used to develop young children's vocabulary in a variety of subjects. Greenwood (1988) has pointed out that learning a list of words is a decontextualized task and risks acquired meanings being vague. Analogy exercises, on the other hand, provide a context and require the learner to engage mentally with the meaning. For example, 'book is to read as television is to...' provides a context to explore a variety of words of like meaning (HuffBenkoski and Greenwood, 1995). In music, inexperienced learners often lack a vocabulary for describing musical experience. Once again, analogy can help. For example, it might be spatial, as in using 'up' and 'down' to describe changes in pitch, or 'figure' and 'ground' to distinguish a musical element from its context (Froehlich and Cattley, 1991; Stollack and Alexander, 1998).

Analogies are not always effective. For instance, Giora (1993: 596) tested one on 13 to 30-year-olds:

> It has often occurred in the history of science that an important discovery was come upon by chance. A scientist looking into one matter, unexpectedly came upon another which was far more important than the one he was looking into. *Such scientists resemble Saul who, while looking for donkeys, found a kingdom.* Penicillin is a result of such a discovery.

The analogy has been highlighted with italics. One possible cause of a lack of effect may be that the topic is readily understood without support. As in providing any support for understanding, it only makes a difference when the topic is relatively difficult to understand. Another possibility is that the analogy is not a good one. The student must know what the analogical model means, must see it as apt and must use it.

Gilbert (1989: 324) also found little evidence of support in using an analogy in two biology units for 14 and 15-year-olds. For example, the analogy for: 'The placental apparatus conducts gas, food, and minerals to the fetus, and wastes away from it' was:

> The embryo is plugged into the mother in somewhat the same way as an electrical appliance is plugged into a socket on the wall. Using this model, we can think of the placenta as being the plug and the umbilical cord as being the electric cord. Instead of electricity, this placental apparatus conducts rivers of gas, food, and minerals to the fetus.

Again, the analogy may not be necessary, may not be good, or may be rendered worthless by the instructional load added to it by the revised text. For instance, it is probable that the reading comprehension demands of the revised text are greater than the original version. These possibilities have to be borne in mind when constructing an analogy.

Kinds of Analogy

Analogies may be classified in a variety of ways. For example, Thiele and Treagust (1994) classified them as *simple, enriched* or *extended*. Simple analogies were those which were statements without elaboration (for example, the spinal cord is like a cable). Enriched analogies included the grounds for the analogy (for example, wind carrying sand acts like a sandblasting machine. Sandblasting machines blow sand at stonework to wear away the dirty surface). Extended analogies apply to several topics (for example, atoms as billiard balls occur in several topics in several sciences).

Curtis and Reigeluth (1984) classified analogies into those that are *structural*, those that are *functional* and those that are both *structural and functional*. With structural analogies, parallels are drawn between appearances, physical organizations or structures (for example, 'the Earth is like an orange'; both appear roughly spherical with a slightly roughened surface and both have 'skins'). With functional analogies, parallels are drawn with the way something operates, behaves or functions (for example, 'the brain is like a computer'; both have means of encoding incoming information, processing and storing it). Some analogies have both properties (for example, the soap dispenser and tube analogy for an electrical circuit can resemble *and* behave like some aspects of a simple electrical circuit; the dispenser can look a little like a battery, the tube outwardly resembles a wire and water circulates through the dispenser and tube as electrical current does through a battery and wire). Curtis and Reigeluth considered this kind of analogy to be particularly effective. It is easy to match the components and that makes it easier to see parallels in the way they function.

The point is that one analogy can have a very different form to another and serve a different function. There is no reason to expect them to be equally effective in these functions, and it is useful to know that functional analogies are potentially effective. At the same time, enriched analogies are likely to be more effective than simple analogies with younger children because the grounds for the analogy are made explicit.

Analogy and Understanding

What is to be understood is often referred to as the *target*. The parallel situation which is to help understand the target is the *analogue*. Analogical mapping between target and analogue is performed to construct the analogy (Duit, 1991). Consider what Curtis and Reigeluth called a structural analogy, such as an orange for the shape of the Earth. The intention is to support the understanding of appearance, organization or structure. The

Earth is the target (T) and the orange is the analogue (A). Structural features can be mapped between the two:

T1: The Earth is roughly spherical;
A1: The orange is roughly spherical.

T2: The surface of the Earth is uneven but this is insignificant on the larger scale;
A2: The surface of the orange is uneven but this is insignificant on the larger scale.

T3: The Earth has a crust;
A3: The orange has a skin.

Because we tend to view the Earth from a local perspective, its spherical nature, the insignificance of its mountains and valleys and the existence of an outer layer can be difficult to grasp. On the scale of an orange, it is easier. As far as these features are concerned, the orange provides a familiar model. The familiarity makes processing less demanding. At the same time, the model provides a mental structure which allows the relevant relationships to be readily inferred. The pores on its skin visibly and palpably do not present major interruptions to the surface so, on the same scale, the Earth's mountains and valleys could be no more significant. In effect, thinking is easier because the orange domain is more familiar and the relationships easier to understand in it.

In the case of a functional relationship, the function or behaviour of the target is modelled by the analogue. The computer as a model for the brain is an example. The brain does not look like the computer and may not be organized like it, nevertheless, they have some functions in common:

T1: encodes information from the senses for processing;
A1: encodes incoming data for processing;

T2: holds and processes information in working memory;
A2: holds and processes data in random access memory (RAM);

T3: stores information for later recall in long term memory;
A3: stores information for later recall on a hard disc drive;

T4: communicates outcomes of processing (e.g. by speech or writing);
A4: communicates outcomes of processing (e.g. by screen or printer).

On the assumption that the learner is familiar with the computer, these functional parallels provide a mental structure for the brain and allow some reasoning about the brain to take place with it. Thus, it is possible to exceed the RAM capacity of a computer so we can speculate about the same possibility with the working memory model.

Another functional example is when the target begins in one state and ends in another and the analogue models the change. One difficulty in understanding an event of this kind is in connecting one state with another. Analogy can help by providing an alternative, more familiar path between mental states drawing on known relationships (Figure 6.3). The situation has to be mentally represented but, instead of attempting to bridge from this to some subsequent state, it is mapped onto another representation (often recalled from memory). This other representation is then articulated according to familiar 'rules' to produce a subsequent state. This subsequent state is then translated into the target's subsequent state (Halford, 1993).

For example, a ray of light changes direction when it travels from air into a block of glass (Figure 6.3). An analogy may be made with a pair of wheels on an axle which run into sand. The reason that the ray of light changes direction can be quite difficult to grasp. But, the reason for the wheels changing direction involves familiar concepts and experience. One wheel (X) enters the sand before the other. The drag of the sand slows it down, but the other wheel is still off the sand and is going faster. This makes the axle slew around and travel in a different direction, much like the ray of light does. A significant amount of research relates to the use of analogy in supporting

Figure 6.3   *A ray of light changes direction on entering a glass block (cross-hatched) from the air; the analogy is with a pair of wheels on an axle that roll into sand (dotted), the first wheel to enter slows and it slews the axle so that the direction of travel is changed.*

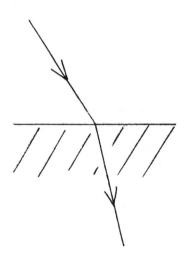
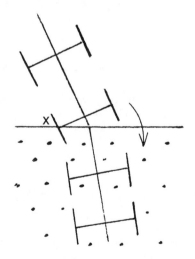

understanding of the natural and physical world and for those with a particular interest in this Duit (1991) and Duit and Glynn (1996) provide useful accounts.

It seems that the retrieval of the basis of an analogy it is not spontaneous, even in adults. When structures *and* functions of a target are modelled by an analogue, the two may be connected in many ways in a learner's memory. This probably increases the likelihood that the target will stimulate a recall of the analogue. It also makes the analogy potentially more powerful since there are more relationships to draw on (Suzuki, 1994). There is, however, more to it than that. For instance, in the case of the *flow* of electricity, it is the correspondence with the *flow* of water that stimulates retrieval. Terms with related meanings may play a significant part in the retrieval process (Thagard, 1992). In mapping, the structure of some existing knowledge is mapped onto the new or less understood target (Gentner, 1989). When it comes to mapping, it is the existence of material correspondences and similar configurations that matter. In the electricity–water flow analogy, wires and tubes carrying the flow would be an instance.

In long explanations, analogies are more effective if presented at the outset (Halpern et al., 1990). Here, they can serve as an advance organizer, giving the student a mental framework to think with and fostering the construction of an appropriate mental representation. This is, of course, what Ausubel's (1968) comparative advance organizer does. It ensures that there is a sound basis to think from at the beginning of the instruction.

Halpern et al. (1990) also compared the relative merits of near and far analogies. Near and far analogies are drawn from similar and different domains, respectively. For example, in an account of the lymph system, they used the movement of water through a sponge as the far domain analogy and the movement of blood through veins as the near domain analogy. The far analogies were more effective in promoting understanding, possibly because they are very unlike the topic under study so attract attention and tend to be recalled more readily. However, being distant, parallels may not be clear and the student may need to dwell on them to a greater degree.

Figure 6.4   *Bridging from known to unknown: the hand senses the compression effects directly, a block compresses a sponge, the block depresses a thin table top, finally, the small depression of a thick table top is shown by the movement of a spot of light reflected from a mirror.*

Learners may, of course, generate their own analogies. The conditions for success are not necessarily like those for the analogy that is given. Wong (1993) found that students (adults in this case) can generate analogies when attempting to understand phenomena such as the behaviour of air in a bicycle pump. These analogies seemed to 'stimulate new inferences and insight' and could help to develop knowledge further. This makes self-generated analogy a potential strategy for supporting understanding, but it assumes that the learner has some idea about what an analogy is. It also opens the possibility that inappropriate or weak analogies will be generated so that understanding may actually be hindered. When this is likely, it would be important to discuss students' analogies as they generate them (Thagard, 1992).

Bridging Analogies

When some action or event is difficult to understand or when misconceptions lead to understanding failure, Clement (1993) has found bridging analogies to be helpful. For instance, he found students had difficulty accepting that a book on a table experiences an upward force from the table (called the reaction of the table). He constructed a chain of experiences intended to bridge from the known to the unknown.

To begin with, the student pushes down on the spring and can feel its response pushing up. This is repeated with a hand on a sponge, then a book replaces the hand and produces the same effect. There is an obvious effect on the hand from the spring. Although less, the effect from the sponge is still noticeable. Since the book depresses the sponge in the same way, it is reasonable to believe that there is an upward push on the book like that experienced by the hand. The book is now placed on a 'table' made from thin board. The 'table' is distorted just like the sponge. Again, it is reasonable to believe that there is an upward force on the book as there was when it was on the sponge. Finally, the book is placed on a real table. Although the depression is not noticeable, it can be made so by reflecting light from a mirror on its surface and watching the reflection as the book is placed on it. Since the real table is also depressed, it is again reasonable to believe that there is an upward force on the book.

The hand on the spring, sponge and thin board 'table' provide the analogies for the book on the real table. The sensation of a hand pushing down on the spring, sponge and thin board may not be in prior experience or may not be available for reflection. Providing the experience ensures that it is available and is in a useful context. At the same time, a feeling of the upward force is likely to be more directly meaningful than using a force meter as an intermediary that requires interpretation. The problem is that, as with bridging explanations, bridging analogies can be difficult to construct for some topics. Most will have to be collected or compiled before teaching and, as they are topic-specific, they will form a part of a teacher's subject-specific, pedagogical knowledge.

Analogy as a Means of Changing Perspectives

Having a particular view of the world shapes the relationships we are likely to infer. In this sense, understanding is perspective-bound (for example, see Wolpert, 1992). Changing the perspective can enable new understandings. For instance, in 1615, William Harvey saw the heart in terms of a bellows-like water pump. This new perspective generated a new way of looking at the function of the heart and its vessels, namely, as a circulatory system (Sutton, 1996). Students often need to adopt another or a particular perspective when approaching a topic in order to understand in the way that subject specialists do. Sutton argues persuasively that perspectives stem from the language, metaphors and analogies of a subject and novices need to assimilate them. In this way, other relationships are enabled through a changed perspective.

This is an important idea. Understanding and reasoning can be supported by analogy in the ways described above. The analogy can reduce processing load but, here, its primary function is as a provider of a new perspective. This perspective-changing role of analogy could play a significant part in enabling particular or authorized understandings in some subjects. Such analogies often stem from the person responsible for the particular perspective in the first place, or from their apologists or popularizers. Darwin's Tree of Life analogy for evolutionary relationships amongst species is an instance. Rouvray (1994) describes the very important role of analogies in the development and progress of science. In particular, he mentions the billiard balls in a box analogy for a gas, beads on a string for polymer molecules, and the solar system for the atom.

In such cases, the analogy may not be familiar to the student and would have to be developed through talk and experience. In other cases, metaphors and analogies become a mundane part of speech and lose their referent power, allusion and meaning. As such, they cease to support in the way they once did. Sutton (1996) feels that understanding is, in part, coming to know this analogical language as it was intended.

Limitations of Support from Analogies

Supporting understanding with analogies is not without its difficulties. One of these arises when the learner does not know the analogical situation well enough to make it immediately useful. A solution is to teach it thoroughly before using it. The less experienced the learner, the more likely this course of action will be needed. In general, it could be good practice to check existing knowledge, if only to bring it to consciousness ready for use.

Analogies are also not without shortcomings. The main one is that no analogy is a perfect match for the target knowledge. This means that there is a danger that an analogy will be overextended and inappropriate aspects will be given to the target. In the electricity–water analogy, when the tube is cut, water runs out. It would not be appropriate to transfer this to the electrical circuit: electricity does not flow from a cut wire. Some limits of the brain–computer analogy have already been described (Chapter 4). One approach to the danger of overextension is to make limitations explicit (Heywood and Parker, 1997).

There is also an order effect which may block alternative interpretations of events. Keane (1997) describes an order effect as one in which 'a particular interpretation of an analogy is adopted because of the order in which domain information is presented. An example is when someone learns British history before American history. This tends to make British history the source of models for American history, rather than the other way around. Keane describes the way politicians use the order effect to their advantage. By drawing an analogy between the drug problem and fighting a war, people tend to think of solutions based on police action and penal legislation rather than alternatives, perhaps based on an 'illness-of-society' analogy.

Analogies are, of course, symmetrical: water flow in pipes could be an analogy for electrical current flow and electrical current flow could be a model for water flow in pipes. In practice, the one generally found to be difficult to understand tends to be the target. However, a good analogy is not available until its source is known to the learner. This means there may need to be some long-term planning to develop a source before the target arises.

Preparing to Offer an Analogy

Generally, Treagust et al. (1992) found that analogy use in teaching tends not to be pre-planned but is a response to non-verbal cues. Analogies in lessons were rare and not used to their best effect. Curtis and Reigeluth (1984) analysed North American science textbooks and found them to be relatively rare (8.3 analogies per book). Newton (1997) came to a similar conclusion for primary science textbooks in the UK. The incidence of analogy can also vary enormously within and between subjects. For instance, Curtis (1988) found that there were about three times as many analogies in science texts as in social studies texts in the USA. On the basis of what has been discussed about analogies, some more or less self-evident steps for teaching with analogy can be offered.

1   Check the student's prior knowledge of the topic in hand to determine if support for understanding is needed.

2   If it is, then consider the topic's difficulty. An analogy may have little to offer the understanding of an easy topic. Check for a stock analogy in books and by asking colleagues.

3   If one is not available, identify clearly the important features of the topic and construct an analogy, preferably one whose basis or source is known to the learner. (This process may not be easy, but it can be a satisfying one.)

4   If the source of the analogy is not well known, prepare a preliminary teaching sequence to make it known or to aid its recall.

5   Introduce the analogy early in the teaching.

6   Exemplify its application.

7   Identify its limitations clearly.

8   Provide practice in using the analogy where relevant.

In the next chapter, various ways of supporting for understanding are brought together and illustrated in the context of the surrogate teacher.

Summary

An analogy is a model drawn from one context and used to support understanding in another context. The difference between the contexts may be small (near analogies and, in the end, homologies) or large (far analogies). Analogies may be classified in a variety of ways and can serve different functions. They support understanding because they enable reasoning about something relatively unknown through something generally well-known. This reduces processing load. At the same time, a novel analogy may draw attention, encourage mental processing of correspondences by the curious and make the analogy memorable. However, this presupposes prior knowledge of the source of the analogy and an awareness that analogical reasoning is expected. In the absence of these, knowledge of the source of the analogy may be provided and the need for analogical reasoning made explicit. Analogies may be overdrawn and so could mislead. The limitations of analogical reasoning need to be made explicit. Analogies can also change perspectives. A changed perspective can enable new kinds of relationships to be inferred. Discussion, experience and time to adjust the viewpoint are likely to be needed.

References

Ausubel, D.P. (1968) *Educational Psychology: A Cognitive View*, New York: Holt, Rinehart & Winston.

Campbell, K.S. (1990) 'The Oral Language Acquisition Analogy in Early Literacy Research', *Educational Research Quarterly* 14: 45–50.

Clement, J. (1993) 'Using Bridging Analogies and Anchoring Intuitions to Deal with Students' Preconceptions in Physics', *Journal of Research in Science Teaching* 30: 1241–57.

Curtis, R.V. (1988) 'When is a Science Analogy like a Social Science Analogy', *Instructional Science* 19: 169–77.

Curtis, R.V. and Reigeluth, C.M. (1984) 'The Use of Analogies in Written Text', *Instructional Science* 13: 99–117.

Davis, P.W. and Davidson, G.V. (1994) 'Language is Like the Human Body: Teaching Concepts Through Analogy', *Educational Technology* 34: 27–32.

Davidson, L. and Scripp, L. (1992) 'Surveying the Coordinates of Cognitive Skills in Music', in R. Colwell, *Handbook of Research on Music Teaching and Learning*, New York: Schirmer, 392–413.

Duit, R. (1991) 'On the Role of Analogy and Metaphor in Learning Science', *Science Education* 75: 649–72.

Duit, R. and Glynn, S. (1996) 'Mental Modelling', in G. Welford, J. Osborne and P. Scott, *Research in Science Education in Europe*, London: Falmer, 166–76.

Froehlich, H.C. and Cattley, G. (1991) 'Language, Metaphor, and Analogy in the Music Education Research Process', *Journal of Aesthetic Education* 25: 243–57.

Gelman, S.A. and Markman, R. (1987) 'Young Children's Inductions From Natural Kinds', *Child Development* 58: 1532–41.

Gentner, D. (1989) 'The Mechanism of Analogical Reasoning', in S. Vosniadou and A. Ortony (eds), *Similarity and Analogical Reasoning*, Cambridge: Cambridge University Press.

—— (1998) 'Analogy', in W. Bechtel and G. Graham (eds), *A Companion to Cognitive Science*, Malden: Blackwell, 107–13.

Gilbert, S.W. (1989) 'An Evaluation of the Use of Analogy, Simile, and Metaphor in Science Texts', *Journal of Research in Science Teaching* 26: 313–25.

Giora, R. (1993) 'On the Function of Analogies in Informative Texts', *Discourse Processes* 16: 591–611.

Goswami, U. (1992) *Analogical Reasoning in Children*, Hove: Lawrence Erlbaum.

Greenwood, S.C. (1988) 'How to Use Analogy Instruction to Reinforce Vocabulary', *Middle School Journal* 19: 11–13.

Halford, G.S. (1993) *Children's Understanding: The Development of Mental Models*, Hillsdale, NJ: Lawrence Erlbaum.

Halpern, D.F., Hanson, C. and Riefer, D. (1990) 'Analogies as an Aid to Understanding and Memory', *Journal of Educational Psychology* 82: 298–305.

Hatano, G. and Inagaki, K. (1994) 'Young Children's Naive Theory of Biology', *Cognition* 50: 171–88.

Heywood, D. and Parker, J. (1997) 'Confronting the Analogy: Primary Teachers Exploring the Usefulness of Analogies in the Teaching and Learning of Electricity', *International Journal of Science Education* 19: 869–85.

HuffBenkoski, K.A. and Greenwood, S.C. (1995) 'The Use of Word Analogy Instruction with Developing Readers', *Teaching Reading* 48: 446–7.

Keane, M.T. (1997) 'What Makes an Analogy Difficult? An Effect of Order and Causal Structure on Analogical Mapping', *Journal of Experimental Psychology: Learning, Memory, and Cognition* 23: 946–67.

Newton, D.P. and Newton, L.D. (1995) 'Using Analogy to Help Young Children Understand', *Educational Studies* 21: 379–93.

Newton, L.D. (1997) 'Teachers' Questioning for Understanding in Science', *British Journal of Curriculum and Assessment* 27–31.

Rouvray, D.H. (1994) 'Similarity Studies: The Necessity for Analogies in the Development of Science', *Journal of Chemistry, Information and Computer Science* 34: 446–52.

Stollack, A. and Alexander, L. (1998) 'The Use of Analogy in Rehearsal', *Music Educators' Journal* 84: 17–21.

Sutton, C. (1996) 'The Scientific Model as a Form of Speech', in G. Welford, J. Osborne and P. Scott, *Research in Science Education in Europe*, London: Falmer, 143–52.

Suzuki, H. (1994) 'The Centrality of Analogy in Knowledge Acquisition in Instructional Contexts', *Human Development* 37: 207–19.

Thagard, P. (1992) 'Analogy, Explanation and Education', *Journal of Research in Science Teaching* 29: 537–44.

Thiele, R.B. and Treagust, D.F. (1994) 'The Nature and Extent of Analogies in Secondary Chemistry Textbooks', *Instructional Science* 22: 61–74.

Thomas, T. (1991) 'Interart Analogy: Practice and Theory in Comparing the Arts', *Journal of Aesthetic Education* 25: 17–36.

Treagust, D.F., Duit, R., Joslin, P. and Landaver, I. (1992) 'Science Teachers' Use of Analogies: Observation From Classroom Practice', *International Journal of Science Education* 14: 413–22.

Wong, E.D. (1993) 'Understanding the Generative Capacity of Analogies as a Tool for Explanation', *Journal of Research in Science Teaching* 30: 1259–72.

Wolpert, L. (1992) *The Unnatural Nature of Science*, London: Faber and Faber.

Zeitoun, H.H. (1984) 'Teaching Scientific Analogies: A Proposed Model', *Research in Science and Technological Education* 2: 107–25.

7 Using Surrogate Teachers

Overview

Text is one of the earliest of learning aids while Information and Communication Technology (ICT) is a more recent addition. The support for understanding which a text might supply is viewed largely through a surrogate teacher (text as tutor) analogy. This analogy is also applied to ICT but, as ICT may function readily in other ways, it is better to view it from a variety of perspectives. These include the computer as a tool, a simulator of the world, and a provider of learning environments. Different people may not learn equally well from different teaching and learning aids so this needs to be taken into account.

A Surrogate Teacher Analogy

A surrogate teacher is something which has the role of teacher. For instance, when instructional radio was introduced in 1932 in the USA, it was described as The Assistant Teacher. Television had a similar role when Samoa was faced with a teacher shortage. In the 1960s, between one-quarter and one-third of the Samoan school day was spent watching televised lessons, and the remaining time was given to activities based on them (Cuban, 1986). Australia and New Zealand have supported education in remote communities in similar ways (Teather, 1989). Distance learning systems are, in effect, teachers for most who must learn at home. These systems can include a wide range of learning aids such as videotapes, computer-based instruction and textual materials to provide what Kaye (1989) has called a 'guided didactic conversation'.

Viewing such materials as teachers suggests ways of making them effective. However, as with all analogies, this one has its limits. These depend on the nature of the surrogate, but some deficiencies may be overcome with support from a teacher. In effect, the teacher and surrogate act in concert, although the teacher usually has overall responsibility for who does what. In practice, surrogate teachers can have a very significant role, particularly in independent learning and amongst older students (Newton, 1993a). In this chapter, text will be used to exemplify the surrogate teacher analogy and illustrate how it could support understanding. The analogy, however, does not capture all that Information and Communication Technology (ICT) may offer and aspects of the use of ICT are also discussed.

Text as Teacher

Text for supporting learning has been used for some 3,000 years and is a feature of most classrooms, yet some view it with distrust. This distrust is often misplaced. Text may be badly written or badly used, but that tells us something about the writer or user, not about the potential of text. With some guiding principles, text may be produced that is likely to support understanding (Newton, 1993a; Chambliss and Calfee, 1998).

Just as the teachers' words have to make sense to the student, there has to be comprehension of the written word. Van Dijk and Kintsch (1983) have described the need to grasp the meaning of words and sentences before they can be used to construct a mental model of the situation being described. Without this fundamental level of understanding, little of value can follow. Mayer (1989) described supporting comprehension as being considerate with the language.

Considerate Text

Considerate text uses words and structures chosen according to the experience and ability of the learner. The difficult part is knowing which words to use and what order to put them in.

Unfamiliar words obviously can increase reading difficulty. Familiar words are often the short words we use in everyday speech: 'dog', 'tree', 'door', 'grass', 'eat', 'hurt', 'run', 'wet' and 'cold' are examples. Long words, such as 'subjunctive', 'corundum', 'efflorescence' and 'hermaphrodite', are not used so frequently and so are less familiar. Similarly, long sentences are generally more difficult to grasp than short ones, particularly when they express abstract ideas. Piling up adjectives and adverbs can also cause difficulty. They increase the demand for working memory capacity and may cause the reader to lose the thread of the argument, just as do too many digressions. The passive voice ('It was said that...') and infinitive subjects ('To be or not to be, that is the question') are other structures that increase demand. Similarly, clauses joined by conjunctions other than 'and' can increase text difficulty (Fatt, 1992).

Counts of language variables like these can indicate the probable difficulty of a text, and there are formulae that capture the relationship. One of the simplest is McLaughlin's SMOG formula:

Reading difficulty $\propto \sqrt{}$ polysyllabic count

The polysyllabic count is the number of words of three or more syllables in thirty sentences, so this formula gauges text according to the proportion of long words (McLaughlin, 1969). Most reading difficulty formulae have been developed for narrative text. Subjects like the sciences, geography and mathematics often have their own specialist language and these formulae do not always assess its difficulty well. For instance, the SMOG formula grossly underestimates the reading difficulty of mathematical text. Suppose the frequency of polysyllabic words in narrative text and in mathematical text were both quadrupled. The narrative text would now be about twice as difficult to read but the mathematical text could be as much as four times as difficult to read (Newton and Merrell, 1994a). Difficulty can be compounded when the language of the text is very different to that of the teacher. For example, there could be problems for children learning about multiplication when a book uses 'multiplied by' when their teacher uses 'times'. Even short and, at first sight, simple words such as 'each' in 'three of each colour' can cause difficulty (Anghileri, 1989).

Such formulae are not precise instruments, but may be rough indicators of relative reading difficulty. Writing to them can make prose unnatural and stilted, but they can draw attention to text which may need attention. However, there are other things that can make a text inconsiderate.

A reader has to knit the given words together to make a whole. This can be made more difficult when words like 'it', 'they' and 'that' cannot be linked unambiguously with what they refer to or appear so far away that the reader cannot recall their referents. Logical relationships between sentences also have to be grasped. Expressions like 'on the other hand' and 'nevertheless' signal logical relationships between sentences and paragraphs. These relationships have to be grasped if meaning is to be established on a larger scale. As might be expected, Chapman (1983) found that the ability to establish textual cohesion increased with age. However, it was still developing in 13-year-old students.

When a text omits the reasons for situations and events, the reader may fail to unify its separate elements. This kind of failure can be due to a lack of prior knowledge which would enable the gaps to be bridged. Consider the passage, 'The cat silently approached the feeding bird. At the last second, as the cat gathered itself for its spring, the cat's bell tinkled. The bird immediately threw itself into the air and escaped'. It might seem reasonable to assume that adults would need nothing more to grasp the passage. For children, on the other hand, such an assumption may not be warranted because words such as 'gathered' and 'spring' can be interpreted in different ways (Kemper, 1983).

Having established that the language of the text is considerate, we now turn to the support it provides for understanding the topic in hand.

Supporting Understanding with Text

A textbook, by itself, generally cannot provide hands-on experience of a topic. It can, however, remind the reader of prior knowledge and supply vicarious experience. It can also provide conceptual structures and carefully thought-out explanations to support the understanding of that experience. In use, the surrogate can be thorough, mindful and infinitely patient.

Activating and Supplementing Prior Knowledge and Scene Setting

As was described in Chapter 5, setting the scene is helpful since it can activate related prior knowledge and draws attention to what is likely to be relevant. What could a text-teacher do? It will probably begin with a title or an introduction. For a title to be useful, it should signal to the reader what the topic will be. Sometimes, titles are cast in the form of questions. Both kinds can be effective, so which to use is a matter of taste and what fits the situation. It seems that readers younger than about 11 years old do not gain a great deal from titles, but an introduction can orient older readers' thoughts towards the topic. Readers are also known to benefit from a sentence referring them to information they are likely to have read earlier. This paragraph began in this way with the intention of activating a relevant context and mental schema (Glover et al., 1988). With older learners, the significance of recalling knowledge during reading may be explained and modelled. After practice in which they recall prior knowledge and link it to the text, such students outperform others on application questions (Spires and Donley, 1998). This suggests that the strategy is one that supports understanding.

There is the risk that the student will read text somewhat passively. Active engagement can be encouraged with textual questions, the equivalent of the teacher's oral, focused questions. Peeck et al. (1982), in a study of Dutch 10-year-olds' learning, asked children to describe the appearance and habits of a fox while a control group did an irrelevant exercise. Both groups then read about a fictional fox with a short, sleek tail and which never ate chickens. The first group recalled more of the fictional fox's incongruous features than the control group. Having activated prior knowledge about the normal fox, incongruities were more readily noticed. Another simple exercise known to be effective is to have readers anticipate what the text will be about. Similarly, three key words may be taken from the topic and the reader has to list as many words as possible that they associate with each of the key words. It is then a short step to ask the reader to construct a concept map for the topic, as described in Chapter 5 (Howard, 1987; Rowe and Rayford, 1987).

Support for the Construction of a Relevant, Initial Representation of a Situation

One way of helping the reader to construct an appropriate mental representation is to provide a resumé. This is a summary or abstract preceding the account of the topic. Two kinds are distinguished: one describes the structure of the text, and the other describes structures in the topic. In practice, both can be included. A reader tends to give more attention to what has been signalled in the resumé so those intended to support understanding should highlight significant relationships and connections that will be described and explained later. Loman and Mayer (1983) concluded that resumés can make conceptual organization and causal links more obvious. Additional support, however, should be given in the body of the text.

The advance organizer was devised by Ausubel (1980) to equip the student with a conceptual structure. He distinguished two kinds: the expositive organizer and the comparative organizer. Working with 13-year-old Canadian students, Kloster and Winne (1989) tested an expositive organizer for supporting the understanding of an account of computer crime and its prevention. The organizer 'described the idea that new inventions give rise to new abuses', and was at a higher level of generality than the account. A comparative organizer, on the other hand, gave an analogy with the misuse of office photocopiers and the attempts to control the abuses. It was at the same level of generality as the account. Both kinds of organizer prepare the reader with relevant structures for what is to follow. It seems that the first kind is of more help to those with little background knowledge of the topic. It provides a broad context as a starting point. The comparative organizer is better suited to those with some prior knowledge (Stone, 1983). It does not offer a context, since the reader can presumably draw on prior knowledge. Instead, it provides a model to which the topic can be related.

Directing Attention to What is Relevant

Advance organizers are not always easy to construct and do not always produce a noticeable affect. You will recall that when a topic is relatively undemanding, adjunct aids of this kind are immaterial. At the same time, they have to be capable of being understood themselves. Further, care is needed with questions and other aids intended to mobilize relevant prior knowledge. They can focus attention on particular aspects of the topic and on particular kinds of knowledge to the exclusion of others (Hartley, 1981; Hamilton, 1985). Stating learning goals or behavioural objectives at the beginning can also direct attention to particular points of the exposition. Once again, if they are to support understanding, they need to refer to it as a specific goal or objective. This means they would be stated in such terms as: 'One important aim of this chapter is to help you understand why ...' or, 'At the end of this chapter, you will be able to write an explanation which gives reasons for …' The underlining of text is another way of drawing attention to particular reasons and causes. Hartley et al. (1980) showed this simple strategy to be surprisingly effective, even with younger children who, presumably, do not benefit to any great extent from titles.

Explaining

Explaining is something the text-teacher should be able to do reasonably well. The information should have been ordered because working memory is a one-task-at-a-time plodder and order supports its way of processing. The grand order of presentation could be world-related, as when a topic is presented in the order in which it is generally found in the world around us. For example, an account of the plant might begin with its leaves, move on to the stem and end with the root. Another order of presentation might be determined by the way concepts are related. For example, energy is a central concept in science so an outline of it might appear first with subsequent discussion referring back to it. Organization is also often learner-related so that logical pre-requisites come first and examples precede the generalization on the grounds that the direction should be from concrete to abstract (Newton, 1990). The order, of course, also matters on a finer scale. Some sequences can make understanding more difficult. Compare:

Alice is taller than John
Ben is taller than Fred
John is taller than Ben
Who is the tallest?

with:

Alice is taller than John
John is taller than Ben
Ben is taller than Fred
Who is the tallest?

In the first of these, the first two elements have to be stored unconnected. The third allows a link to be made. In the re-ordered piece, the second element can be assimilated into the first, then the third assimilated in the combination. Ordering elements so that relationships can be readily inferred reduces demands on working memory. The careful juxtaposition of elements of information that are to be related may facilitate the process of inferencing.

After that, support for understanding lies in the conceptual structures provided for the reader. As with a live teacher, these may be literal, analogical or both. What has been said in the preceding chapter about these applies here as well. Similarly, the need to bridge gaps in events and be explicit about relationships, reasons and causes is relevant. As in oral explanation, care must be taken not to add instructional load to an already demanding situation.

In explaining conceptual structures likely to be compatible with existing knowledge, the text writer might:

- begin by reviewing underlying concepts to ensure that they are available to the reader;
- provide a succinct statement of the new conceptual structure;
- provide some examples, highlighting relevant features;
- provide some relatively close non-instances, clearly marked as such, and show why they are non-instances;
- provide some practice with the structure.

Some conceptual structures, such as 'humane' and 'police state', can be vague and ill-defined. In this event, one or two highly typical exemplars would be described in the place of a succinct definition. Subsequent examples are then judged for the extent to which they overlap these exemplars. Concepts such as 'inverse' and 'infinite' cannot be treated in this way. Several instances and non-instances are not available, at least at the introductory level. Instead, a description accompanied by some examples may have to do.

Brooks and Dansereau (1983) have given a procedure for teaching theories. Paraphrased, this is:

- Describe the theory succinctly, confining attention to the essential elements. What is it? What does it do?
- Describe the origins of the theory briefly. How did it arise?
- Describe the significance of the theory. What difference has it made?
- Describe the evidence for and against the theory.
- Describe briefly competing theories and similar theories.
- State further relevant information.

Why do such procedures work? First, they order the information. Second, irrelevancies are kept to a minimum. Third, they highlight what is significant. Fourth, they distinguish it from other ideas. These simplify and clarify what has to be mentally manipulated, reducing demand and instructional load. If in addition what has been said about oral explaining is incorporated, this will further reduce instructional load.

Redundancy is the extent to which the content is predictable. Most texts could be made more concise without injuring the meaning or amount of information in it. However, the process may make the text so spartan that it becomes difficult to grasp, particularly by inexperienced readers. Increased redundancy can make it longer but more meaningful (as was illustrated by Beck et al.'s (1991) study in Chapter 5).

Some prior knowledge, of course, is not compatible with the conceptual structures that are to be taught. How these might be dealt with orally and in text is discussed in the next chapter.

Concluding

The development of an explanation or argument could occupy a considerable space and take time to read. The reader may need to be reminded of its various elements and how key features relate to one another. This is commonly done in a summing up statement. Summaries are known to stimulate recall and integration of ideas in a backward-looking processing of the facts, ideas and relationships presented in the text. When placed at the beginning, like a resumé, they tend to focus attention on the ideas they mention at the expense of other information. At the end, this effect is not so pronounced and the learning of so-called incidentals is not so greatly reduced (Newton, 1990). Hartley and Trueman (1982) found that less able students can benefit particularly from concluding summaries. Presumably, such students have some difficulty in the process of updating or integrating an explanation or argument as it proceeds.

Mental Engagement

Beck et al. (1995) have described how students may read text in a cursory manner and fail to process it actively. They review ways of increasing students' engagement. For instance, the situation in which the reading occurs can affect the outcome. Reading in a group, with a partner, to the teacher, or aloud in class tend to result in greater engagement. The content, form and style of a text will also influence a student's engagement, as does interest. Schank (1988) described what makes a text interesting: the unexpected, a personal relatedness and finding that the text is about something already found to be interesting.

Making text attractive by simply adding material that is known to interest the reader, such as anecdotes, can be counter-productive. The reader tends to remember these to the detriment of recall of the important ideas. Merely grafting on extras like this is an uncertain way of engaging the reader in what matters. Instead, Beck et al. (1995: 225) decided to give the text engaging features. Text is often impersonal so they revised a sample to give it a 'voice'. For example, 'The British lawmaking body was and still is called Parliament', became, 'The British called their lawmaking body Parliament.' Similarly, 'Britain thought the colonists should pay the share of the cost of the French and Indian War' became, '"It's only fair to ask the colonists to pay their share of the cost of the French and Indian War", they said'. They also produced revisions of these texts with a greater coherence, providing missing information, making connections explicit and referents clear, as described in Chapter 5. Testing them on 9-year-olds showed that the voiced version was more effective in producing a better grasp of the issues than the original version. The text that was made coherent was much more effective than either of these, but the version that was both voiced and coherent was most effective, both on immediate testing and on re-testing a week later.

In addition to strategies which produce a more engaging explanation, adjunct aids may be integrated or added. The most common such aid is to ask questions. These may be dispersed throughout the exposition and relate to the elements of the discussion nearby. As such, they can have the function of focused questions, induce processing when it is needed and support learning (McDaniel and Donnelly, 1996). On the other hand, questions which appear in a block, after a topic has been expounded, cannot have this function. Nevertheless, comprehension questions placed after the text are known to improve subsequent problem solving (Felker and Dapra, 1975). It is likely that they initiate integration and structuring of information and so enhance understanding. Post-questions may also provide practice, consolidate and extend learning, and assess its quality. If both dispersed and block questions are available, gains might be optimized.

Other intra-textual activities require the reader to underline key points, invent a title for the paragraph, think of an analogy, draw a map of relationships or translate it into pictorial form (or from pictures into words). It should not be forgotten that summaries, too, can be treated in a cursory manner and may need to be modified in ways that engage the reader. For example, the reader might be asked to paraphrase the summary, judge the validity of an inference made from it, rearrange a scrambled summary or supply key words for a summary. However, these only help if what is to be understood is taxing to begin with.

Illustrations in Text

Like words, pictures are vehicles of communication. Ellis and Beattie (1986) describe a pictorial letter from a North American Ojibwa girl to her lover. The boy and girl are represented by their totemic symbols, a mud puppy and bear, respectively. The girl beckons to the boy from her tent. Lakes and paths are also shown and an encampment of Christians is depicted nearby. The message is an invitation and a description of the place of meeting. The picture uses a two-dimensional surface to show the physical relationship between material bodies. This is something that it can do well and often in a less demanding way than a verbal account (Newton, 1983; Marcus et al., 1996). A verbal description of the same situation would have to be presented in a linear fashion. The account would be relatively long and have to include a description of the physical relationships between the various bodies. Maintaining these in working memory to construct a mental representation of the overall situation could easily exceed its capacities. The picture is one solution.

The effectiveness of a picture in supporting young children's initial grasp of a complex situation was described in Chapter 5. Another example of the supportive role of the picture comes from an experiment performed by Hayes and Henk (1986). They tested the effect of analogy on knot tying. One group of students (15 to 17 years old) were given written instructions on how to tie a bowline knot, accompanied by a set of step-by-step illustrations. Another group's instructions included an analogy. In both pictures and text, the act of tying the knot was related to a rabbit guarding his territory. In effect, the sequence of acts to check out its territory paralleled the steps involved in tying the knot. In the original version, there is little to suggest what the next step should be. The analogy, however, provides a well-connected sequence of actions for knot-tying and was found to be 'an enduring framework for remembering it'. The pictures, on the other hand, offered a very significant level of support for understanding what mechanical actions were to be performed.

Hegarty and Just (1993) watched the eye movements of adult students as they read text about how a set of pulleys worked. When the text referred to an element of the pulley system, the gaze was transferred briefly to the relevant part of the accompanying picture. In effect, there was an interplay between the text and picture in which each filled in the gaps in the information left by the other. The reader interprets the text with the help of the picture and the picture with the help of the text, a process Sipe (1998) refers to as transmediation. This interaction produces an understanding of the object of instruction. In the situation tested by Hegarty and Just, students took longer to read the material when they had only the text than when they had both text and picture. This points to the efficiency of the combination in supporting a coherent mental representation of the situation.

Sweller (1994), however, warns that there are occasions when illustrations are counter-productive. When a learner is given an illustrated explanation, the learner reads and represents the explanation in working memory. The accompanying illustration must also be processed and integrated with the representation. This increases the demand for resources and, if the demand is already high, can hinder understanding. His effective solution was to integrate text and diagram, thereby reducing the demand. The effect was confirmed by Mayer et al. (1996). They found that a 600 word description of the cause of lightning was ineffective when tested on college students. The researchers translated it into a sequence of annotated pictures with captions as a summary of each. They now observed that the students could apply their learning to solve new problems, indicating an understanding of the cause of lightning. Success was attributed to a successful integration of the pictorial and verbal information, a reduction in cognitive load and the generative ability of structured knowledge (Wittrock, 1989; Clark and

Paivio, 1991; Sweller and Chandler, 1994). Integrated illustrations of this kind are not uncommon in text and may serve as the visual organizers mentioned in Chapter 5.

Once again, the value of illustrations depends on the nature of the demand for mental resources. If this is trivial, either the picture or the text may be of little value. For example, Sweller describes his attempt to integrate text with a picture of the human circulatory system only to find that the text was a distraction and the task was so undemanding that his students could understand it from the diagram alone. If the demand is already very high, pictures could become an additional burden unless the presentation is restructured to give them a useful role.

As representations of the world, pictures need not include every detail of a scene. By omitting non-essential details in a picture, the student is more likely to direct attention to what is relevant. It is, of course, possible to go too far so that learners with limited experience may not recognize the simplified figure presented (Constable et al., 1988; Newton, 1990).

Non-spatial properties and attributes, such as temperature, are not so easily shown in pictures. One solution is to use two-dimensional space to represent non-spatial attributes. Showing temperature on a sheet of paper could be achieved by, for example, using different colours or showing thermometers of different sizes next to the objects. Thermometers could be reduced to lines of different length. The graph takes this further by using different directions for representing different attributes. Whether someone understands a graph depends on whether they know its metaphorical nature and the conventions of graph drawing.

The Ojibwa girl indicated her invitation with a beckoning hand. To show happiness, a smile might be sufficient (although young children put smiles on most drawings of people, whatever the situation). To understand the intention, you must know the convention. Sometimes, there may not be a convention. How are mental torment, satisfaction and pins and needles to be shown? At the same time, pictures cannot show physical properties, such as hot or cold, magnetism, electrical charge, compression, density and other non-visible attributes. But motion is also difficult to depict unambiguously because the picture can show only a frozen moment in time. For some of these, conventional symbols may be available, such as an arrow for a push in a particular direction. Others may be shown with pictorial metaphors. Pictorial metaphors take something of the desired attribute in a real world situation and use it in the target situation. For example, tyres leave tracks in snow or mud, and something similar appears as parallel 'whizz' lines to depict motion, musical notes may indicate music, and splat marks show impact. Experience is needed to understand the significance of such pictorial devices otherwise they may not be interpreted as intended. For instance, over 30 per cent of 8-year-olds interpreted whizz lines incorrectly (Newton, 1990). Other devices are not perceived with the relative intensity expected.

Close C-lines (CCC) behind an object, for instance, indicate a relatively slow movement, in accordance with what would be seen with a flashing strobo-scope. Well spaced C-lines (C C C) indicate a faster motion. Many younger children see the latter as meaning a slower movement than the former. Unless care is taken to ensure that pictorial metaphor is perceived as intended, it may add to difficulty rather than alleviate it. This may be one occasion when children's comics, which tend to use pictorial metaphor a great deal, have a useful role in developing a grasp of its meaning (Newton, 1985).

Visual organizers often use the flat paper surface to arrange concepts and ideas spatially so that relationships may be discerned more readily. These include story maps, Venn diagrams, webs, cause–effect frameworks, charts and flowcharts (Tarquin and Walker, 1997). Tables of data have a similar function. When the pattern is simple and clear in tabulated data and the form of the table is familiar to the reader, the table is generally better under-stood than the graph (Newton, 1993b; Natriello, 1997). Of course, the intention may be to develop graphing comprehension abilities so a graph might still be included. In all these cases, as with representational pictures, their effectiveness lies in their ability to display relationships spatially.

Text and Teaching

The text can be used as a teacher who cannot be distracted and does not forget its plan. Its memory for detail is limitless, its patience is boundless and it can repeat its lesson as needed. But some of these are also weaknesses. The route it offers is relatively inflexible. Even when a book has a branching structure, there is a limit to the number of branches. While it can repeat itself, it can only say what it has already said. In addition, the text is not sensitive to the situation. It does not know what the reader already knows and cannot adjust to it. The writer must either assume the worst and attempt to tell all or make a guess at what the 'average' student might know. (Of course, since text writers are often teachers, this guess may not be wide of the mark.) Being, in essence, a blind and deaf teacher, the text cannot notice a failure to understand or, if it anticipates it, respond very flexibly to it. It also relies on the reader's cooperation in using its aids to understanding and generally it does not provide direct experience of a phenomenon, situation or event. Of course, the teacher may be similarly constrained, as when describing historical events, remote places or phenomena that are not directly accessible to the senses. The quality of the vicarious experi-ence a book offers depends partly on the skill of the writer. I recall learning of exotic animals from books and then being disappointed by how small they are when seen in the flesh. The books had described their appearance well but, presumably, without anything for the reader to judge their size.

Textual materials seem to have acquired a reputation as being a poor second best and as encouraging memorization. There are things they cannot do well and an over-reliance on textual resources, particularly amongst inexperienced learners, risks learning not being well-grounded in experience. But limitation does not mean worthless. The availability of textbooks is positively related to learner achievement and is a major contributor to success in many, less industrial societies (Westbury, 1989). Any lesson is only as good as the teacher makes it, surrogate or otherwise. A textbook in which the author has given attention to considerate, coherent and well-ordered text, incorporating strategies for useful mental engagement, should not be ignored. In some ways, such as its grasp of the subject, the kind of information it provides, its unfailing memory, its patience, the way it can repeat its lesson and enable individuals to work at their own pace, it may even be better than the teacher. When the teacher is aware of a text's shortcomings, it may be supported and used to advantage, but that takes forethought.

Books are not limited to the role of surrogate teacher. They may be a tool, as in the case of a dictionary or atlas, or a model, as with the pop-up book that opens to form a castle with moving parts. A variety of roles is also seen in the use of ICT to support learning.

Supporting Understanding with Information and Communication Technology (ICT)

According to Molenda et al. (1998), printed materials are the most commonly used resources for supporting learning worldwide. Audio is less common, video comes next, and finally there is ICT. Even when ICT is available, it may not be used (Crook, 1994). Hurd (1987) has described some of the reasons given by teachers in the USA: lack of know-how, cost and poor quality of materials, and inconvenience. These are remarkably like the reasons given for not using film in the 1950s (Cuban, 1986). Nevertheless, the use of ICT to support learning in a variety of subjects is increasing (Molenda et al., 1998). Claims for its potential can be enthusiastic and extravagant. For instance, Brna, P. and Dicheva, D. (1998) are enthusiastic about the 'exciting opportunities' that ICT offers. Papert (1980) has gone further and believes that there will be no schools in the future, only computers. Similarly, Perelman (1992) argues that ICT has made home study an affordable and feasible alternative to schools. This is remarkably reminiscent of Edison's claim that film would replace the textbook (Molenda et al., 1998) but, perhaps, history really has no lessons. Certainly, there are those who see ICT as offering a quick, relatively cheap and teacher-proof way of mending and extending education (Dillon, 1998).

ICT Doing What Other Resources Can Do

ICT could do much that a book does, presenting text and pictures screen by screen, together with adjunct aids to learning. For instance, Cavalier and

Klein (1998) described ICT support for teaching 10 and 11-year-olds about prospecting for minerals. The topic had a story format, and the children were told on the screen that they would accompany a prospecting team on a field trip. Reasons for learning about prospecting were given. Versions which stated the learning objectives ('At the end of this unit, you should be able to...') and which offered advance organizers (in this case, a general, descriptive overview) were prepared. A total of 140 'screens' was used to present information about modern prospecting. These included screens with practice exercises and feedback on the children's learning dispersed through the narrative. The feedback comprised either 'You're right!' or provision of the correct answer. Progress through the information was screen by screen at a pace determined by the learner. Cavalier and Klein found that, for this material, the provision of instructional objectives gave rise to significantly better post-test scores. Knowing that children cannot always work at a computer alone, they included a comparison of working in pairs and working alone and found that those working alone spent more time on the instruction and practice.

Without stretching the imagination too far, the same kind of lesson could have appeared in a textbook, probably with similar results. When textbooks are in short supply and the children have to share them, we might similarly expect it to affect their learning behaviours. A like view could be taken of the observation that the animation of diagrams with motion cues on a computer provides significantly greater understanding than still pictures (Park, 1998). Presumably, this could also be achieved using a video recorder. This is not to undervalue the studies; the effect of variation and the conditions under which ICT is used have to be tested. However, beyond novelty value, is it worth using ICT to support learning in this way when a textbook or videotape could have the potential to be just as effective?

The Effectiveness of ICT as a Teacher

There have been many studies of the effectiveness of ICT in supporting learning. Some have found it to be effective and others have not (for example, Kulik et al. (1983) and Levine (1994)). Emerson and Mosteller (1998) reviewed such research. They report effect sizes that are often small (Cohen, 1969) and show little advantage for ICT over 'traditional', presumably teacher and book, approaches. Add to this the observation that reading from a screen tends to be slower than from a book and, in any case, some students learn better by listening (Steinberg, 1991), and ICT may not offer much that is new. The problem has to be seen more in terms of when can ICT be useful rather than to expect it to be effective everywhere. At the same time, some of its use has not been particularly well-informed. What is needed is a playing to the strengths of a resource, whether it is text, software, video or audiotape. ICT can provide various kinds of support and some cannot be replicated by other surrogates, such as a textbook. These may include teaching strategies that foster very specific kinds of learning. For instance, Emerson and Mosteller do include in their review evidence of medium effect sizes when using ICT to support older students' reasoning. Its potential lies in what ICT does well.

Interactivity

One thing ICT can do is offer a higher degree of interactivity than the textbook or tape and this has, as Neuman (1995) put it, 'become the focus of irrepressible optimism'. This interactivity can, of course, be gratuitous, facile and educationally pointless. Steinberg (1991) has drawn an analogy between ICT and a musical instrument. The better the musical instrument, the greater its potential for making good music but the realization of that potential depends on the ability of the player. Interactivity means that the computer or learner initiates an action to which the other responds. Some degree of interactivity is possible with other resources. For instance, a textbook can ask a question in the hope that the reader will respond. The computer, however, can ask that question, wait until there is a response, comment on it, provide remedial instruction if necessary, retest learning and then return the learner to the main body of instruction. It might also gauge the mental attributes of the learner on the basis of the responses and tailor subsequent instruction to suit that learner's preferences and needs. In this way, instruction is individualized and mental engagement required and judged. Of particular relevance is the possibility of promoting mental engagement that results in reasoning and inferencing. ICT is likely to support understanding to the extent that it does this.

The nature of the interaction is governed by how the learner is modelled. If the learner is seen as a sponge and an absorber of knowledge, the form of interaction supported by the computer will tend to reflect that. If the learner is seen as arriving with some knowledge and needing to relate the new material to it, then the interaction is likely to include an attempt to bring that knowledge into consciousness, check its quality and support connection making. Similarly, in problem solving, the computer might monitor the learner's responses, anticipate common misconceptions and intervene when the attempted solution goes off track. The extent to which it can do so depends on the sophistication and quality of the model of the learner. Given that, Emerson and Mosteller (1998) claim that ICT offers some particular benefits. It can be used in a flexible way, the materials can be engaging and motivating, worthwhile kinds of feedback and interaction are possible, it can provide information through a variety of channels and facilitate access to alternative representations of it and links to other information, and it allows the learner to work at his or her own pace. It can also allow the teacher to shape the instruction and the learner to have some control over it although they have found that there are better results when the learner's control is limited to, for instance, practice and reviews of the information.

Support also comes from the mental engagement that arises in response to the computer's questioning and other demands, particularly when these are directed towards stimulating the recall of existing knowledge, directing attention to what is relevant in it, supporting the noticing of relevant connections with the new information, and checking on the outcome. When knowledge or its development is inadequate, the computer can support some digression to make good the deficiencies. In short, ICT supports understanding when it provides information and certain kinds of mental engagement that foster inferencing.

A high level of interactive capability gives the computer-teacher the potential to work alone with a learner. Ridgeway (1988) has pointed to a danger in this. Interaction between people while learning is an important aspect of schooling. It supports the understanding of people. At the simplest level, a child will find that the computer is infinitely patient and tolerant of abuse but this should not be generalized to relationships with people (Cuban, 1986). Body language, another feature of human interaction, may also be a neglected experience if ICT was to dominate the classroom. Equally, how satisfying is machine-generated praise? At another level, learners are potentially able to represent a problem situation in many ways. If the computer does not recognize all of them, is there a risk that a child will learn to narrow thinking to the expected and conventional? Will this impoverish learning (Dillon, 1998)? These questions might have arisen before had the textbook been a better teacher-substitute than it is. When a substitute takes control of the teaching there can be resistance to it, as happened in Samoa in the 1970s. Since then, the role of educational television has been to supplement or enrich teachers' lessons (Westbury, 1989). What it amounts to is: if a really good surrogate teacher of any kind was available, should we use it?

The answer to this has to be that it depends on the circumstances. Such a teacher might be used to good effect with children, but not all the time. There are also other ways of using it which still involve the teacher. Older students may have to rely on it through necessity. For instance, when the number of students is large, it may be used to reduce an excessive burden on the teacher. Such an application, The Modified Socratic Dialogue, is described by Longstaffe (1994). Questions are set for students relating to their lectures. He calculates that a question which takes the 100 students only ten minutes each to complete is worth between 50 and 100 contact hours over the estimated three years of its life. ICT should not be seen as a quick, technological fix for educational problems; it could bring with it as many problems as it solves. Nor should it be assumed that, because it is used, it is of value. As in all teaching, if understanding is to be fostered, the presentation and discourse have to be managed to that end. It is better to see surrogates as a team teacher rather than as a substitute for a teacher, particularly in the earlier stages of education. However, this does not mean that ICT should be seen as an add-on (Somekh and Davis, 1997). It should have a clear part to play in the instruction and be aimed at achieving specific objectives. Since knowing the objectives helps a student approach learning appropriately, these need to be stated.

There are other ways of viewing ICT. Papert (1980) was concerned that a surrogate teacher analogy would carry with it the implication that the computer controls the situation, rather than the learner. He sought ways of enabling the learner to take control through 'microworlds'. In a microworld, the computer provides an environment where the learner explores, tests ideas and solves open-ended problems. Turtle Logo was one of these. The learner gives instructions to a computer and hence controls a floor robot or, for instance, the completion of patterns on a screen (for example, see McFarlane, 1997). Patterns of instructions may be stored and incorporated in other sets of instructions. In a sense, the computer is less of a teacher and more of a learner. The student is meant to acquire or discover new skills and knowledge about, for example, mathematical concepts in the process of directing the robot to do some task. Even the humble pocket calculator may provide a microworld in which the learner explores the properties of numbers in an open-ended way. According to Crook (1994), the approach has not been uniformly successful, possibly because some teachers take the view that, 'simply using it is enough'.

ICT may also be used as a simulator of real world events. A simple example would be the unfolding of events in a house. Children might access the house at different dates and interpret what they see, make predictions and test them (Whitbread, 1997). Typically, the learner interacts with events, solves problems or shapes the outcome. This may involve a conscious or unconscious grasp of the factors that shape events through experience that the computer provides. Used in this way, ICT is a surrogate for the event rather than for the teacher. It provides vicarious experience for the student to learn from. The computer's version of the event, however, generally stems from a model which is relatively simple when compared with what could happen in the real world. On the one hand, this is a shortcoming of ICT as simulator but, on the other, the simplification can focus attention on what matters.

Another way of looking at ICT is as a box of tools. For instance, it can relieve the learner from the burden of calculation and from some of the tiresome aspects of re-drafting text (Crook, 1994). The potential to support understanding comes from the software's ability to reduce mental processing load. McFarlane (1997) described children developing the basic experience of graphing then using the computer to carry out the labour-intensive activity of producing the figure as the child gives it instructions. A new activity, such as drawing a graph, can occupy so much of a child's conscious processing capacity that the purpose of the graph is lost (Newton and Merrell, 1994b). When the intention is that the child should learn to collect information and read a graph which captures its essence, the computer allows the children to focus on that. In this way, the computer can help in capturing and handling data, in drawing a graph, in arriving at a conclusion, in structuring story making, in providing a pallet and enabling the manipulation of images (Steinberg, 1991; McFarlane, 1997; Somekh and Davis, 1997).

Multimedia

Multimedia packages contain different kinds of resources. These may be, for instance, text, audiotape and videotape and the support that each provides might be considered alone. Hartley (1988) applied principles for producing effective text to the production of instructional audiotapes. He added spoken summaries and headings, simplified the language, rearranged the elements and numbered them. The tests showed that these can lead to better recall of content, just as they can do with text. Instructional video can also be a useful medium for supporting learning (Newton, 1993c). It can present information in much the same way as a teacher (and could be a video record of a teacher giving a lesson), but it can also present kinds of experience which otherwise would not be possible in the classroom. However, like the textbook, the videotape is blind and deaf to learners' behaviour. It does not know if users are paying attention or if they are confused. They may engage in the presentation at a relatively low level and in a passive way (Kozma, 1991). This means that it is advisable to support them before, during and after a showing. Relevant prior knowledge may be mobilized, the structure of the information to be presented can be provided, the tape may be stopped at intervals while the students write key words from what they have seen so far, and some form of summary may be needed at the end, perhaps in the form of a concept map (Newton, 1990).

The effect, however, may be greater than the sum of the parts. Mayer and Moreno (1998) argue that a multimedia approach allows branches of working memory to be used in parallel, alleviating the limited mental capacity of any one branch. They showed that animated pictures (drawing on visual working memory capacity) in conjunction with spoken narrative (drawing on auditory working memory capacity) produced better retention and problem solving than animation or text alone (both drawing on visual working memory capacity). In this instance, they achieved the effect using a computer to manage the media. Computer management of media allows rapid access to the various components of the package and enables a variety of paths through it but the management system, or hypermedia environment, has to be well-made, otherwise it can cause difficulties. Most readers can follow a path through a book but the multiplicity of roads, paths and byways that are possible in a computer-managed system can make the overall structure difficult to grasp and learners become lost in hyperspace. They need a practical model of the structure of the package so that coherent mental structures of the topic in hand can be constructed (Astleitner, 1997).

It is possible that the kinds of learning that result from different media are different. Neuman (1992) found no differences in inferencing in story reading amongst 10-year-olds when the inferences were elicited by textual and video presentations. On the other hand, Orellano (1996) found that 10 to 12-year-olds given text subsequently wrote longer compositions than those given text and a picture depicting what the text described. This was seen as arising from the more open nature of text which tended to stimulate elaboration. There may, of course, be pictures that are capable of stimulating elaboration as well, but the point is that mental processing stimulated by different media may be different. Further, in a review of the wider field, Kozma (1991) concluded that what people learn depends on their cognitive style and learning preferences. In other words, some media suit some learners more than others (Riding and Raynor, 1998).

ICT and Teaching

Like the textbook, ICT could be a surrogate teacher and support understanding. If it only replicates what the text does and does not do it better, the textbook is likely to be a more convenient and cheaper resource. ICT can, however, manage various media, provide learning environments and be a learning tool. These may offer something for understanding that other resources do not do well. If an integrated use was made of its potential, from interactive surrogate teacher to learning tool, a way of thinking of ICT might be 'computer as classroom'. In effect, ICT would then act as teacher, provider of experience and provider of tools for making sense of that experience, not separately but in an integrated way. This, however, would only be as good as its designer. In the meantime, Aldrich et al. (1998) advise teachers to judge software by the extent to which it:

- facilitates inferencing by directing attention to what matters;
- makes visible what are normally invisible processes;
- allows learners to manipulate and annotate information and create their own examples and solve problems;
- enables learners to create and combine new representations in different media;
- allows learners to experiment and test their ideas about the topic.

The next chapter examines understanding failure in spite of support from the teacher and the learning resources.

Summary

Teaching is not the sole preserve of the teacher. Teaching resources can also have this role and might support understanding if they do what the teacher would do. In practice, there will be some things they cannot do well. For example, one is the extent to which they can recognize understanding failure and respond adequately to it. At the same time, there will be things they do very well. For instance, a textbook is patient and has a good memory, and a computer programme can allow a learning path that is shaped by or for a particular student. A reliance on such resources, however, risks dehumanized teaching.

From another perspective, the learner can be given control of the resource. The resource provides an environment that the learner explores and shapes. It might also provide vicarious experience of the world through simulations of events and phenomena. These are explored and manipulated until what governs them is understood. A resource may also be seen as a toolbox for freeing mental capacity for what matters and for helping the organization of thought. In practice, we may take different views of the function of such resources according to the needs of the situation and the learner.

References

Aldrich, F., Rogers, Y. and Scaife, M. (1998) 'Getting to Grips with Interactivity: Helping Teachers Assess the Educational Value of CD-ROMS', *British Journal of Educational Technology* 29: 321–32.

Anghileri, J. (1989) 'An Investigation of Young Children's Understanding of Multiplication', *Educational Studies in Mathematics* 20: 367–85.

Astleitner, H. (1997) 'Effect of External Learning Aids on Learning with Ill-Structured Hypertext', *Journal of Educational Computing Research* 17: 1–18.

Ausubel. D.P. (1980) 'The Facilitation of Meaningful Verbal Learning in the Classroom', in J. Hartley (ed.), *The Psychology of Written Communication*, London: Kogan Page.

Beck, I.L., McKeown, M.G., Sinatra, G.M. and Loxterman, J.A. (1991) 'Revising Social Studies Text from a Text-Processing Perspective: Evidence of Improved Comprehensibility', *Reading Research Quarterly* 26: 251–76.

Beck, I.L., McKeown, M.G. and Worthy, J. (1995) 'Giving a Text Voice Can Improve Students' Understanding', *Reading Research Quarterly* 30: 220–38.

Brooks, L.W. and Dansereau, D.F. (1983) 'Effects of Structural Schema Training and Text Organisation on Expository Prose Processing', *Journal of Educational Psychology* 75: 811–20.

Brna, P. and Dicheva, D. (1998) 'Editorial', *British Journal of Educational Technology* 29: 3–4.

Cavalier, J.C. and Klein, J.D. (1998) 'Effects of Cooperative Versus Individual Learning and Orienting Activities During Computer-Based Instruction', *Educational Training Research and Development* 46: 5–17.

Chambliss, M.J. and Calfee, R.C. (1998) *Textbooks for Learning*, Malden: Blackwell.

Chapman, L.F. (1983) 'A Study in Reading Development', in B. Gillman (ed.), *Reading Through the Curriculum*, London: Heinemann.

Clark, J.M. and Paivio, A. (1991) 'Dual Coding Theory and Education', *Educational Psychology Review* 3: 149–210.

Cohen, J. (1969) *Statistical Power Analysis for the Behavioural Sciences*, New York: Academic Press.

Constable, H., Campbell, B. and Brown, R. (1988) 'Sectional Drawings from Science Textbooks: An Experimental Investigation into Pupils' Understanding', *British Journal of Educational Psychology* 58: 89–102.

Crook, C. (1994) *Computers and the Collaborative Experience of Learning*, London: Routledge.

Cuban, L. (1986) *Teachers and Machines*, New York: Teachers' College Press.

Dillon, P. (1998) 'Teaching and Learning with Telematics', *Journal of Information Technology for Teacher Education* 7: 33–49.

Ellis, A. and Beattie, G. (1986) *The Psychology of Language and Communication*, London: Weidenfield and Nicolson.

Emerson, J.D. and Mosteller, F. (1998) 'Interactive Multimedia in College Teaching, Part 1: A Ten-Year Review of Reviews', in Branch, R.M. and Fitzgerald, M.A. (eds), *Educational Technology Yearbook*, Englewood Cliffs, NJ: Libraries Unlimited, 43–58.

Fatt, J.P.T. (1992) 'Text-Related Variables in Textbook Readability', *Research Papers in Education* 6: 225–45.

Felker, D.B. and Dapra, R.A. (1975) 'Effects of Question Type and Question Placement on Problem-Solving Ability From Prose Material', *Journal of Educational Psychology* 67: 380–4.

Glover, J.A. et al. (1988) 'Effects of Across Chapter Signals on Recall of Text', *Journal of Educational Psychology* 80: 3–15.

Hamilton, R.J. (1985) 'A Framework for the Evaluation of the Effectiveness of Adjunct Questions and Objectives', *Review of Educational Research* 55: 47–85.

Hartley, J. (1981) 'Eighty Ways of Improving Instructional Text', *IEEE Transactions on Professional Communication* PC-24, 17–27.

—— (1988) 'Using Principles of Text Design to Improve the Effectiveness of Audiotapes', *British Journal of Educational Technnology* 19: 4–16.

Hartley, J. , Bartlett, S. and Braithwaite, A. (1980) 'Underlining Can Make a Difference – Sometimes', *Journal of Educational Research* 53: 205–14.

Hartley, J. and Trueman, M. (1982) 'The Effects of Summaries on the Recall of Information from Prose: Five Experimental Studies', *Human Learning* 1: 63–82.

Hayes, D.A. and Henk, W.A. (1986) 'Understanding and Remembering Complex Prose Augmented by Analogic and Pictorial Illustration', *Journal of Reading Behavior* 18: 63–78.

Hegarty, M. and Just, M.A. (1993) 'Constructing Mental Models of Machines from Text and Diagrams', *Journal of Memory and Language* 32: 717–42.

Howard, R.W. (1987) *Concepts and Schemata*, London: Cassell Education.

Hurd, S. (1987) 'Factors Influencing Computer Use in Economics', in W.A. Kent and R. Lewis, *Computer Assisted Learning in the Humanities and Social Sciences*, Oxford: Blackwell.

Kaye, A.R. (1989) 'Distance Learning Systems', in M. Erhaut (ed.), *The International Encyclopedia of Educational Technology*, Oxford: Pergamon, 286–91.

Kemper, S. (1983) 'Measuring the Inference Load of a Text', *Journal of Educational Psychology* 66: 614–22.

Kloster, A.M. and Winne, P.H. (1989) 'The Effects of Different Types of Organisers on Students' Learning from Text', *Journal of Educational Psychology* 81: 9–15.

Kozma, R.B. (1991) 'Learning with Media', *Review of Educational Research* 61: 179–211.

Kulik, J.A., Bangert, R.L. and Williams, G.W. (1983) 'Effects of Computer-Based Teaching on Secondary School Students', *Journal of Educational Psychology* 75: 19–26.

Levine, T. (1994) 'A Computer-Based Program Can Make a Difference', *Studies in Educational Evaluation* 20: 283–96.

Loman, N.L. and Meyer, R.E. (1983) 'Signalling Techniques that Increase the Understanding of Expository Prose', *Journal of Educational Psychology* 75: 402–12.

Longstaffe, J.A. (1994) 'Modified Socratic Dialogue: An Easier Way into Computer Aided Learning', *CTI Medicine* 5: 9–10.

McDaniel, M.A. and Donnelly, C.M. (1996) 'Learning with Analogy and Elaborative Interrogation', *Journal of Educational Psychology* 88: 508–19.

McFarlane, A. (ed.) (1997) *Information Technology and Authentic Learning*, London: Routledge.

Marcus, N., Cooper, M. and Sweller, J. (1996) 'Understanding Instructions', *Journal of Educational Psychology* 88: 49–63.

Mayer, R.E. (1989) 'Systematic Thinking Fostered by Illustrations in Scientific Text', *Journal of Educational Psychology* 81: 240–46.

Mayer, R.E., Bove, M., Byrman, A., Mars, R. and Tapangco, L. (1996) 'When Less is More: Meaningful Learning from Visual and Verbal Summaries of Science Textbook Lessons', *Journal of Educational Psychology* 88: 64–73.

Mayer, R.E. and Moreno, R. (1998) 'A Split-Attention Effect in Multimedia Learning', *Journal of Educational Psychology* 90: 312–20.

McLaughlin, G.H. (1969) 'SMOG Grading – A New Readability Formula', *Journal of Reading* 12: 639–46.

Molenda, M., Russell, J.D. and Smaldino, S. (1998) 'Trends in Media and Technology in Education and Training', in R.M. Branch and M.A. Fitzgerald (eds), *Educational Technology Yearbook*, Englewood Cliffs, NJ: Libraries Unlimited, 2–10.

Natriello, G. (1997) 'Picture This: Graphs, Figures, and Photographs in Academic Papers', *Teachers College Record* 99: 1–8.

Neuman, S.B. (1992) 'Is Learning from Media Distinctive? Examining Children's Inferencing Strategies', *American Educational Research Journal* 29: 119–40.

Neuman, W.R. (1995) 'The Psychology of the New Media', *Educom Review*, January: 48–54.

Newton, D.P. (1985) 'Children's Perception of Pictorial Metaphor', *Educational Psychology* 5: 179–85.

—— (1990) *Teaching with Text*, London: Kogan Page.

—— (1993a) 'Teaching Packages and Their Evaluation Through a Surrogate Teacher Model', *Educational and Training Technology International* 30: 375–85.

—— (1993b) 'Learning from Tables', *Educational Psychology* 13: 89–106.

—— (1993c) 'Using Instructional Video', *Education Today* 43: 31–4.

Newton, D.P. and Merrell, C.H. (1994a), 'Words That Count: Communicating with Mathematical Text', *International Journal of Mathematics Education in Science and Technology* 25: 457–62.

—— (1994b) 'Helping Children Notice Co-Variation in Tables: The Effect of Some Strategies', *Research in Education* 51: 41–50.

Newton, L.D. (1983) 'The Effect of Illustrations on the Readability of Some Junior School Textbooks', *Reading* 17: 43–54.

Orellano, E.R. (1996) 'Comparative Study of the Information Developed from Messages Containing Picture and Text', *Instructional Science* 24: 357–75.

Papert, S. (1980) *Mindstorms*, Brighton: Harvester Press.

Park, O. (1998) 'Visual Displays and Contextual Presentations in Computer-Based Instructions', *Educational Training Research and Development* 46: 37–50.

Perelman, L.J. (1992) *Schools Out*, New York: Avon Books.

Peeck, J., van den Bosch, A.B. and Kreupeling, W.J. (1982) 'Effect of Mobilising Prior Knowledge on Learning from Text', *Journal of Educational Psychology* 78: 34–8.

Ridgeway, J. (1988) 'Of Course ICAI Is Impossible...Worse Though, It Might Even Be Seditious', in J. Self, *Artificial Intelligence and Human Learning*, London: Chapman and Hall, 28–48.

Riding, R. and Rayner, S. (1998) *Cognitive Styles and Learning Strategies*, London: Fulton.

Rowe, D.W. and Rayford, L. (1987) 'Activating Background Knowledge in Reading Comprehension Assessment', *Reading Research Quarterly* 22: 160–75.

Schank, G.T. (1988) 'Interestingness: Controlling Inferences', *Artificial Intelligence* 12: 273–97.

Sipe, L.R. (1998) 'How Picture Books Work', *Children's Literature in Education* 29: 97–108.

Somekh, B. and Davis, N. (1997) *Using Information Technology Effectively in Teaching and Learning: Studies in Pre-Service and In-Service Teacher Education*, London: Routledge.

Spires, H.A. and Donley, J. (1998) 'Prior Knowledge Activation: Inducing Engagement with Informational Texts', *Journal of Educational Psychology* 90: 249–60.

Steinberg, E.R. (1991) *Teaching Computers to Teach*, Hillsdale, NJ: Lawrence Erlbaum, 2nd edn.

Stone, C.L. (1983) 'A Meta-Analysis of Advance Organiser Studies', *Journal of Experimental Education* 5: 194–9.

Sweller, J. (1994) 'Cognitive Load Theory, Learning Difficulty, and Instructional Practice', *Learning and Instruction* 4: 285–312.

Sweller, J. and Chandler, P. (1994) 'Why Some Material is Difficult to Learn', *Cognition and Instruction* 12: 185–233.

Tarquin, P. and Walker, S. (1997) *Creating Success in the Classroom*, Englewood Cliffs, NJ: Teaching Ideas Press.

Teather, D.C.B. (1989) 'Australia and New Zealand', in M. Erhaut (ed.), *The International Encyclopedia of Educational Technology*, Oxford: Pergamon, 503–8.

Van Dijk, T.A. and Kintsch, W. (1983) *Strategies for Discourse Comprehension*, New York: Academic Press.

Westbury, I. (1989) 'The Role of Textbooks', in M. Erhaut (ed.), *The International Encyclopedia of Educational Technology*, Oxford; Pergamon, 476–80.

Whitbread, D. (1997) 'Developing Children's Problem Solving', in A. McFarlane, A. (ed.), *Information Technology and Authentic Learning*, London: Routledge, 13–37.

Wittrock, M.C. (1989) 'Generative Processes of Comprehension', *Educational Psychologist* 24: 345–76.

8 Failing to Understand

Overview

Reasons for not understanding are reviewed and the effect of misconceptions, in particular, is considered. Misconceptions vary in nature, consequence and tenacity. At their worst, they may generate understanding failure in whole topics and may be difficult to address. Some possible origins of misconceptions are outlined and some theories and strategies for dealing with them described. The need to consider the possibility that some conceptions may be replaced while others coexist with the new conceptions is suggested. Some implications of this for treating misconceptions are considered.

Failure to Understand

Failure to understand could occur for a variety of reasons. There may be a failure to construct an adequate, coherent mental representation of the information in a situation. The learner may simply not know understanding is expected and so does not attend in a way that makes it possible. He or she may be unable to construct a mental representation because of a lack of relevant prior knowledge, excessive mental demand, not knowing what is relevant, or failing to notice relevant relationships within the new information and between it and prior knowledge. There could be a failure to manipulate a mental representation or relate it to others because of a lack of 'rules' for governing the relationship. There could even be a failure to recognize a mental representation as being the state that was to be understood or achieved, as when a solution to a problem is found but is not recognized as such.

How to support understanding in such circumstances was the subject of earlier chapters. But what of those occasions when learners develop understandings that satisfy them yet are unacceptable to the academic community or are otherwise unsound? This kind of understanding 'failure' can exist in very different domains of thought. For example:

- In biological science, some believe that acquired characteristics, such as rough hands can be inherited over several generations (Clough and Wood-Robinson, 1985). As a child, Peter Ustinov avoided drinking water after eating fish in case the bits rejoined in his stomach (Ustinov, 1977). In physical science, a common belief is that a force is needed to maintain motion in the absence of friction.

- In history, children tend to consider earlier people as somewhat stupid (Knight, 1990). Another source of misconceptions arises from words which mean different things at different times. For instance, 'revolution', 'industry' and 'middle class' have changed in meaning over the years. Applying these conceptions anachronistically could lead to plausible but unacceptable understandings of past events. This applies also to ethical and moral conceptions.

- In geography, Flat Earth misconceptions are well known, but some people think of Africa as being totally in the southern hemisphere, Edinburgh as being directly north of London, and that volcanoes release lava from the centre of the Earth (Bisard et al., 1994). Misconceptions about the weather are not uncommon, too. Some believe that lightning never strikes the same place twice, yet, at the same time they accept that lightning strikes mountains more frequently than low lying areas (Aron et al., 1994).

- In mathematics, novel situations commonly cause difficulties in applying algorithms (Dehaene, 1997). For example, errors in subtraction occur when children attempt to apply a half-understood rule to situations such as $27-19$, resulting in the answer 12. So-called buggy arithmetic is not uncommon and is not confined to subtraction (Bruer, 1994; Woodward and Howard, 1994).

- In gambling, there is often an inability to consider events as independent, even when they are. In tossing dice, if a six and four come up this time, they are thought less likely next time. The result is that the gambler chooses different numbers. This may arise from experience of a world where every effect has a cause (Savoie and Ladouceur, 1995).

- In environmental health, people may believe we are experiencing an epidemic of cancer from exposure to synthetic chemicals. These chemicals are seen as inherently toxic while natural substances are benign. When widespread, public misconceptions of this nature can influence government policy (Hrudely, 1990).

- In public health, there are dietary misconceptions. For instance, saturated fats may be thought to have more fat than unsaturated fats; you may substitute margarine for butter and so reduce your fat intake, and you can tell by looking at foods whether or not they are high in fats (Auld et al., 1994).

- In popular psychology, there are common misconceptions like IQ does not predict academic success and less academically able children are generally gifted in non-academic areas. There is also a belief that having convicts talk to children about the error of their ways persuades the children to go straight, in spite of evidence to the contrary (McCutcheon et al., 1993).

- In teaching, 'authentic learning' is a term used to describe activity closely related to the situation in which the knowledge would tend to apply. Since knowledge is considered to be tied to the situation in which it is acquired, this situating of cognition is likely to aid its application. Cronin (1993) describes some misconceptions teachers in the USA have about authentic learning. For example, some argue that approximations to the real world are not valid or worthwhile ('if you can't take 'em to Spain, they might as well not learn Spanish at all'). There may be a belief that it needs extensive training to use it effectively ('if you haven't got your chef's licence, then you'll have to starve'). Others may say that only complex situations are valid because that is what the world is like ('If you want to learn to play the piano, you must start by mastering Chopin'). Cronin argues that each of these is unfounded but, unfortunately, those who believe them do not try authentic learning.

Some understanding failure is simply due to factual error. For example, it seems reasonable to believe that pencil lead contains lead; so lead, being a metal, will conduct electricity and so there is nothing special in finding that a pencil lead does, indeed, conduct electricity. In reality, pencil lead contains graphite, a non-metal. The word 'lead' is a hangover from the days when real lead was used in pencils. It is likely that an error of this kind is easy to correct: a statement of the correction and the reason for it is likely to suffice.

Perhaps a little more difficult to correct are some law-like ideas, such as 'all wild animals are dangerous'. After all, a belief of this kind has survival value, and even when someone is given contrary examples, such as the butterfly, the frog and the sparrow, they may still feel a need for caution.

Some personal theories about how the world works can shape a wide range of understandings. Misconceptions of this kind are generative in that they are frequently used to explain, predict or justify situations and events. For instance, the belief that a force is needed to maintain motion even in the absence of friction will make its owner expect rocket engines to be kept on in space, otherwise the rocket will slow and stop. On the Earth, too, such a student's understanding of many situations in dynamics would lead to very significant errors.

This means that the impact of misconceptions ranges from a minor and local failure to a major and widespread disability, according to the nature of the misconception. No one is immune to misconceptions, and not all are serious. Some, however, have the potential to underpin (mis)understandings across a wide field and so can have significant consequences. Probably most problematic are those that are deep rooted, work adequately in a limited range of circumstances and can be used across a wide domain. Unfortunately, these also tend to be the ones most difficult to change. How does someone come to have such conceptions?

Origins of Misconceptions

Misconceptions may arise in a variety of ways. They may, for instance, stem from misinformation, inattentiveness, selective attention, misinterpretation, a lack of aural or visual acuity or be generated by ambiguous information. For example, after hearing a Bible story, a child referred to 'Jesus and His Twelve Icicles'. Discounting the first cause of misinformation (on the assumption that the child was not misinformed) any one of the others might be responsible for this. The application of an inappropriate analogy may also generate misconceptions about regularities in the world (as, perhaps, when a child uses a common inflection as an analogy and announces that something is 'deaded'). Some particularly problematic misconceptions are probably acquired through direct but limited experience with the world. For instance, experience tends to teach us that light objects and hollow things generally float in water when really what matters is a 'light for its size in comparison to water' property. The light–hollow rule is probably based on years of observation, and it can be difficult to have someone abandon such a rule on the basis of one or two lessons. It is the same with the common misconception that a force is needed to maintain an object's motion in the absence of friction. In the world we know, we have probably never experienced motion without friction. To keep a bicycle moving on a level road you have to keep turning the pedals. Unsurprisingly, experience like this usually leads to a generalization that a force is always needed to maintain motion. Such misconceptions provide frameworks for understanding the world and for making predictions about events in it.

At the same time, some frameworks may have innate foundations. That we arrive in the world with some fundamental, ready-made ideas about it might, at first, seem odd but evolutionary psychologists like Cosmides and Tooby (1992) argue that the mind, like the other organs of the body, has evolved in response to selective pressures of the environment. Those born with advantageous mental attributes would be more likely to survive and pass them on. During the last Ice Age, which ended about 10,000 years ago, we might expect an advantage in, for instance, knowing something about the behaviour of rigid objects. This could help in throwing a projectile, as animals are unlikely to wait while you think about it. Certain fundamental expectations about the world seem to exist in the mind of a child within its first year of life. Babies show surprise at seeing an object stay in mid-air after losing its support. Similarly, they seem intrigued by objects which apparently occupy the same place or that are hidden behind a screen but are not there when the screen is removed (Wynne, 1996; Dehaene, 1997).

Reasoning about life in the Pleistocene era, Cosmides and Tooby speculated about the mental units or modules that would be advantageous. Such modules might prepare the mind for language, the physical and natural worlds and human relationships. This is not to say that children come pre-wired with a knowledge of a particular language or of formal physics or formal psychology. Instead, they may be equipped with what underpins languages, so that it is possible to acquire one easily at a certain stage of development. Similarly, modules for supporting human relationships would help someone gauge another's thoughts and mental states (Whiten, 1991). According to Spelke (1991) and Vosniadou (1994), we may be born with a belief in the essential continuity and solidity of things and that there can be no action at a distance. In the biological world, we may be equipped with a readiness to divide the world into, for instance, living and non-living, and we know that the two are not subject to the same rules (Mithen, 1996). Numerosity is another example. While we may have precise knowledge about small numbers, our grasp of large numbers tends to be vague. Anything more in the Pleistocene world would be unlikely to confer additional survival value (Dehaene, 1997). At the same time, natural selection does not have to favour knowledge that is logical, correct or scientifically acceptable, only that which aids survival. This means that any innate inclinations could conflict with what we want to teach. Further, they could sustain a whole body of understandings developed and reinforced from birth.

Mithen (1996), for example, sees the mind as equipped with intuitive knowledge relating to language and to social, technical and natural world matters. Another, more general purpose unit that enables reflection upon mental representations is postulated (Sperber, 1994). Ideas can flow between specialized and general purpose modules. There are interesting parallels with Gardner's theory of multiple intelligences. Gardner (1983), coming from a different direction, concluded that we are endowed with multiple, specialized intelligences rather than merely a general purpose intelligence. He proposed linguistic, musical, logical-mathematical, spatial, bodily-kinaesthetic and personal intelligences. Some parallels with the modules of evolutionary psychologists are apparent. Further, Gardner emphasized the potential for interaction between the intelligences, exemplified by the important role of metaphor and analogy in our thinking. Not all would agree with Sperber or Mithen's architecture (see, for instance, Fodor, 1984). Nevertheless, the possibility of innate, hard-wired knowledge has to be considered, along with other sources, when planning to treat misconceptions. Such knowledge, or the structures it generates, may be practically useful yet still conflict with formal knowledge.

Theories about Dealing with Misconceptions

Some misconceptions are relatively easy to change. Difficulty is more likely to occur in treating those that are well-founded in experience or which may be based on innate knowledge.

The Replacement Theory

As the name suggests, this theory treats the process as one of replacing existing mental structures with others. Vosniadou (1992, 1994) sees this as a gradual process involving the enrichment and revision of ideas.

Enrichment is the simplest form of change. It amounts to the 'addition of new information to an existing theoretical framework'. This is a relatively easy form of conceptual change. For example, children do not find it difficult to learn that the Moon has craters, given what they know of the Moon. Generally, this additional knowledge does not conflict with prior knowledge.

Revision is necessary when new information conflicts with prior knowledge. This is easier for a specific theory than for a framework. The example Vosniadou gives is when children assume there to be air and water on the Moon by analogy with the Earth. They soon revise that theory when they learn that astronauts must take their own air and water with them. On the other hand, children can find it very difficult to believe that the Earth is a sphere, contradicting direct but limited experience. They are likely to believe that the world is flat. Since all objects fall down, staying on the ground is no problem. However, anyone on the 'underside' of the world must fall off since objects fall 'down'.

Vosniadou describes how children's conceptions of the Earth can be found in several cultures and follow similar patterns of change as formal knowledge develops. The conceptions move from initial mental models of the Earth as a flat, rectangular sheet, to a flat disc, through hybrid, synthetic models, such as a flattened sphere, to a more scientific model (Figure 8.1). Note, however, that there is a reluctance to abandon earlier ideas. The flattened disc is a compromise between a rectangular sheet and a 'round' Earth, and the truncated sphere maintains a flat Earth on a sphere. It is as though the child has expectations about what is correct and is reluctant to abandon them. Similar effects are observed with beliefs about the cause of day and night. Initial ideas often involve the sun moving behind distant features, such as hills, or below the horizon. The target idea is that of a rotating Earth which brings people into daylight. Synthetic, compromise models develop in which, for instance, the sun moves down, past a spherical Earth until it is out of sight from an observer on the top. Johnson (1998) has similarly noted intermediate states in a longitudinal study of 11 to 14-year-old's particulate theories of matter.

Figure 8.1   Earth Theories

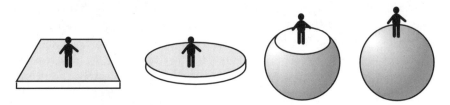

Disconnected/Mini Theories

DiSessa (1993) sees knowledge of the world as fragmented ('knowledge in pieces') and composed of small knowledge structures he called phenomenological primitives. They are primitive in that they usually are unquestioned, superficial derivations from experience. Notions of force, resistance and equilibrium are examples but these words do not necessarily mean quite the same as they do in formal physics (Kozma and Russell, 1997). Misconceptions arise when these pieces figure in reasoning. An example is the belief that an object moves because of the impetus it possesses. This is based on pieces of knowledge such as 'force is a mover' and 'dying away'. Experience has taught that these are 'valid' pieces of knowledge with explanatory value so they are used to underpin explanations to do with motion.

Vosniadou (1994) believes that such knowledge is not fragmented but forms coherent structures or frameworks. These frameworks provide radically different explanations of the world. She argues that it is not an inappropriate assemblage of knowledge fragments that causes the problem but the presuppositions that underpin the misconceptions. These presuppositions are what are difficult to change, not the misconceptions themselves (White, 1993).

Multiple Representations Theory

Caravito and Hallden (1994) subscribe to the view that we have a range of theories about the world. Initially, this may be very limited and one or two may be deployed regularly. As experience increases, the number increases and they are used in more discriminating ways. For instance, shown a piece of wood and asked if it will float, someone is likely to draw on a relatively simple generalization they acquired early to the effect that wooden objects float. Shown a more complex body, they might switch to a 'light for its size' theory of flotation. Asked about the depth to which it will sink, they may have to rely on a more formal scientific theory. Each theory of the world co-exists and is triggered by the situation. As experience grows, some theories may be found more useful, more encompassing, more relevant than others, and so the relative frequency with which each is deployed could change with time.

One problem is that learning situations are often of a kind that trigger theories based on misconceptions. If we show someone an object and ask if it will float, that person may have several relevant theories. We want them to apply the one that is generally acceptable. The situation is, at least superficially, like many that have been met in the past. Unfortunately, the person dealt with those by using an inappropriate theory, although it gave the correct answer on most, if not all, of those occasions. The tying together of situation and knowledge makes it likely that the inappropriate theory will be recalled and applied again. The practical difficulty here is in inducing that person to recall and apply the new and more appropriate theory.

According to these views, knowledge may be changed, dislodged or supplanted, it may be fragmented, or it may co-exist and compete with new knowledge. Some kinds of knowledge may be more difficult to change than others. For example, understandings may be based on immutable, hard-wired knowledge. Counter-intuitive understandings may simply have to co-exist with them. On the other hand, what is innate may be predispositions that produce more or less plastic understandings, susceptible to change (Carey and Spelke, 1994; Karmiloff-Smith, 1995). Faced with such possibilities, strategies for dealing with misconceptions have to allow for a variation in the kind and origin of the misconception.

Strategies for Dealing with Misconceptions

As there are several kinds of misconception, it is probably a mistake to believe they all are susceptible to the same treatment. Some may be readily overcome and, in effect, are replaced by more acceptable conceptions. Those that are well-integrated with existing knowledge structures or based on innate conceptions may be less susceptible to change. What may happen is that learners develop another conception beside the first and, preferably, begin to use the new one in certain contexts. They may, however, continue to use the earlier conceptions in everyday contexts. This suggests that, as well as strategies which *replace* misconceptions, there needs to be strategies which *displace* misconceptions. The latter are likely to be needed for deep-rooted, well-integrated ideas.

Diagnosis, Integration, Differentiation, Exchange (and Constraining)

Hewson and Hewson (1984) have described a general teaching strategy with the aim of changing misconceptions. This approach has four components: diagnosis, integration, differentiation and exchange. Diagnosis is a necessary prerequisite. The nature of any misconception and what underpins it has to be determined. This can be time-consuming because the precise nature may be different for different learners. Where there is no conflict between what is to be learned and prior knowledge, integration is used. This is much like Vosniadou's enrichment approach, and is a familiar strategy to most teachers. Given a lack of conflict, it seems justified. However, where there is cognitive conflict, the learner may pay lip service to the new conception but revert to the old one in explanations and applications.

Sometimes, conceptions are confused. For example, heat and temperature are different concepts, but are commonly used almost synonymously. This probably arises from and is reinforced by popular usage. People usually say that it is a hot day and that the bath is hot when, strictly speaking, they are referring to the temperature. In this instance, differentiation is used to distinguish between such concepts. Differentiation establishes the differences so that conceptions can be used in appropriate situations. A graphic organizer for supporting this process was described in Chapter 5.

Exchange is to be used when the new information is not consistent with prior knowledge. The aim is to replace the inadequate conception with one considered to be more appropriate. This is similar to Vosniadou's process of revision, noted above. An approach derived from Piagetian principles is to confront the misconception with contrary experience. If a child believes that balloons filled with air drift upwards, they can test the idea with a set of balloons. This is an instance of initiating cognitive conflict in the mind of the learner. The belief is that the learner will attempt to resolve the conflict and, as a result, revise their conceptions. A number of strategies are based upon initiating cognitive conflict. Of course, the assumption is that a learner will attempt to resolve the conflict. This may be true for some learners, but there are others who seem able to tolerate inconsistency (Beveridge, 1985). In effect, new and old knowledge co-exist.

Refutational Text

This is text which cites and refutes common misconceptions about the topic in hand (Guzzetti, 1990). William of Occam (*c*.1300–1349) once refuted the impetus theory of motion by describing the flight of two arrows which pass one another closely at their highest point as they move in opposite directions (Figure 8.2). He pointed out that the equal and opposite 'forces' driving the arrows, if they existed, would cancel out at that point and the arrows would fall vertically to the ground. That they do not fall shows that the impetus theory is incorrect.

Instead of avoiding misconceptions, a textbook could describe and refute them and demonstrate the superiority of the alternative view. Guzzetti (1990) did not find this to be very effective and decided that, once again, incongruity and cognitive conflict were not always sufficient for change. On the other hand, Hynd et al. (1994) found it to work. It may be that refuting

Figure 8.2 *Occam's refutation of the view that forces accompany moving objects until consumed: if arrows from the left and right are accompanied by the forces which sent them, these equal and opposite forces would cancel at the top when the arrows become parallel to one another, leaving the arrows to fall as shown. Since the arrows simply pass one another at the top, the forces must not accompany the arrows.*

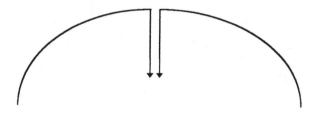

misconceptions in this way may be effective for some topics (perhaps where incongruity is not great or contrary views are not deeply embedded in mental structures) but inadequate for others.

Activating Prior Learning

Bringing prior knowledge into consciousness is not, in itself, a useful strategy for bringing about conceptual change. It may even make the situation worse since a misconception may have been resurrected and is now ready to be used. However, if the activation reveals misconceptions and these are refuted, this can be an effective strategy (Guzzetti et al., 1993).

Peer Group Discussion

Co-operative learning is often considered to be an effective way of developing knowledge. Nevertheless, it has been found wanting when it comes to supporting conceptual development and it may even propagate the misconceptions you want to address. (Levin and Druyan, 1993; Hynd et al., 1994; Snyder and Sullivan, 1995). Lonning (1993) was able to show that it could work provided that it was carefully structured and the teacher monitored and guided the discussion.

Demonstration

Physically demonstrating the inadequacy of a view has been found to be effective. In the case of Occam's refutation, some means of setting up a version of it would be needed. Once again, the effect has been ascribed to the cognitive conflict it engenders but it is not always a feasible option (Guzzetti et al., 1993).

Question–Answer–Explanation Worksheets

Question–answer–explanation worksheets have been found to be largely ineffective in treating misconceptions (Guzzetti et al., 1993), perhaps because of the nature of the questions. In the case of learned misconceptions, focused questions of the kind described in Chapter 5, may have some effect, particularly if they address what underpins the misconception (Newton, 1997).

Analogy and Example

Generally, analogy and multiple example have been found to be effective in supporting conceptual change, particularly where it bridged from what learners readily accept (the anchor) to the target knowledge (Brown, 1992, 1993, 1994). Not everyone has found it to be effective but the basis and purpose of examples and analogies must be known to the learner or made explicit.

Prediction

Hameed et al.(1993) and Saxana (1992) have demonstrated that prediction can help learners acquire new conceptions. A situation is presented in which a prediction based on a misconception will lead to an error. The event then shows this to be an error, and so presents conceptual conflict. The situation does not always have to be a real-world event, and useful effects have also been observed with simulations, such as those presented using ICT.

Displacement

Most of these strategies tend to focus on conceptual change, exchange or replacement. I suggest that, in addition, some strategy is needed in the event of misconceptions that resist change strongly and tend to co-exist with the desired conception. It may not be clear which conceptions are susceptible to replacement and which are not. A strategy which begins with and extends a replacement approach is, therefore, likely to be economical since it may change what can be changed and could lead into a treatment for the more difficult cases. For instance, Hewson and Hewson's exchange approach might be attempted first, confronting ideas with direct experience. Guzzetti et al. (1993) recommends that a combination of strategies has more effect than any one alone so this may be followed by, for instance, refutational text. This will either begin the process of replacing or changing the misconception, or else support the establishment of the desired one in parallel with it.

One approach that shows some promise of displacing misconceptions is the use of analogy. Analogy allows a mental movement away from the representations of a domain where the misconception is a problem to a different but parallel representation in another domain (for example, White, 1993).

For example, mass and density are often confused. Smith et al. (1992) drew an analogy with sugar dissolved in water. The amount of sugar and water is like the mass of a substance and the degree of sweetness of the solution is like the density. Chi (1992) and Ohlsson (1992) suggest another approach. They advocate that the new conception be taught initially without regard to the biologically rooted misconception. Only when facility with the conception has developed would it be set against the misconception. The delay allows the power of the new idea to become apparent.

The difficulty with co-existing conceptions is that everyday situations are likely to cue the misconception. Everyday situations are those that have tended to legitimize it in the past so the misconception comes to mind first. The task is to displace it from its prime position. One strategy may be to use examples and partially completed solutions and explanations which constrain the learner to use the new conception. This would be progressively extended to encroach on those everyday situations which commonly cue the misconception. The aim is to establish a pattern of recall and use of the new conception in the misconception's domain. Resnick (1994) recommends a similar approach using 'organized sequences of designed situations that will tune learners adaptively to kinds of natural situations'. This alone, however, may be insufficient. Other strategies, such as focused questioning and forced prediction, may need to be involved. It will take time and patience and the old conception may remain alive but the intention is that it is used on fewer and fewer occasions.

No single method may be universally effective and even teaching itself can give rise to misconceptions (Adeniyi, 1985). Some teaching strategies popularly thought to establish understanding do not work well when it comes to changing or displacing conceptions. For instance, discovery methods where learners are left to construct their own understanding unsupported, is one of these (Driver, 1994). The variability of effect may have several causes. The quality of instruction may be variable, there are different kinds of conceptions which may be susceptible to different kinds of treatment, reasoning skills and ability will vary from learner to learner, and motivation, attitudes and metacognitive skills must play a part in determining what actually happens in a given situation (Dagher, 1994; Pintrich et al., 1993; Lawson et al., 1993; Mason, 1994). This broader picture is the subject of the next chapter.

Summary

This chapter has looked at the occasions when learners bring with them prior knowledge which conflicts with what is to be learned. There are various kinds of faulty prior knowledge, and they may not be susceptible to the same treatment. Not all prior knowledge is problematic, but of that which is, some can be very difficult to deal with. It is important to address the knowledge which underpins the misconception rather than treating only surface features of it. Some faulty knowledge may be susceptible to change and replacement. Strategies that may help include engendering cognitive conflict by, for instance, direct experience, practical demonstration and having the learner predict the outcome of an event. Activating prior knowledge and direct refutation of it, analogy and example are also known to help. Peer group discussion which airs misconceptions and allows an opportunity to notice inconsistencies and their limitations may help but can also spread misconceptions unless carefully guided. Since it is possible that misconceptions and new conceptions may co-exist, some attempt to displace the former from dominance may be needed. The aim is to have situations cue the new conception rather than the misconception. Clusters of strategies are likely to be more effective than one alone, and the process may take time.

References

Adeniyi, E.D. (1985) 'Misconceptions of Selected Ecological Concepts Held by Some Nigerian Students', *Journal of Biological Education* 19: 311.

Aron, R.H., Francek, M.A., Nelson, B.D. and Bisard, W.J. (1994) 'Atmospheric Misconceptions', *The Science Teacher*, January: 31–3.

Auld, G.W., Achterberg, C.L., Getty, V.M. and Durrwachter, J.G. (1994) 'Misconceptions About Fats and Cholesterol: Implications for Dietary Guidelines', *Ecology of Food and Nutrition* 33: 15–25.

Beveridge, M. (1985) 'The Development of Young Children's Understanding of the Process of Evaporation', *British Journal of Educational Psychology* 55: 84–90.

Bisard, W.J., Aron, R.H., Francek, M.A. and Nelson, B.D. (1994) 'Assessing Selected Physical Science and Earth Science Misconceptions', *JCST*, September–October: 38–42.

Brown, D.E. (1992) 'Using Examples and Analogies to Remediate Misconceptions in Physics: Factors Influencing Conceptual Change', *Journal of Research in Science Teaching* 29: 17–34.

—— (1993) 'Refocusing Core Intuitions', *Journal of Research in Science Teaching* 30: 1273–90.

—— (1994) 'Facilitating Conceptual Change Using Analogies and Explanatory Models', *International Journal of Science Education* 16: 201–14.

Bruer, J.T. (1994) *Schools of Thought*, Cambridge, MA: Bradford Books.

Caravito, S. and Hallden, O. (1994) 'Re-Framing the Problem of Conceptual Change', *Learning and Instruction* 4: 89–111.

Carey, S. and Spelke, E. (1994) 'Domain-Specific Knowledge and Conceptual Change', in L.A. Hirschfeld and S.A. Gelman (eds), *Mapping the Mind*, Cambridge, MA: Cambridge University Press, 169–200.

Chi, M.T.H. (1992) 'Conceptual Change Within and Across Ontological Categories', in R. Giere (ed.), *Cognitive Models of Science*, Minneapolis, MN: University of Minnesota Press, 129–60.

Clough, E.E. and Wood-Robinson, E. (1985) 'Children's Understanding of Inheritance', *Journal of Biological Education* 19: 304–10.

Cronin, J.F. (1993) 'Four Misconceptions About Authentic Learning', *Educational Leadership*, April: 78–80.

Cosmides, L. and Tooby, J. (1992) 'Cognitive Adaptations for Social Change', in J.H. Barkow, L. Cosmides and J. Tooby (eds), *The Adapted Mind*, Oxford: Oxford University Press, 163–228.

Dagher, Z.R. (1994) 'Does the Use of Analogies Contribute to Conceptual Change', *Science Education* 78: 601–14.

Dehaene, S. (1997) *The Number Sense*, London: Allen Lane.

DiSessa, A. (1993) 'Towards an Epistemology of Physics', *Cognition and Instruction* 10: 105–225.

Driver, R. (1994) 'The Fallacy of Induction in Science Teaching', in R. Levison (ed.), *Teaching Science*, London: Routledge, 41–8.

Fodor, J.A. (1984) *The Modularity of the Mind*, Bradford: MIT Press.

Gardner, H. (1983) *Frames of Mind*, New York: Basic Books.

Guzzetti, B.J. (1990) 'Effects of Textual and Instructional Manipulations on Concept Acquisition', *Reading Psychology* 11: 49–62.

Guzzetti, B.J., Snyder, T.E., Gamas, W.S. and Glass, G.V. (1993) 'Promoting Conceptual Change in Science: A Meta-Analysis of Instructional Interventions from Reading Education and Science Education', *Reading Research Quarterly* 28: 116–61.

Hameed, H., Hackling, M.W. and Garnett, P.J. (1993) 'Facilitating Conceptual Change in Chemical Equilibrium', *International Journal of Science Education* 15: 221–30.

Hewson, P.W. and Hewson, M.G.A. (1984) 'The Role of Conceptual Conflict in Conceptual Change and the Design of Science Instruction', *Instructional Science* 13: 1–13.

Hrudely, S.E. (1990) 'Principles and Misconceptions in Environmental Health', *Research Journal Water Pollution Control Federation*, May–June: 211.

Hynd, C., McWhorter, J.Y., Phares, V.L. and Suttles, C.W. (1994) 'The Role of Instructional Variables in Conceptual Change', *Journal of Research in Science Teaching* 31: 933–46.

Johnson, P. (1998) 'Progression in Children's Understanding of a 'Basic' Particle Theory: A Longitudinal Study', *International Journal of Science Education* 20: 393–412.

Karmiloff-Smith, A. (1995) *Beyond Modularity*, Bradford: MIT Press.

Kozma, R.B. and Russell, J. (1997) 'Multimedia and Understanding', *Journal of Research in Science Teaching* 34: 949–68.

Knight, P. (1990) 'A Study of Teaching and Children's Understanding of People in the Past', *Research in Education* 44: 39–53.

Lawson, A.E., Baker, W.P., Didonato, L., Verdu, M.P. and Johnson, M.A. (1993) 'The Role of Hypothetico-Deductive Reasoning and Physical Analogies of Molecular Interaction in Conceptual Change', *Journal of Research in Science Teaching* 30: 1073–82.

Levin, I. and Druyan, S. (1993) 'When Sociocognitive Transaction Among Peers Fails: The Case of Misconceptions in Science', *Child Development* 64: 1571–91.

Lonning, R.A. (1993) 'Effect of Co-Operative Learning Strategies on Student Verbal Interactions and Achievement During Conceptual Change Instruction in 10th Grade General Science', *Journal of Research in Science Teaching* 30: 1087–1101.

Mason, L. (1994) 'Analogy, Metaconceptual Awareness and Conceptual Change', *Educational Studies* 20: 267–91.

Mithen, S. (1996) *The Prehistory of the Mind*, London: Phoenix.

McCutcheon, L.E., Furnham, A. and Davis, G. (1993) 'A Cross-National Comparison of Students' Misconceptions About Psychology', *Psychological Reports* 72: 243–7.

Newton, L.D. (1997) 'Teachers' Questioning for Understanding in Science', *British Journal of Curriculum and Assessment* 8: 28–32.

Ohlsson, S. (1992) 'The Cognitive Skill of Theory Articulation', *Science and Education* 1: 181–92.

Pintrich, P.R., Marx, R.W. and Boyle, R.A. (1993) 'Beyond Cold Conceptual Change', *Review of Educational Research* 63: 167–99.

Resnick, L.B. (1994) 'Situated Rationalism: Biological and Social Preparation for Learning', in L.A. Hirschfeld and S.A. Gelman (eds), *Mapping the Mind*, Cambridge, MA: Cambridge University Press, 474–93.

Savoie, D. and Ladouceur, R. (1995) 'Evaluation et Modification de Conceptions Erronées au Sujet des Loteries', *Revue canadienne des sciences du comportement* 27: 199–213.

Saxana, A.B. (1992) 'An Attempt to Remove Misconceptions Related to Electricity', *International Journal of Education* 14: 157–62.

Smith, C. Snir, Y. and Grosslight, L. (1992) 'Using Conceptual Models to Facilitate Conceptual Change', *Cognition and Instruction* 9: 221–83.

Snyder, T. and Sullivan, H. (1995) 'Co-operative and Individual Learning', *Contemporary Educational Psychology* 20: 230–35.

Spelke, E.S. (1991) 'Physical Knowledge in Infancy', in S. Carey and R. Gelman (eds), *Epigenesis of Mind: Studies in Biology and Culture*, Hillsdale, NJ: Erlbaum, 133–69.

Sperber, D. (1994) 'The Modularity of Thought and the Epidemiology of Representations', in L.A. Hirschfeld and S.A. Gelman (eds) *Mapping the Mind*, Cambridge, MA: Cambridge University Press, 39–69.

Ustinov, P. (1977) *Dear Me*, London: Heinemann.

Vosniadou, S. (1992) 'Knowledge Acquisition and Conceptual Change', *Applied Psychology: An International Review* 41: 347–57.

—— (1994) 'Capturing and Modeling the Process of Conceptual Change', *Learning and Instruction* 4: 45–69.

White, B. (1993) 'ThinkerTools: Causal Models, Conceptual Change, and Science Education', *Cognition and Instruction* 10: 1–100.

Withen, A. (1991) *Natural Theories of Mind*, Oxford: Blackwell.

Woodward, J. and Howard, S. (1994) 'The Misconceptions of Youth', *Exceptional Children* 61: 126–36.

Wynne, K. (1996) 'Infants' Individuation and Enumeration of Actions', *Psychological Science* 7: 164–53.

9 The Total Learning Environment

Overview

Support for mental processing and mental engagement is often insufficient by itself: students may still fail to perform as expected. This chapter points to the total mental environment that shapes learning behaviours. Interaction between the many components of the mental environment gives rise to particular approaches to learning. Some associated learning behaviours are described. This sets the scene for subsequent chapters.

More Than One Hurdle

It is a mistake to imagine that providing for mental engagement is, in itself, a sufficient condition for ensuring that understanding will follow. The various strategies that foster understanding may provide a gentle slope up to one significant hurdle but there are others to cross. For instance, the learner must be willing to make an inference. There is sometimes a tendency to ignore such hurdles. Petraglio (1998) has drawn attention to this:

> The model of a learner who is cleansed of inappropriate attitudes and motivations continues to lie at the heart of constructivist education. Such a learner is not merely predisposed to efficiency and logic, but is affectively compliant with the educator's desires. This reflects many of the constructivists' somewhat sentimental presumption that students are fairly bursting with enthusiasm to learn if only the educators would let them.

Of course, many are not.

Each of us has a variety of attitudes, motives, emotions and other such attributes which cannot be divorced from a mental engagement in learning. Far from being like sparkling shopping trolleys just waiting to be filled with goods, we may be reluctant to start, difficult to steer, full of boxes that resist the intrusion of more, even when they have been carefully shaped to fit. What people actually do about their learning is not completely determined by what we do to make it easier. Learning behaviour is shaped by the total mental environment and, like an iceberg, a lot of it is out of sight (Lewin, 1938; Higgins, 1999)

The Total Mental Environment

The total mental environment includes the student's, the teacher's and the situation's characteristics. While these bear directly upon the learning outcome, the effect is also mediated by the participants' perceptions of them (Figure 9.1). For instance, if students perceive a strategy as exposing them to ridicule and therefore as being threatening, they are likely to be very reluctant participants. If a teacher perceives this response as a willful, bloody-minded lack of co-operation, the environment could become somewhat tense. In this event, the prospect of the strategy achieving its anticipated ends is greatly reduced. The components of the total learning environment have the potential to be highly interactive. You (1993) saw parallels between the elements of the learning environment and the chaos theory butterfly: just as a tiny flick of the butterfly's wing may bring about a hurricane, a small change in one of the elements can be catastrophic for the quality of learning.

The factors which might shape the learning environment seem limited

Figure 9.1 An Interactive View of Learning

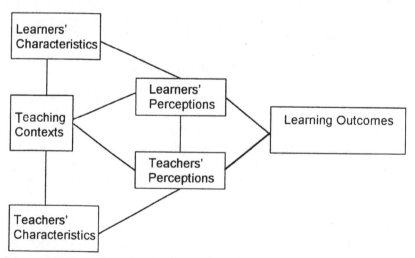

Source: MacAulay (1990), Gibbs (1992a, 1992b, 1995)

only by the imagination. Figure 9.2 shows some of the characteristics of its three major components. In the case of the student, the relative strength of the characteristics will vary with age and the individual. For instance, an older student is more likely to be governed by career aspirations than a young child. Similarly, their metacognitive skills are likely to be very different. Differences like these need to be reflected in teaching approaches (Knowles, 1980). In addition, two older students who have the same career aspirations are likely to bring different prior knowledge, amongst other things, to the situation.

Each teacher brings to the classroom subject knowledge and teaching expertise. How well a teacher knows a subject will shape the activities provided, the questions asked and the answers accepted. Similarly, the teaching strategies, explanations, analogies and ways of organizing and managing activities that a teacher knows, both general and subject-specific, will affect the quality of instruction. At the same time, a teacher has interests and feelings that can shape instruction. Again, these interact to produce the unique piece of instruction that a particular teacher provides. These characteristics are not necessarily fixed.

The context of instruction supplies other factors which affect learning outcomes. For instance, the physical surroundings where the learning takes place are likely to affect the recall and use of that knowledge at a later date. If certain situations are perceived by a learner to be authentic, that is, like the real life situation in which the knowledge is normally used, learning is likely to be applied more readily in similar situations in the future (Petraglio, 1998).

Taken together, the direct action, indirect action and interaction of such characteristics produces the learning behaviours we observe (Biggs and Moore, 1993). To illustrate, in the USA, Wentzel (1998) found that some 11-year-olds' perceptions of the support they had from teachers predicted the children's classroom interest. Levels of interest were also associated with academic performance. However, this is not to say that there is a simple causal chain from the first to the last. Academic performance may enhance interest, and higher levels of interest could lead to more interaction with the teacher and greater perceptions of teacher support. Of course, perceptions of teacher support may be realistic. Greater support could lead to both higher interest and academic performance.

Alexander and Murphy (1998) looked for patterns in trainee teachers' characteristics on entering an educational psychology course. In particular, they focused on their relevant prior knowledge, interest in the subject and strategic processing (the strategies used in reading educational psychology text such as, self-questioning, re-reading, reflection and summarizing). These, they believed, would be significant determinants of success. They identified:

- a cluster of students with strong prior knowledge, relatively low interest and moderate use of strategic processing (which they called strong-knowledge);

Figure 9.2   Some Characteristics of the Main Components of the Learning Environment

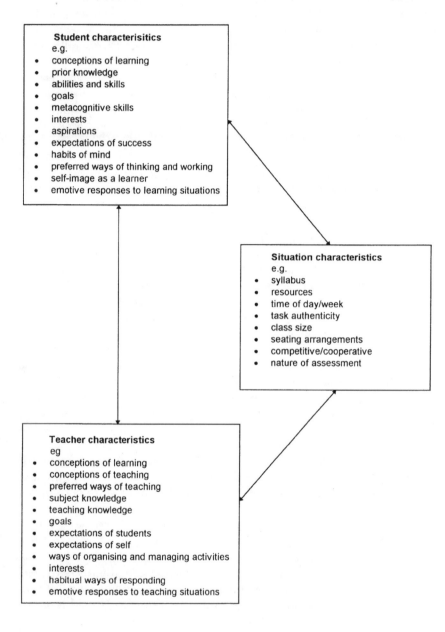

- a cluster of students with moderate prior knowledge, a high level of interest and high use of strategic processing (which they called learning-orientated), and;
- a cluster of students with a low level of knowledge, moderate interest and least use of strategic processing (which they called low-profile).

While we might expect that no course will be enlightening for all students, we would probably hope that the group with favourable characteristics would keep them and be reinforced by others who have seen the light. At the end of the course, Alexander and Murphy re-tested their students and now found four clusters:

- a cluster of students with strong knowledge, relatively low interest and moderate use of strategic processing (strong knowledge);
- a cluster of students with moderate knowledge, a high level of interest and relatively high use of strategic processing (learning-orientated);
- a cluster of students characterized by low knowledge, moderate interest, and high strategy use (which they called effortful processor), and;
- a cluster of students with low knowledge, moderate interest, and low strategy use (which they called non-strategic reader).

Only 18 per cent of the strong knowledge group remained in that cluster while 46 per cent became non-strategic readers. Thirty-nine per cent of the learning-orientated group remain in that cluster, but 26 per cent of them joined the non-strategic readers. On the positive side, 25 per cent of the low profile group became learning-orientated and 12 per cent became a part of the strong-knowledge group. This serves to illustrate the fluidity or malleability of at least some student characteristics during a course. It also shows how a given learning environment can result in different outcomes. Alexander and Murphy go on to suggest that there are two paths to academic success, a strong prior knowledge which, presumably, guides learning, and a combination of at least a moderate level of prior knowledge, interest and willingness to invest effort in learning through strategic processing. This leaves open, of course, the cause of factors like interest and a willingness to invest effort.

Learning Behaviours

Marton and Saljo (1976) found that some learners adopt a surface or shallow approach to learning in which information is treated as unconnected facts to be memorized. What is often needed for understanding is a deep approach in which inferencing establishes relationships and builds mental structures (Marton and Saljo, 1976; Saljo, 1982; Gibbs, 1992a).

A tendency to use a surface approach may even increase as a student progresses through a chosen course (Volet et al., 1994). This seems more common in the sciences than in the arts and amongst those learners who do not intend to follow the subject at a higher level (Ramsden, 1983). For some of these, the course may serve as a rite of passage: it is the qualification which is valuable, not the understanding (Wildy and Wallace, 1992). For others, the course may be interesting and engaging but the quantity of learning is so great that they adopt what seems like a survival strategy. Others may respond emotionally to particular forms of assessment in a dysfunctional way. Their strategy for reducing anxiety may be to store as much information as possible.

What learners do about their learning depends on many factors and the way they interact. On the one hand, there can be some consistent tendencies over a period of time. Someone may approach learning fairly consistently in the same way, even when some variables in the situation change markedly. Changing the variables in the context may change the approach to learning. For example, Ollerenshaw et al. (1997) found that undergraduate surface learners showed much higher comprehension of novel technical material when learning from multimedia than from text alone, and their scores almost equalled those of the achieving, deep learners. This demonstrates that it may be possible to shape situations so that learners adopt the desired approach. At the same time, it cannot be assumed that different cultural groups will tend to behave in the same way, as Biggs (1992) demonstrated when comparing Anglo-Chinese and Australian students across a wide age range.

In one form or another, the existence of surface and deep approaches has been confirmed by other researchers. Some have added other approaches (for instance, Tait and Entwistle, 1996; Geisler-Brentsein et al., 1996). Biggs (1987) added a motivational element, the achievement orientation. On this basis, a student could be achievement-orientated and have either a deep or shallow approach (Andrews et al., 1994). In both cases, the learners are motivated to achieve. Further, Volet and Chalmers (1992) argue against a surface–deep dichotomy and provide evidence of some sort of continuum between the two. Working in the Netherlands with adult students of law, economics, sociology, management sciences, psychology, language and litera-ture, and philosophy, Vermunt aimed to integrate the various conceptualizations of learning approaches (Vermunt, 1998, published in Dutch in 1992). His comprehensive model of what shapes learning approaches is shown in Figure 9.3.

Learners prior knowledge obviously includes far more that just subject-related matter. Amongst other things, learners develop conceptions (and misconceptions) about learning objectives and tasks that relate to the nature of the expected learning, what it is, how it comes about and the extent to which it is broadly worthwhile. These figure in what Vermunt calls mental models of learning and, for a given person, they form a more or less 'coherent whole of learning conceptions...about the learning process'.

Figure 9.3   Various Factors which bear upon the Learning Approach

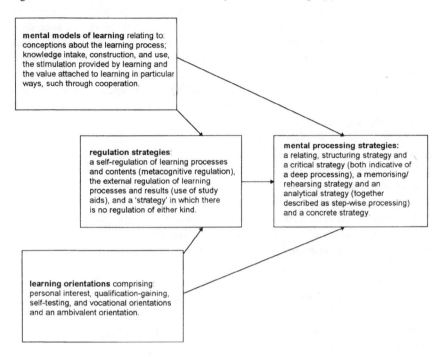

People have different goals, intentions, motives, expectations, worries and doubts about engaging in learning. A personal interest may orient someone towards a subject, as might a desire for the award associated with it. For others, it could be an opportunity to prove themselves, measure themselves against others, compete and succeed or it could simply be the route to a particular kind of employment. These are not mutually exclusive. For instance, someone could be both interested in the subject and vocationally oriented. These constitute learning orientations in which motivation plays a significant part.

Regulation strategies control mental activities such as monitoring learning, noting when learning fails and doing something about it. Self-regulation relates to the actions initiated and maintained by the student to support and extend learning. It includes planning and self-direction towards learning objectives determined by the student. It also includes, 'the knowledge, views, conceptions and beliefs people have about learning processes'. Together, such activities are often referred to as metacognitive processes. However, a learner can be regulated externally as when a teacher, text or some other surrogate supports the learning with a variety of learning aids, strategies and assessments.

Mental processing strategies are the ways in which learners deal with the content of the topic to be learned. They might look for relationships in an attempt to understand a topic. These structures could be ideas which enable them to judge critically the worth of other ideas about the topic. Another strategy is to analyse the topic into more or less discrete units and take each in turn in a stepwise fashion. Others might attempt to make the subject concrete by looking for examples of its operation and by applying the ideas in other contexts. On the other hand, students may try to memorize the topic and acquire it by rote learning, point by point. These approaches are not mutually exclusive. For instance, a student could use both a relating strategy and a concrete strategy.

The learning approaches Vermunt identified arise from combinations of the elements described in the model. In particular, he found:

- a meaning-directed approach, associated with relating and structuring, critical processing and self-regulation of learning;
- a reproduction-directed approach associated with memorizing and rehearsing and the external regulation of leaning;
- an application-directed approach associated with the use of knowledge, and;
- an undirected approach associated with a lack of regulation, cooperation with other learners and ambivalent learning orientation.

The first two parallel the deep and surface approaches. Vermunt suggested that the application-directed approach, a tendency to elaborate and apply the learning elsewhere, may develop after one of the others. The undirected approach is described as similar to Tait and Entwistle's (1996) 'apathetic approach'.

A meaning-directed approach is more likely to lead to understanding than a reproduction approach. The latter is more likely to support the acquisition of memorized content. The application-directed approach may, of course, support understanding in application contexts, but it does not necessarily mean that what is being applied is understood as a coherent mental structure that has been related to existing knowledge. Instead, there may be an understanding of how the knowledge might be legitimately used. The variation amongst the students was large and many showed an inclination to undirected or reproduction approaches.

Vermunt argued that mental models of learning and learning orientations show some stability when compared with regulation and processing strategies. Of course, this may not be true of students who are obliged to study a wide range of disparate subjects not of their own choosing, as in school. For them, approaches may vary from subject to subject and even lesson to lesson. He also found that students who are more likely to adopt a strategy supportive of understanding tended not to use adjunct learning aids like those provided in textual materials. External regulation was not a significant feature of their success. Similarly, Beishuizen et al. (1994) found that such students did not benefit particularly from advice on the regulation of their learning while studying a block of text. Instead, they tended to create their own structures and work in their own ways. Those with more surface approaches, on the other hand, benefited from an advance organizer and advice on structuring. It seems likely that some adult students may have developed their own regulatory habits over the years so that adjuncts aids may be ignored. It could also be that a routine offering of adjunct aids tends to technify and impersonalize the learning experience and even appear patronizing, leading to its rejection. This may not, however, apply to all adults or to younger learners.

In Holland, it has been argued that higher education should give specific attention to learning approaches, discouraging undirected approaches and fostering meaning-directed ones. Busato et al. (1998) found the undirected approach to be associated with less academic success. The meaning-directed approach tended to be the one associated most with higher academic success, but the variation was large. This assumes that what counts as academic success needs meaning-directed approaches. At the same time, it also could be that some important element of the learning environment has not been taken into account. What is needed is, of course, a controlled test to see if a learning approaches programme is effective.

Because Vermunt found his four approaches to show some consistency over time, he referred to them as learning styles. This term is, however, used to describe a variety of learning tendencies and Murray-Harvey (1994) has demonstrated that these can be quite unrelated. Curry (1987) described approaches and styles in terms of relative stability. In the inner core are those that are relatively slow to change, such as the cognitive styles of Riding (Riding and Cheema, 1991). Around these are styles with more fluidity but, nevertheless, they show some consistency over time. Some aspects of Vermunt's model might fit here. Outside are styles of low stability, such as the learning preferences of Price et al. (1991). Other bases for classification are possible (see Murray-Harvey, 1994) and this reinforces the point that learning style can refer to a variety of tendencies.

One such tendency that is probably nearer the core of Curry's onion is field independence. Field independent learners tend to be analytical and able to restructure what is to be learned. Field dependent learners tend to depend on their physical and social background, rely on others for support and are less autonomous in their learning. Several studies have shown that field independence tends to be associated with higher academic achievement. Field dependent learners are also more likely to have learning difficulties in independent situations such as distance learning (Luk, 1998). Riding has included a verbalizer–imager dimension (Riding and Cheema, 1991). This takes into account the degree to which learners tend to benefit from information presented verbally and presented pictorially. When learning styles from the stable core are involved, economy of effort would suggest that it is probably better to adapt the learning environment to the student than expect the student to change style. On the other hand, there could be some benefit in the learner acquiring some facility in coping with less considerate learning materials. In practice, providing for a mixed group of learners will usually mean preparing materials which offer the same information in a variety of ways.

Summary

The total learning environment has to be considered in supporting under-standing. Its main components are the characteristics of the student, the teacher and the situation. The interaction between these produces the observed learning behaviour of the student. Various learning approaches or styles have been observed. For instance, there are meaning-directed, repro-duction-directed, application-directed and undirected approaches. Each of these represents a different assemblage of mental models of learning, learning orientations, regulation strategies and cognitive processing strate-gies. These approaches show some degree of stability although they are not necessarily immutable. Learners may benefit from instruction which accom-modates a range of learning approaches and, if necessary, facilitates the change of maladaptive approaches.

The hurdles depend on how learners respond to the learning environ-ment. Learners are different and they change with time. Subsequent chapters look at this learner variability in the context of some components of their learning environment. In particular, the mental models of learning compo-nent is illustrated by conceptions of learning (and especially of understanding); learning orientations are described in motivation; and some aspects of the regulation of learning appear as metacognition.

References

Alexander, P.A. and Murphy, P.K. (1998) 'Profiling the Differences in Students' Knowledge, Interest, and Strategic Processing', *Journal of Educational Psychology* 90: 435–47.

Andrews, J., Violato, C., Rabb, K. and Hollingsworth, M. (1994) 'A Validity Study of Biggs' Three-Factor Model of Learning Approaches', *British Journal of Educa-tional Psychology* 64: 179–85.

Beishuizen, J., Stoutjesdijk, E. and Van Putten, K. (1994) 'Studying Textbooks: Effects of Learning Styles, Study Task, and Instruction', *Learning and Instruction* 4: 151–74.

Biggs, J.B. (1992) *Why and How do Hong Kong Students Learn?*, Hong Kong: Univer-sity of Hong Kong.

—— (1987) *Student Approaches to Learning and Studying*, Victoria: Australian Council for Educational Research.

Biggs, J.B. and Moore, P.J. (1993) *The Process of Learning*, Melbourne: Prentice Hall, 3rd edn, 447–82.

Busato, V.V., Frans, J.P., Elshout, J.J. and Hamaker, C. (1998) 'Learning Styles: A Cross-Sectional and Longitudinal Study in Higher Education', *British Journal of Educational Psychology* 68: 427–41.

Curry, L. (1987) *Integrating Concepts of Cognitive Learning Style: A Review with Attention to Psychometric Standards*, Ottawa: Canadian College of Health Science Executives.

Geisler-Brentstein, E., Schmeck, R.R. and Hetherington, J. (1996) 'An Individual Difference Perspective on Student Diversity', *Higher Education* 31: 73–96.

Gibbs, G. (1992a) *Improving the Quality of Student Learning*, Bristol: Technical and Educational Services.

—— (1992b) 'Improving the Quality of Student Learning Through Course Design', in R. Barnett (ed.), *Learning to Effect*, Buckingham: Society for Research in Higher Education/Open University.

—— (1995) 'Research into Student Learning', in B. Smith and S. Brown (eds), *Research, Teaching and Learning in Higher Education*, London: Kogan Page.

Higgins, S. (1999) in D. Moseley et al., *Effective Pedagogy using Information and Communication Technology in Literacy and Numeracy in Primary Schools*, Newcastle-upon-Tyne: Newcastle University.

Knowles, M.S. (1980) *The Modern Practice of Adult Education*, Chicago: Association Press/Follet.

Lewin, K. (1938) *The Conceptual Representation and the Measurement of Psychological Forces*, Durham, NC: Duke University Press.

Luk, S.C. (1998) 'The Relationship Between Cognitive Style and Academic Achievement', *British Journal of Educational Psychology* 68: 137–47.

MacAulay, D.L. (1990) 'Classroom Environment: A Literature Review', *Educational Psychology* 10: 239–53.

Marton, F. and Saljo, R. (1976) 'On the Qualitative Differences in Learning', *British Journal of Educational Psychology* 62: 184–92.

Murray-Harvey, R. (1994) 'Learning Styles and Approaches to Learning: Distinguishing Between Concepts and Instruments', *British Journal of Educational Psychology* 64: 373–88.

Ollerenshaw, A., Aidman, E.V. and Kidd, G. (1997) 'Is an Illustration Always Worth Ten Thousand Words? Effects of Prior Knowledge, Learning Style and Multimedia Illustations on Text Comprehension', *International Journal of Instructional Media* 24: 227–38.

Petraglio, J. (1998) 'The Real World on a Short Leash: The (Mis)Application of Constructivism to the Design of Educational Technology', *Educational Technology Research and Development* 46: 53–65.

Price, G.E., Dunn, R. and Dunn, K. (1991) *Productivity Environmental Preference Survey (PEPS manual)*, Lawrence, NZ: Price Systems.

Ramsden, P. (1983) 'Institutional Variations in British Students' Approaches to Learning and Experiences in Teaching', *Higher Education* 12: 275–86.

Riding, R. and Cheema, I. (1991) 'Cognitive Styles – An Overview and Integration', *Educational Psychology* 11: 193–215.

Saljo, R. (1982) *Learning and Understanding*, Gothenberg: University of Gothenberg.

Tait, H. and Entwistle, N.J. (1996) 'Indentifying Students at Risk Through Ineffective Study Strategies', *Higher Education* 31: 97–116.

Vermunt, J.D. (1998) 'The Regulation of Constructive Processes', *British Journal of Educational Psychology* 68: 149–71.

—— (1992) *Leerstijlen en Sturen van Leerprocessen in Het Hoger Onderwijs*, Amsterdam: Swets and Zeitlinger.

Volet, S.E. and Chalmers, D. (1992) 'Investigation of Qualitative Differences in University Students' Learning Goals', *British Journal of Educational Psychology* 62: 17–34.

Volet, S.E., Renshaw, P.D. and Tietzel, K. (1994) 'A Short-Term Longitudinal Investigation of Cross-Cultural Differences in Study Approaches using Biggs' SPQ Questionnaire', *British Journal of Educational Psychology* 64: 301–18.

Wentzel, K.R. (1998) 'Social Relationships and Motivation in Middle School: The Role of Parents, Teachers, and Peers', *Journal of Educational Psychology* 90: 202–09.

Wildy, H. and Wallace, J. (1992) 'Understanding Teaching or Teaching for Understanding', *American Educational Research Journal* 29: 143–56.

You, Y. (1993) 'What Can We Learn From Chaos Theory? An Alternative Approach to Instructional Systems Design', *Educational Technology Research and Development* 41: 17–32.

10 Knowing What Counts

Overview

The development of conceptions of learning and some of their consequences are described. That such conceptions are learned in particular
contexts is emphasized. Some ways of supporting the development of
conceptions of understanding and of modifying misunderstandings
about understanding are mentioned.

Conceptions of Learning

Conceptions of learning are an important element of a student's make-up.
As Vermunt (1998) demonstrated, they are one of the learner's attributes
that are associated with his or her learning approach. While we can expect
someone's subject knowledge to matter, the impact of misconceptions is
often relatively localized. Thinking that electricity comes from one terminal
of a battery, through the wire to a bulb where it is consumed will tend to
matter in the topic of electricity. Learning about sound, light, erosion or the
causes of the Great War is not likely to be adversely affected.

Conceptions of learning are more fundamental and may underpin whole
areas of learning behaviour. For instance, if students in mathematics see
learning as memorization and facility with procedures and algorithms, they
may take them as goals across mathematics as a whole. If a teacher has the
same view, the activities, the questions and the accepted answers are also
likely to reflect that. This is not to say that memorization and procedural
facility are not useful or unnecessary, but understanding is more than these
and can be of greater value. Different conceptions of learning could bring
about different approaches to teaching and learning.

The difference between those who think memorization counts and those
who think understanding counts is likely to be apparent. Learners, however,
could agree that understanding counts yet not agree on what it is. In this
case, learning goals may differ in subtle ways. Some possibilities and their
origins are now described.

137

Children's Conceptions of Understanding

Even young children are able to infer relationships. For instance, Das Gupta and Bryant (1989) examined children's ability to compare an initial and final state of an event. They found that 4-year-olds were successful in inferring a causal link between the two. The sophistication of such inferences develops with age, and Maurice-Naville and Montenegro (1992) identified three 'levels'. In explaining the decay of a log, at 8 or 9 years children generally did not give an account of the continuous process of the event although they recognized that decay was the cause. Children about a year older could do so. Later, they could also state relationships between one stage of decay and the next.

During lessons, children are often asked if they understand. The question seems a ready probe for checking a variety of mental structures. Rogers (1969) was of the opinion that children can indicate whether or not they understand. Markman (1977), however, has found that 6-year-olds only knew they had failed to understand when there was evidence of it. Further, when studying the effect of different kinds of lesson on the level of conceptual understanding in science, 10-year-olds were asked to rate their understanding on a scale ranging from 'very well' to 'not at all' (Cavalcante et al., 1997). Correlations between these ratings and post-test performances were low, regardless of type of lesson (explanation withheld versus explanation provided). These children proved to be poor judges of their own understanding and generally overestimated it.

Why should such children overestimate their understanding? There are a number of possibilities. An obvious one is that the child may have misperceived, misheard or misconstrued the situation to be understood. In effect, he or she has constructed an understanding of something else. Equally, the child's mental structure may contain an erroneous assumption or connection which has passed unnoticed. Another possibility is that a child may have successfully constructed a mental representation but has drawn on misconceptions about the world. Understandings based on misconceptions have been mentioned in earlier chapters but they do not exhaust the possibilities.

Another is that a child may have a mental representation that is in many ways acceptable but is too simple. In history, for example, they may be unable to de-centre and see a situation from the other participants' points of view (Pendry et al., 1997). Consequently, in learning about the decline of the Roman Empire, they may have a representation in which they see the empire as being overthrown in a battle with barbarians in the fifth century (Lee et al., 1996). In science, they may know that a bow will bend more when pulled harder, but they have not grasped the quantitative essence of Hooke's Law that doubling the pull doubles the extension.

One possibility is that children may conceive of understanding as knowing what the words mean or being able to recall facts, but not knowing what counts as understanding in a particular context is another prospect.

When children are asked in history why the remnants of the Spanish Armada sank, they may describe the way hollow, wooden vessels sink when filled with water. In science, on the other hand, they may say it was due to the captains' inadequate seamanship. These are rational but inappropriate responses given the contexts.

The last possibility is particularly interesting. Formal knowledge is divided into more or less self-consistent domains. While memorization does not pass for understanding in any domain, what counts as understanding and explanation in one domain may not pass in another. For instance, if a car suffers a burst tyre and plummets from a cliff, a lawyer would be interested in who was responsible for the maintenance of the tyre or the road; a scientist's attention is more likely to be on the properties of the materials and physical conditions involved; a historian is likely to be more interested in motives and events which brought this about. From the vast number of possible inferences, different sets are appropriate for each of the domains (Hewstone, 1989). In effect, different understandings of the same event count in different contexts.

What is appropriate has to be learned. For instance, some pre-schoolers think they can read – until they go to school. There, they learn that what they thought was reading is not what counts. Learning what counts is not usually the subject of formal instruction but is acquired through a process of enculturation (Bishop, 1988; Becher, 1989). Margaret Mead (1932) described Manus children's reasons for the floating away of a canoe. To begin with, they ascribed it to the tide or said it had not been tied up. Later, like their parents, they attributed it to a water spirit. Enculturation taught them what was an acceptable explanation. In school, enculturation is a cognitive socialization in which children learn acceptable epistemic forms in various divisions of knowledge (Gellatly, 1997; Collins and Ferguson, 1993). It is provided by, for example, a teacher's discourse, the kind of questions asked, the answers accepted and the contents of books and other surrogate teachers.

Although children's ability to construct an understanding may be present at an early age and, by 10-years-old, they may be able to recognize understanding in general, they may not be clear about the kind of understanding expected in a given subject. When asked to choose explanations for the sinking of the ships of the Spanish Armada, many chose them without regard to whether the context is science or history. Obviously, a teacher would steer children to appropriate explanations but this shows that it is needed at this age (Newton and Newton, 1999).

Enculturation, which teaches a child what is expected, is largely an informal process that takes time. This means that children may not know what passes for understanding and, left to themselves, may produce what others perceive to be unsuitable explanations in a given domain. At the same time, if there is an imbalance in this enculturation, children could develop unbalanced conceptions of understanding. If, for instance, non-causal description dominated science lessons, children may tend to associate it with successful understanding. As a consequence, they may not infer causal relationships in that subject and be satisfied with a descriptive understanding (Newton and Newton, 1999).

A lack of understanding can have causes other than a failure to construct a relationship. A child may construct a relationship that is valid but is irrelevant to the domain, the relationship may be descriptive when it should be causal, and it may be relevant but built on a misconception. Such children are likely to have an unjustified confidence in their understanding. This is not to say that children who lack the ability to differentiate between what counts in different subjects cannot understand. Rather, they may pursue the wrong kind of understanding in a some contexts. These possibilities could lead to the failure of a child in those contexts because the child has not yet learned what counts in them.

Older Learners' Conceptions of Understanding

History and science graduates conceptions of understanding in history and science have been compared to look for differences in the effects of the enculturation process (Newton and Newton, 1998). As might be expected, the processes produced conceptions of understanding that are nearer to those of university lecturers in these subjects. Nevertheless, some significant differences between students and lecturers can exist.

First, lecturers do not always agree about what counts as understanding in their subject. In science, there were those who saw it as knowing why the world is as it is. They believed this involves constructing a mental picture of events. There were others who saw it as facility in acquiring and applying laws and procedures. New graduates were also divided. In history, for instance, some saw understanding as perceiving trends and patterns in events while others emphasized the essential uniqueness of events. This means that there is the possibility of a mismatch between the conceptions of a particular lecturer and those of their students. Franz et al. (1996) also noted the potential for mismatch in a study of first-year university students in Australia. Such mismatches are particularly important when it comes to setting and marking assignments; that is, making judgements about student achievement and abilities (Newton and Newton, 1998).

Science sixth formers (17-years-old) were found to be, in some respects, much like their graduate counterparts in their conceptions although they placed a greater store on learning factual information. On the other hand, they undervalued the relevance of simplification and prediction. History sixth formers' conceptions of understanding were different to those of history graduates in that the sixth formers tended to see history as a well-structured domain where logical reasoning leads to the truth of an event. The sixth formers also tended to be more confident about predicting the course of an event and tended to see more relevance in the acquisition of factual information. Both groups, however, did have conceptions of understanding which probably seemed to them to be quite adequate. As new students, they could arrive at university with views which may limit their success, at least initially. The amount to be learned and the need to pass the examination can also have significantly more bearing on learning than any desire to understand. As mentioned earlier, one graduate, when questioned about strategies for supporting understanding, commented that understanding was a luxury (Newton and Newton, 1998).

Teachers' Conceptions of Understanding

There is also another potential problem. Teachers have often specialized in a limited range of subjects and so are encultured more in those than in others. Outside that range of subjects, they may hold inappropriate conceptions of understanding. In fact, the evidence indicates that they may hold inappropriate conceptions *within* their specialism as well. This means that they may propagate such views through the lessons they give and so shape children's enculturation adversely – which is back to the beginning (Newton and Newton, 1997). Teachers may also see children's minds as, in essence, receptacles with doors that may be open or closed to incoming information. This model can ignore the personal and active nature of learning (Strauss and Shilony, 1994).

Conceptions of Learning are Learned

The process of acquiring conceptions of learning in particular contexts has been called enculturation, but it is nevertheless a process of learning. Although born with the capacity to understand, the relationship between a particular context and the kind of inference that counts in that context has to be learned. Much of that learning may be unconscious. The learner may be unaware of a developing understanding of what counts but the mental structures that result, such as Vermunt's mental models of learning, help to shape learning behaviour for good or ill. Just as in learning subject content, an understanding of what counts could be perfectly adequate or may be more or less inadequate. Like subject knowledge misconceptions, some errors may be trivial and some may be serious. Equally, some may be easy and others may be difficult to change. Again, both subject knowledge misconceptions and learning misconceptions may arise from unconscious learning.

Failure to understand may arise from inappropriate goals generated by inadequate conceptions of learning. Suspicions should be aroused when failure is relatively general in a domain and shows a consistent pattern that points to inappropriate goals. This is more likely with younger learners and those that are new to a subject.

What someone believes to count in a domain might be elicited by questioning. Bringing conceptions into consciousness so they can be discussed may be a starting point but this is not always easy. Even some lecturers in a subject would pause when asked what counts as understanding in their field. The response, 'Oh, I haven't really thought about it', is not uncommon, reflecting the unconscious processes which produce their conceptions. With younger learners, this is probably not a feasible approach. But, it may be possible to support the process of enculturation in a deliberate way by, for example, modelling thought patterns for children, scaffolding thinking and making explicit why some responses are appropriate and others are inappropriate. For example, in history a teacher might specify what counts for a particular event with, 'Here, we are interested in why the people on the *Mayflower* wanted to go to North America'. In science, the generality of the understanding is emphasized with, 'So why did the lamp come on? What is it that makes any lamp come on?' Modelling could also highlight the goal in other ways: 'Now then, let me see. What I'm trying to do is understand why this happens…This means I will have to know…' Discriminating between the learning goals in different contexts may also prove useful. Ultimately, the features and distinctions should come from the children: 'So, what kind of answer do you think I want? Will it be one that tells me…or one that…?'

In most cases, the process of enculturation should tend to make older students' conceptions of understanding, if not perfect, at least more suited to the task in a particular domain than those of young children. The evidence did support this. Nevertheless, learners' perceptions of the learning goals of a course may lead them to see a surface approach as better suited to their ends (Heywood, 1989; Gibbs, 1992, 1995; Volet et al., 1994). While a non-patronizing form of modelling may continue with older learners, they may be more capable of discussing learning and pointing out the features that count. Exemplars or case studies illustrating what the teacher or lecturer sees as counting may also be useful at the beginning of a course. What is to count needs to be discussed, particularly when courses are given and assignments and examination papers are marked by a number of people. In other words, there is a need for teachers to externalize and reflect on their conceptions of learning (Franz et al., 1996).

Nevertheless, even when conceptions of learning match needs, learners may still have a shallow, reproduction or undirected approach to learning when a deep or meaning-oriented approach is what is expected of them. Among other things, motivation and feelings are also important in shaping learning behaviours, and these are the subject of the next chapter.

Summary

Conceptions of learning, and of understanding in particular, help to shape learning behaviours. If, for instance, a child thinks that understanding means only knowing what the words mean, their learning approach could be inappropriate. Enculturation teaches a child what kind of understanding is appropriate in different domains. Since this is likely to take time, there is the possibility that a learner will aim for an understanding that, though legitimate, is not appropriate for the context. Exemplification, modelling and being specific about learning goals are approaches that might aid the process of enculturation and adjust inappropriate conceptions of learning. Views on what counts or what should have the greatest emphasis may vary amongst teachers, and the implications of this for practice have to be considered.

References

Becher, T. (1989) *Academic Tribes and Territories*, Milton Keynes: Open University Press.

Bishop, A.J. (1988) *Mathematical Enculturation*, Dordrecht: Kluwer.

Cavalcante, P.S., Newton, L.D. and Newton, D.P. (1997) 'The Effect of Different Kinds of Lesson on Conceptual Understanding in Science', *Journal of Research in Science and Technological Education* 15: 185–93.

Collins, A. and Ferguson, W. (1993) 'Epistemic Forms and Epistemic Games: Structures and Strategies to Guide Enquiry', *Educational Psychologist* 28: 25–42.

Das Gupta, P. and Bryant, P.E. (1989) 'Young Children's Causal Inferences', *Child Development* 60: 1138–46.

Franz, J. et al. (1996) 'Students' and Lecturers' Conceptions of Learning: An Interdisciplinary Study', *Teaching in Higher Education* 1: 325–39.

Gellatly, A. (1997) 'Why the Young Child has Neither a Theory of Mind nor a Theory of Anything Else', *Human Development* 40: 32–50.

Gibbs, G. (1992) 'Improving the Quality of Student Learning Through Course Design', in R. Barnett (ed.), *Learning to Effect*, Buckingham: Society for Research in Higher Education/Open University.

—— (1995) 'Research into Student Learning', in B. Smith and S. Brown (eds), *Research, Teaching and Learning in Higher Education*, London: Kogan Page.

Hewstone, M. (1989) *Causal Attribution*, Oxford: Blackwell.

Heywood, J. (1989) *Assessment in Higher Education*, Chichester: John Wiley.

Lee, P.J., Ashby, R. and Dickinson, A.K. (1996) 'Progression in Children's Ideas about History', in M. Hughes (ed.), *Progression in Learning*, Clevedon: Multilingual Matters, 50–81.

Markman, E.M. (1977) 'Realizing That You Don't Understand', *Child Development* 49: 168–77.

Marton, F. and Saljo, R. (1976) 'On the Qualitative Differences in Learning', *British Journal of Educational Psychology* 62: 184–92.

Maurice-Naville, D. and Montenegro, J. (1992) 'The Development of Diachronic Thinking: 8–12 Year-Old Children's Understanding of the Evolution of Forest Disease', *British Journal of Developmental Psychology* 10: 365–83.

Mead, M. (1932) 'An Investigation of the Thought of Primitive Children, With Special Reference to Animism', *Journal of the Royal Anthropological Institute* 63: 173–90.

Newton, D.P. and Newton, L.D. (1997) 'Teachers' Conceptions of Understanding Historical and Scientific Events', *British Journal of Educational Psychology* 67: 513–27.

—— (1998) 'Learning and Conceptions of Understanding in History and Science: Lecturers and New Graduates Compared', *Studies in Higher Education* 23: 43–58.

—— (1999) 'Knowing What Counts as Understanding in Different Disciplines: Some 10-Year-Olds' Conceptions', *Educational Studies* 25: 35–54.

Pendry, A., Atha, J., Carden, S., Courtenay, L., Keogh, C. and Ruston, K. (1997) 'Pupils' Pre-Conceptions in History', *Teaching History* 86: 18–20.

Ramsden, P. (1983) 'Institutional Variations in British Students' Approaches to Learning and Experiences in Teaching', *Higher Education* 12: 275–86.

Rogers, C. (1969) *Freedom to Learn*, Columbus, OH: Merrill.

Strauss, S. and Shilony, T. (1994) 'Teachers' Models of Children's Minds and Learning', in L.A. Hirschfeld and S.A. Gelman, *Mapping the Mind*, Cambridge: Cambridge University Press, 455–73.

Vermunt, J.D. (1998) 'The Regulation of Constructive Processes', *British Journal of Educational Pscyhology* 68: 149–71.

Volet, S.E., Renshaw, P.D. and Tietzel, K. (1994) 'A Short-Term Longitudinal Investigation of Cross-Cultural Differences in Study Approaches Using Biggs' SPQ Questionnaire', *British Journal of Educational Psychology* 64: 301–18.

11 Motivated to Understand

Overview

Student motivation can make the difference between success and failure when supporting understanding. Motivation is not a simple matter and what makes one person want to understand may be very different to what makes another want to understand. Various aspects of motivation are described with particular emphasis on perceptions of value, expectancy of success and emotions associated with learning. The implications for supporting understanding are discussed in each case.

Motivation to Learn

Understanding often needs student's active, mental engagement with the topic in hand. Simplification, clarification, consideration and other support for understanding can be a waste of time otherwise. In the real world, it would be naive to assume that all students are willing and interested participants in learning, each seeking understanding and enlightenment. Galloway et al. (1998: 26–7) found that about a half of Years 7, 9 and 11 students (12, 14 and 16-year-olds) showed signs of 'maladaptive motivation' in mathematics and English. This could be one cause of low educational achievement. At the same time, low educational achievement could also contribute to maladaptive motivation. Those who are motivated to learn tend to pay attention, volunteer answers, ask for guidance, persist, and complete tasks beyond what is merely acceptable (Okolo et al., 1995). Without favourable inclinations, little attempt may be made to establish mental relationships or a coherent, generative mental structure of the topic in hand. Subsequent failure is likely to depress those inclinations further. In this context, motivation is about why learning behaviour occurs (or does not occur) and how it comes to have a particular form. Motivation towards the task in hand may be weak or strong and, at the same time, favourable or unfavourable. An indifferent or negative motivation on the part of the student could be disastrous for attempts at fostering understanding. It helps if a student is highly motivated to learn.

The problem is that motives are shaped by a number of things. Some stem from inside and some from outside the person. For instance, an innate curiosity in the environment helps an animal learn about its surroundings and so could have survival value. An interest in novelty may stem from this. People, however, also take into account what the likely outcome of their actions will be, not just in the material sense but in terms of personal mental outcomes such as a feeling of well-being. In this sense, a given situation will afford different outcomes to different people, according to their personal realities. For instance, experience may have taught someone that he or she tends to be unsuccessful in learning a language. If it is felt that the reason is beyond his or her control, motivation to engage in language learning is likely to be low or even negative. Human behaviour can also be influenced by a need for affiliation and positive regard. People are likely to avoid learning situations if there is a risk of embarrassment or humiliation. A teacher, however, may set a learning goal with a substantial incentive so that the risk is, nevertheless, taken.

There are many factors, internal and external, that could prompt a student to engage in learning or avoid it, so it is not surprising to find several accounts of learning motivation. No one view of motivation may be adequate by itself.

Accounts of Learning Motivation

Early theories tended to account for motivation by referring to instincts and drives. People were thought to respond to these like a machine would respond to the throw of a switch. However, learning behaviour involves such things as beliefs, desires, intentions, expectations, commitment, goals, persistence, volition, self-confidence, emotions and topic difficulty. As far as people are concerned, whatever underpins learning behaviour does not show itself in a simple and straightforward way, other than perhaps amongst infants. Instead, it is mediated by thoughts and emotions and this has to be taken into account if we are to elicit the kind of motivation that will support understanding.

McClelland (1961) argued that we all have more or less of a need to achieve, and this underpins behaviour in situations that call for achievement. Atkinson (1978) hypothesized that there are really two tendencies. The first is a tendency to strive for success, so learners appraise a topic for what it has to contribute to that. The tendency depends on the strength of the success motive and the value and chance of success as perceived by the learner. However, there is also a tendency to avoid failure. A tendency to avoid failure is determined by the strengths of the motive to avoid failure and the disincentive value and probability of failure. Whichever is the greater of these two tendencies will determine the behaviour.

On this basis, those students with a dominant need to achieve will tend to avoid tasks where the chance of success is low. But tasks where the chance of success is high tend to be easy and so offer little in the way of achievement. Consequently, we should expect such students to engage in tasks of intermediate difficulty. On the other hand, those dominated by a fear of failure could be expected to attempt lots of easy tasks. They offer little risk and anxiety. Difficult tasks should also be attractive because the outcome is certain and failure in such circumstances is understandable, excusable and not a source of anxiety. These responses have had some confirmation, particularly in the case of the first group of students, but it is apparent that it is not the full picture.

Atkinson, however, mentioned the importance of the value of the task for the student, and Feather (1982, 1992) has emphasized the need for an outcome that students value. It is not uncommon to find students who see no point in what is proposed or else value competing behaviours more highly and do not even approach learning, let alone engage in it. At the same time, they must expect some success if they do engage in it (Vroom, 1964; Newsom, 1990). Perception of value and expectancy of success are both needed for such students to engage willingly in learning. Eccles and Wigfield consider these to be the primary determinants of learning behaviour, and if one or the other is zero, there will be no engagement (Wigfield, 1994). Pintrich and De Groot (1990) have suggested a third element for inclusion: emotions. Even though someone who values a learning task and feels there is a reasonable chance of success may believe that it will be boring or a source of anxiety or be emotionally unpleasant in another way. This triad (Figure 11.1) will now be explored and various motivational factors related to it.

Values

The value of a learning task is what it has to offer the learner. To have value,

Figure 11.1 A Triad of Motivational Concerns

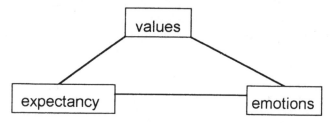

the task must offer something the learner desires, wants, needs, believes to be important or sees as worthwhile. For instance, it might offer a material reward such as a longer break (or a chance to avoid a punishment such as a shorter break). In this case, the task is simply a means to an end and has no intrinsic value. Desirable behaviour is rewarded, undesirable is not. Rewards acceptable in teaching situations include tokens, such as stars used with young children and points collected to be exchanged for some other reward in the case of adults.

What is on offer does not have to be material. Engaging in the task could bring praise or approval from a highly regarded person or group of people, such as teachers or parents. Success might also bring respect and approval in the long term, as for winners of a Nobel Prize. The need for affiliation may be involved when students engage in a task because someone they admire does so. Some lifelong interests begin in this way. Similarly, a teacher's obvious interest and enthusiasm may attract students to a task. Enthusiasm can be catching. A student may adjust his or her mental state, perhaps involuntarily, towards that of the teacher just as someone is inclined to match another's posture.

A task might also be a challenge which offers students the opportunity to feel success, to be better than others or to show they can do it. They may not always enjoy the route but, knowing success is likely (although not so likely that the achievement is trivial) students engage in the task for these outcomes. It can, however, result in intense competition amongst students which means that many must fail and failure could be attributed to causes beyond their control. Competition is likely to be a feature of some societies more than of others. Similarly, attributing success to ability is more likely to occur in Western than in Asian societies. In the latter, it is more likely to be attributed to effort (Hawkins, 1994). Nevertheless, in general, learners value tasks in which they do well (Wigfield, 1994).

Another source of value is what a task offers in terms of satisfaction of curiosity, interest, an understanding of the world in its broadest sense, and enhanced feelings of competence. Such rewards come from within the student and elicit an intrinsic or self-motivation (Zimmerman, 1994). For instance, if students are aware of the personal relevance of a topic, they are more likely to value it. Personal relevance has several forms. For example, there is what it has to offer in terms of a feeling of satisfaction at the potential for competent action. This includes opportunities for self-understanding and learning about the human condition and what the task might contribute to the learner's overall view of the world and his or her place in it (Newton, 1989).

A variety of circumstances may lend value to a learning task. There may be a material reward at its successful completion, commonly referred to as an extrinsic motivation for doing the task. There may be opportunities for affiliation and the rewards that might bring, commonly referred to as social motivation. Some tasks may offer a chance to achieve, compete and prove oneself, generally referred to as achievement motivation. Any motive which is acceptable in the classroom and results in understanding is likely to be welcome but a positive, intrinsic motivation is what teachers particularly value. It has the potential for generating high-quality and sustained engagement in learning and can lead to high levels of learning (Alexander and Murphy, 1998). As Covington (1992: 20) has put it, 'learning becomes valued for what it can do to benefit the individual' and learners 'may seek out answers or information simply to satisfy their curiosity'. Self-motivation of this kind has distinct advantages over others in that it is particularly supportive in the self-regulation of learning. The teacher cannot and probably would not want to stand over a student and direct his or her learning all the time. Learners often have to be self-regulating, activate their own thinking and find the motivation to persist with a task.

In this respect, the work of Deci et al. (1991) on self-determination is relevant. Students are more likely to engage in a task if they feel that they are in control and able to develop it in a direction which satisfies their needs for self-determination (Okolo et al., 1995). Deci believes that the need to feel competent, independent and to affiliate underpins much of a learner's behaviour. These three needs fuel an attitude of self-determination to accomplish a goal. However, Deci allows that these needs are mediated by a learner's thoughts and feelings about a particular situation. Attributions regarding the causes of success and failure will affect behaviour to the extent that someone feels competent and able to operate independently. The extent to which someone feels in control of the situation is reflected in his or her attitude of self-determination. Some earlier work by de Charms (1976) illustrates this well. De Charms ascribed learning behaviour to the degree of control learners have over the situation. If they have no control, they tend to behave defensively, irresolutely and avoid challenge. There is little to satisfy the need for human relationships, the need to feel competent and the need for autonomy that underpin an attitude of self-determination. Only external sources of motivation, such as threats or promises, keep these 'pawns', as de Charms called them, on task. On the other hand, if the learner feels in control, there tends to be a feeling of potency, positive motivation and a willingness to accept challenge. These 'origins', in de Charms' terminology, are more likely to show intrinsic motivation towards the task.

Implications for Supporting Understanding

When supporting understanding, the aim is often to help someone construct a coherent structure of the subject under study. No structure of this kind stands in isolation but is a part of some larger network of relationships. Some of these relationships tie the topic to the needs it satisfies and the reasons for its existence. These relate to interest, satisfaction, self-understanding, practical utility, competence and place in the natural, physical and human world. Often, students are unlikely to have this fuller network as prior knowledge. Such students may fail to see that relevance of what is asked of them and see no value in engaging in it. If they see no value in it, they are unlikely to engage in it willingly or will do so in only a shallow way. Understanding does not have much of a chance in such circumstances.

We must ensure that the relevance of a topic is apparent to the student. I do not see this as a task that is altogether distinct from supporting understanding because it amounts to taking the topic in hand and embedding it in its wider context. In other words, the structure that we often want students to construct has been taken from a larger web. Some of its threads need to be restored. These threads relate to what makes the topic relevant and satisfy human needs. This could be achieved by:

- setting the scene in a way which highlights human needs that the topic could satisfy;
- eliciting prior knowledge that is relevant to the topic, including the ways in which it satisfies human needs;
- asking questions which relate to topic relevance.

For instance, in science, a topic on genetics might be preceded by a discussion of beliefs about inheritance before Gregor Mendel, an outline of Mendel's work, inheritance as it is seen today and some of the practical possibilities of genetic manipulation and their significance. Subsequent tasks would be to explore the science of inheritance at an appropriate level. The intention is to bring in the element of human endeavour, showing Mendel as a person much like some people we know but who spent a lot of time and effort in making sense of the problem of inheritance.

However, this approach needs to be used with care. Dewey (1913) warned against merely adding spice to instruction; the spice tends to be what is remembered. Seductive details, as they have become known, are interesting but unimportant as far as the main message is concerned. For instance, writing of Nelson's love affairs in an account of his naval strategies is entertaining but irrelevant. Seductive details are often recalled at the expense of main ideas (Harp and Mayer, 1998; Schraw, 1998). Harp and Mayer prepared an account of the cause of lightning and sprinkled it with snippets of information such as describing how golfers are prime targets for lightning. They found that psychology undergraduates tended to remember 'what lightning causes' rather than 'what causes lightning'. In other words, these snippets diverted them from the real purpose of the instruction to an incidental one.

Making relevance explicit can risk diverting attention from the target. Nevertheless, in some circumstances, the risk is worth taking, particularly when students see no value in what is expected of them and their learning is poor as a consequence. The tests show that the diversion of attention is not complete, and some knowledge of the main theme is retained. In this context, making relevance explicit is worthwhile. Nevertheless, care is needed to minimize its potentially adverse influence on learning. One way could be to demarcate it clearly and overtly from the main theme by signalling a change of focus: 'Now we are going to have a look at...'. This would be followed by a new setting of scene and eliciting of prior knowledge as it relates to the main theme.

Many people immediately recognize utility as supplying value to a task and, while it may be tempting to play that card frequently, an overuse puts at risk those occasions when practical utility is debatable. For instance, learning about history may be difficult to justify in terms of practical utility but it offers opportunities to know about why the world is the way it is today, amongst other things. In such circumstances, ways of highlighting other sources of value can be at a premium.

Smith and Lloyd (1972) have advocated a contemporary history approach so that students would see the relevance of history more readily. They believe that people expect some understanding of current affairs and a satisfaction of their curiosity about the past. Early history is approached through contemporary history, as when the Magna Carta was discussed in connection with its bearing upon more recent events. They claim that society wants guidance on current issues and, at the same time, has a curiosity about the past and the way earlier events have shaped the contemporary world.

Intrinsic motivation might be achieved by careful scene setting in which the relevance for the student is made explicit and is discussed and agreed. Covington (1992) has pointed out that goals can serve as surrogates for motivation. Setting a learning goal might highlight an opportunity to increase competence and self-efficacy, but the gains should be apparent to and valued by the student. In practice, the goal often has the form of solving some problem. Problems offer a challenge which we tend to assume students will want to meet. Some do, particularly if they see relevance for their own lives, but others shy away from an activity that offers a high probability of failure. Problems which may be solved in a number of ways and at different levels increase the likelihood that fewer students will feel threatened by them.

Being realistic, when an interest in the subject is thin, other forms of motivation may need to be elicited to induce students to engage in learning. Offering external rewards for a productive mental engagement might be one way but the danger is that they become an expectation and the learning task becomes secondary (McGraw, 1978). Once engaged on the task, interest in what was seen as boring can develop. External rewards would be faded out in that event. Authentic activity, it may be recalled, was that which enabled learning to take place in a context like that where it would be used. Providing authentic activities is a strategy which tends to be associated with supporting learning in context. Students may see authentic learning situations as particularly relevant to human needs since they relate to real life in more obvious ways. Like real life, however, authentic activity can be relevant and uninteresting. It may help if the teacher draws students' attention to the way their interest develops even though the topic seemed an uninteresting one at the outset.

Another source of value which could be overlooked in highly structured classroom climates is control over learning. Okolo et al. (1995) recommends that students be given a degree of choice over the activity when that is possible, that their perceptions and awareness of their control be enhanced, and that individual differences in learning characteristics be taken into account in the choices provided. This does not mean that students have complete control over what they do, but it may be possible for some topics to offer alternative routes to the same goal. For example, evidence of learning could come from writing, a test or an oral presentation. It may be possible to allow the student to choose which they want to do. Some students are not always aware of the freedom they have even within the constraints of a prescribed activity. Similarly, differences in prior knowledge and preferred ways of learning have to be considered. Those with little prior knowledge benefit from structure to guide them into the task. Those with a higher level of prior knowledge may already have that structure. At the same time, not everyone performs well in the same circumstances. Some benefit more from information presented verbally, others find diagrams particularly helpful. While we may cater for this variety, there will be occasions when students' channels of communication should be widened. Students may benefit from some guidance on choosing a learning path, but this need not eliminate all student control of the task.

What a young child values is unlikely to be quite the same as an adult. It is important to distinguish between the various kinds of value that a task has and emphasize that which a particular learner sees as relevant. For young children, relevance is likely to stem from what they know well about their world. Home, family, school and local community are likely to be more meaningful to them than remote concerns. This could be widened with older students.

Expectancy

Expectations of success can come from prior experience or, to be more precise, from the student's perceptions of that experience. In particular, how they attribute past success and failure will figure in their expectancy. If success is attributed to controllable causes, they may feel more inclined to engage in the task. Repeated failure, on the other hand, can lead to helplessness, particularly if this is attributed to causes beyond the student's control (Galloway et al., 1998).

Weiner (1986) explained differences in students' responses to a given learning situation in terms of the causal attributions they make. Success and failure tend to be attributed to antecedents such as luck, topic difficulty, ability and effort (Earl Wilson once illustrated this with: 'Success is just a matter of luck. Ask any failure.'). These antecedents are classified according to their locus of causality (internal or external), their stability (stable, unstable) and their controllability (controllable, uncontrollable). Ability, for instance, is often seen as internal, stable and uncontrollable. If failure is attributed to a lack of ability, then the student is likely to believe that nothing can be done about it. Situations that are similar in the future are likely to be met without enthusiasm; there is little expectation of success. Effort, on the other hand, is commonly seen as internal, unstable and controllable. If failure is ascribed to a lack of effort, this is in the student's control and more effort might be made in the future. The possibility of positive motivation is greater in this case and an expectation of success is more likely. Drew and Watkins (1998) have demonstrated with Hong Kong university students that when attribution is to causes seen as beyond the learner's control, there is a tendency to adopt a surface approach to learning and a tendency for academic achievement to be depressed.

There are a number of sources of attributions. For instance, if most students appear to do little preparation but do well in a test, someone who spent hours on preparation yet achieved little is likely to ascribe this to a lack of ability. A teacher who praises a student for hard work even though that work was weak risks reinforcing a lack of ability attribution. On the other hand, a student who tends to receive grades with no consistent pattern could ascribe it to luck. Ability and luck are out of the student's control, so why be positive about the next topic?

After seeing what the task entails, a student may feel capable of succeeding and confident enough to take the task on. Various studies have shown that a positive academic self-concept, the ideas and attitudes a learner holds about him or herself, tends to be associated with a deep approach to learning and better academic achievement (Drew and Watkins, 1998). Bandura (1977, 1982) and Schunk (1991) believe that it is perceptions of self-efficacy that are important. Self-efficacy is a student's judgement about his or her ability to perform a given task well (Gist and Mitchell, 1992; Zohar, 1998). If a student believes he or she has the ability to organize and perform the actions needed for success, that is, to cope with the task, that student is likely to be positive about engaging in it and show an intrinsic motivation towards it.

Past experience, encouragement, attributions and observation of the behaviour of others contribute to judgements of self-efficacy. Someone who has consistently experienced success in a particular area tends to have a higher self-efficacy than others. The earlier experience is likely to have equipped them with enough of the mental wherewithal to organize and perform the actions needed. If, however, they recall that they were worried, anxious and concerned, they may ascribe it to a lack of ability and may lower their estimate of their self-efficacy. Encouraging someone who doubts he or she has the necessary self-efficacy can sometimes persuade them that their assessment is wrong, so that they willingly engage in the task. Being in a group who describe a task as feasible can similarly persuade students to be more positive about their own self-efficacy. Of course, if the likelihood of failure remains high, this is risky. Persuasion relies on some credibility.

Matters to consider in expectancy are to do with the past record of success and failure, its causal attribution, and the self-concept particularly in relation to self-efficacy.

Implications for Supporting Understanding

One of the main problems with raising an expectation of success is that it is potentially very damaging if failure repeatedly follows. This means that raising expectations should generally be followed by some success, otherwise a teacher's credibility risks becoming so low that future approaches are likely to be rejected. It also risks confirming students' beliefs that potentially controllable causes, such as effort, matter little. This means that goals set for students have to be considered carefully so that they are neither trivial nor beyond what they can achieve (Borich and Tombari, 1997). It is recommended that:

- Goals be near, clear, specific, realistic and achievable (Elliot and Dweck, 1988; Johnson and Johnson, 1990). What will count as success should be clear to the students. Some quick success may make the point that it is not impossible and could bolster feelings of self-efficacy particularly for those inclined to be negatively motivated.
- Self-efficacy be supported by realistic persuasion and modelling. Here, modelling is provided by a group of students that believes in its ability to plan and execute a course of action to complete the task. Placing someone with low self-efficacy in such a group can help him or her.
- Whenever possible, the task is organized so that there is a degree of learner control over what is done and how it is done. Often the same end can be achieved in a number of ways. This allows students to adopt approaches they prefer and that are within their competences, increasing a feeling of self-efficacy.
- Effort is rewarded rather than attributing success only to ability. This is intended to focus causal attribution on what is in the student's control. If what governs success is felt to be in the hands of the student, there is at least the possibility of success. Avoid messages which attribute failure to mental processes beyond the learner's control. For example, when the task is to make a self-propelled buggy, praise for a failed buggy's appearance confirms the student's belief in a lack of capability. Although

kindly meant, 'Never mind, just read your book, instead', does the same and often publicly.

• Tests of learning are designed carefully so that they enhance future expectations of some success (see also below).

Precisely how reasonable expectations might be raised depends on the cause of the existing expectation and the stage of development of the learner. For instance, young children commonly attribute success and failure to effort rather than ability, so suggesting that they are likely to be successful if they make the effort is more likely to be accepted than if they were older students.

Emotions

Ingleton (1995) argues that the risk of shame and humiliation is such that it is a significant concern for some students, and Sogunro (1998) adds the risk of feeling inferior or inadequate. Particularly when students attribute the cause of what is perceived as failure to themselves, self-worth, self-esteem and self-image are at risk. This alone can be sufficient to lead to task avoidance (Geisthardt and Munsch, 1996). Certainly it is not uncommon for those who take the risk to signal their concern, with words such as, 'It might be a silly question but ...' How we think of ourselves and what others think of us is important.

Covington (1992) argues that a student aims to maintain a positive self-image of competency. The disposition to defend this self-image constitutes the self-worth motive. It is fuelled by, for instance, a need to believe in our own competence and the need for the approval and respect of others. The learning environment is a potential threat to this self-image. While success may bring pride, failure could bring shame and humiliation. Understandably, this is a source of worry and anxiety. It means that students, young and old, can be anxious about particular tests and examinations (Sogunro, 1998; Zohar, 1998). A small degree of anxiety may prompt a student to engage in the task in order to avoid the risk to the self-image but, in the extreme, anxiety can occupy the student's mind to the extent that productive thinking is radically reduced.

Implications for Supporting Understanding

The problem with anxiety is that it has a number of causes. Students may be anxious because they have not made the effort and are not prepared for the test. On the other hand, some may know the subject but anxiety stems from an inability to organize thoughts, plan and answer test questions. Others, may know the subject and the necessary test skills but anxiety occupies their thoughts to the exclusion of subject knowledge: they are unable to retrieve and organize under examination conditions. There may also be some who do not know the subject, perform badly and attribute failure to anxiety. By claiming this to be beyond their control, self-esteem is saved. What may work for one student does not for another. Some strategies for dealing with anxiety have been suggested but, probably because the precise reason for each person's anxiety is not always known, results have been mixed (Covington, 1992; Sogunro, 1998). These include:

- Rational-emotive therapy in which any irrational basis for the anxiety is refuted. Failure often looms larger than success in students' minds and it may help if balance is restored and misconceptions about the consequences of failure removed.
- Test-taking instruction in which students are advised on planning and organizing an answer and making the best use of the time available.
- Study-skills instruction in which students are taught ways of monitoring learning and remedying deficiencies (see also Chapter 12).
- De-sensitizing students to tests by giving them so frequently that they no longer provoke excessive anxiety.
- Having students take physical activity before assessment and learn relaxation techniques.
- Encouraging students to over-prepare for a test by learning beyond the level needed to be successful.

As Covington (1992) points out, these strategies aim to reduce the threat so that students may succeed. Some students will still fail and attribute it to causes beyond their control. In the end, they may become helpless and give up. The risk of learned helplessness may be reduced by increasing the likelihood of some success. Some possible courses of action are:

- Placing easier test items first to give some initial success and thereby allay test anxiety.
- Using custom testing in which a computer presents the test items. If the student fails on a response, easier questions are presented until the level suited to the student is found. A variation is to move in the other direction and present questions until the student begins to fail. This identifies the upper boundary of the student's knowledge, but also gives him or her the satisfaction of answering more questions correctly than incorrectly.
- Using self-adaptive testing in which the student selects the starting level of difficulty. Those who are anxious tend to begin with easier questions but, nevertheless, progress to more difficult ones.
- Using untimed tests to reduce some of the pressure on the student. Highly anxious students tend to make more errors under time pressure than low anxiety students (Covington, 1992).

Again, Covington (1992) describes these approaches as not suited to all students. Indeed, removing stress and anxiety for some students can also depress achievement.

Motivation training is an attempt to develop a positive orientation towards learning. For instance, motivation might be improved if a learner's self-concept is better. Teenagers in an Australian private school were given an achievement motivation training programme intended to change habits, attitudes, beliefs and expectations. Some positive results were obtained in that there was evidence of a deeper approach to learning and an increased achieving orientation amongst some students. Unfortunately, the achievement motivation of low-performing students became worse and, for the others, the improvement did not persist. There are several possible reasons for the disappointing results, but probably the lesson is that motivation is very complex and attending to only one of its aspects is not, in itself, sufficient.

Summary

In order that support for understanding may have a chance, motivation to learn should be taken into account. In particular, this means that what a task offers in terms of value, expectancy and emotion has to be considered. For practical purposes, an expectancy–value–emotion view of motivation captures several important features of motivation and, at the same time, acknowledges the problem of reaching first base with negatively motivated students. But we do not simply respond to motivation like a moth to a flame. Being burnt makes a difference. We attribute success and failure to a variety of causes, some of which we see as being in our control. If we believe we can and want to do something about it, we are likely to do so, particularly if we can see a way of doing it. While each student is likely to differ from another in what they value, what they expect and how they respond emotionally, some general approaches may serve as starting points for eliciting positive motivation to learning. Nevertheless, a sensitivity to individual differences appears to be essential as what shapes motivation can be beliefs about the self. A lack of forethought could even make a negative motivation worse.

If students see personal value in a task, there is a reasonable chance that it will elicit a positive orientation towards it. To ensure that students are at least aware of the task's potential value, it should be made explicit. It may not be sufficient to point out the relevance that a task has or has had for someone else. The student must see the task as personally valuable. Intrinsic motivation is prized because it has the potential for supporting self-regulated learning. An expectancy of success depends on a variety of things, such as, past experience and how it has been interpreted, the extent to which someone believes he or she can devise a successful course of action and the possibility of working with confident others. Emotions may also be a source of negative motivation and may occupy mental space that could be used for marshalling thoughts about the task in hand. There are some ways of addressing problems caused by emotions but they need to be matched to the underlying cause.

References

Alexander, P.A. and Murphy, P.K. (1998) 'Profiling the Differences in Students' Knowledge, Interest, and Strategic Processing', *Journal of Educational Psychology* 90: 435–47.

Atkinson, J.W. (1978) *Personality, Motivation and Achievement*, Washington, DC: Hemisphere.

Bandura, A. (1977) 'Self-Efficacy: Toward a Unified Theory of Behavioral Change', *Psychological Review* 84: 191–215.

—— (1982) 'The Self and Mechanisms of Agency', in J. Suls (ed.), *Psychological Perspectives on the Self: Vol. 1.* Englewood Cliffs, NJ: Prentice Hall, 3–40.

Borich, G.D. and Tombari, M.L. (1997) *Educational Psychology: A Contemporary Approach*, New York: Longman.

Charms, R. de (1976) *Enhancing Motivation: Change in the Classroom*, New York: Irvington.

Covington, M.V. (1992) *Making the Grade: A Self-Worth Perspective on Motivation and School Reform*, Cambridge: Cambridge University Press.

Deci, E.L., Vallerand, R.J., Pelletier, L.G. and Ryan, R.M. (1991) 'Motivation and Education: The Self-Determination Perspective', *Educational Psychologist* 26: 325–46.

Dewey, J. (1913) *Interest and Effort in Education*, New York: Houghton Mifflin.

Drew, P.Y. and Watkins, D. (1998) 'Affective Variables, Learning Approaches and Academic Achievement', *British Journal of Educational Psychology* 68: 173–88.

Elliott, E.S. and Dweck, C.S. (1988) 'Goals: An Approach to Motivation and Achievement', *Journal of Personality and Social Psychology* 54: 5–12.

Feather, N.T. (1982) 'Expectancy-Value Approaches', in N.T. Feather (ed.), *Expectations and Actions: Expectancy-Value Models in Psychology*, Hillsdale, NJ: Lawrence Erlbaum, 395–420.

—— (1992) 'Values, Valences, Expectations, and Actions', *Journal of Social Issues* 48: 109–24.

Galloway, D., Rogers, C. Armstrong, D. and Leo, E. (1998) *Motivating the Difficult to Teach*, London: Longman.

Geisthardt, C. and Munsch, J. (1996) 'Coping with School Stress: A Comparison of Adolescents with and without Learning Disabilities', *Journal of Learning Disabilities* 29: 287–96.

Gist, M.E. and Mitchell, T. (1992) 'Self-Efficacy: A Theoretical Analysis of its Determinants and Malleability', *Academy of Management Review* 17: 183–211.

Harp, S.F. and Mayer, R.E. (1998) 'How Seductive Details do their Damage', *Journal of Educational Psychology* 90: 414–34.

Hawkins, J.N. (1994) 'Issues of Motivation in Asian education', in H.F. O'Neil and M. Drillings, *Motivation: Theory and Research*, Hillsdale, NJ: Lawrence Erlbaum, 101–14.

Ingleton, C. (1995) 'Gender and Learning: Does Emotion Make a Difference?' *Higher Education* 30: 323–35.

Johnson, D.W. and Johnson, R.T. (1990) *Learning Together and Alone: Co-operation, Competition and Individualisation*, Englewood Cliffs, NJ: Prentice Hall.

McClelland, D.C. (1961) *The Achieving Society*, Princeton, NJ: Van Nostrand.

McGraw, K. (1978) 'The Detrimental Effects of Reward on Performance', in M. Lepper and D. Greene (eds) *The Hidden Costs of Reward*, Hillsdale, NJ: Lawrence Erlbaum.

Newsom, W.B. (1990) 'Motivate, Now!' *Personnel Journal*, 51–5.

Newton, D.P. (1989) *Making Science Education Relevant*, London: Kogan Page.

Okolo, C.M., Bahr, C.M. and Emmett Gardner, J. (1995) 'Increasing Achievement Motivation of Elementary School Students with Mild Disabilities', *Intervention in School and Clinic* 30: 279–86.

Pintrich, P.R. and De Groot, E.V. (1990) 'Motivational and Self-Regulated Learning Components of Classroom Academic Performance', *Journal of Educational Psychology* 82: 33–40.

Purdue, N.M. and Hattie, J. A. (1995) 'The Effect of Motivation Training on Approaches to Learning and Self-Concept', *British Journal of Educational Psychology* 65: 227–35.

Schunk, D.H. (1991) 'Self-Efficacy and Academic Motivation', *Educational Psychologist* 26: 207–32.

Schraw, G. (1998) 'Processing and Recall Differences Among Seductive Details', *Journal of Educational Psychology* 90: 3–12.

Smith, G.C. and Lloyd, H.A. (1972) *The Relevance of History*, London: Heinemann.

Sogunro, O.A. (1998) 'Impact of Evaluation Anxiety on Adult Learning', *Journal of Research and Development in Education* 31: 109–21.

Vroom, V.H. (1964) *Work and Motivation*, New York: Wiley.

Weiner, B. (1986) *An Attribution Theory of Motivation and Emotion*, New York: Springer-Verlag.

Wigfield, A. (1994) 'The Role of Children's Achievement Values in the Self-Regulation of Their Learning Outcomes', in D.H. Schunk and B.J. Zimmerman (eds), *Self-Regulation of Learning and Performance*, Hillsdale, NJ: Lawrence Erlbaum, 101–26.

Zimmerman, B.J. (1994) 'Dimensions of Academic Self-Regulation', in D.H. Schunk and B.J. Zimmerman (eds), *Self-Regulation of Learning and Performance*, Hillsdale, NJ: Lawrence Erlbaum, 3–24.

Zohar, D. (1998) 'An Additive Model of Test Anxiety', *Journal of Educational Psychology* 90: 330–40.

12 The Self-Regulation of Learning

Overview

The nature of the self-regulation of learning is outlined and related to metacognition. Self-regulation is illustrated and its effects commented on. Metacognitive skills depend on age, experience and practice but some skills may be taught or developed. Self-regulation of motivation is another possibility that is considered.

The Self-Regulation of Learning

The emphasis so far has been on what the teacher can do for the learner. Learners, however, are not usually helpless. 'Humans have the ability to monitor and control their conscious cognitive processes' (Redding, 1990: 27). If they fail to understand they may, for instance, persist or try a new approach. In short, they may initiate actions themselves which help them understand (Flavell, 1979). They regulate, control and sustain learning so that their learning goals may be achieved (Zimmerman, 1989; Schunk, 1994).

This do-it-yourself process depends on metacognition. Metacognition is often used to describe people's knowledge and control of their cognitive activity (Brown, 1987; Cheng, 1993). It covers a variety of mental activities, some of which have been described by Flavell (1987). He lists metacognitive knowledge relating to people (for example, someone's beliefs about his or her ability to cope with verbal material, the relative capabilities of people and the reliability of memory); metacognitive knowledge relating to the task (for example, knowing that highly non-redundant text can take time and mental effort to grasp); and metacognitive knowledge relating to strategies (for example, planning or re-reading after comprehension failure). He also described metacognitive experiences such as puzzlement when trying to understand and satisfaction on success. Some of this mental activity may not be open to conscious reflection.

Jacobs and Paris (1987: 255) prefer to focus on what is conscious and deliberate. They define metacognition as 'any knowledge about cognitive states or processes that can be shared between individuals. That is, knowledge about cognition that can be demonstrated, communicated, examined, and discussed'. They describe two main components: the self-appraisal of cognition and the self-management of thinking. The first relates to declarative, procedural and conditional knowledge. Declarative knowledge, as the terms suggests, is that which can be stated. Knowing that re-reading facilitates memory is an example. Knowing how to skim-read or summarize text is an instance of procedural knowledge. Conditional knowledge is contained in the tying together of a situation and an action, such as knowing that when someone needs to learn the relationships between areas of knowledge, a mind-mapping activity on paper could be helpful. The self-management of thinking refers to mental activities such as planning, evaluating, regulating, monitoring and plan and strategy revision.

Self-regulation is a mental process that draws on metacognitive knowledge and strategies to achieve its end. For instance, students' conceptions of learning can be seen as a part of their metacognitive knowledge; if they see learning as the acquisition of as much information as possible, they are likely to be concerned with how much they have acquired rather than its quality. With that goal in mind, they select a way of learning, appraise progress and take some action if the quantity learned seems insufficient. Metacognitive experience, such as feelings of satisfaction, may also serve to indicate that the goal has been achieved, at least in the way it was conceived by the student.

Examples of Self-Regulatory Strategies

Assuming that learners have an adequate conception of understanding in the domain concerned, how does self-regulation support understanding? The first thing is that the conception lets them know what counts as understanding. (They may, of course, opt for memorization but they would know that it is a different outcome.) The second is mental engagement. Self-regulation may shape the form of any mental engagement and monitor its effect. If understanding fails and that failure is noted, strategies may be deployed to remedy the matter. Thus, self-regulation may involve an awareness that prior knowledge is inadequate, and a specification of the requisite knowledge and the nature of the action taken to acquire that knowledge are needed. Equally, it could involve asking where understanding failed and elaborating upon the information prior to that in order to make good the missing connections. Or, it could amount to using a mind-mapping strategy for displaying the connections within a topic or with existing knowledge so that a coherent, integrated structure is developed. Self-regulation serves a function that is very like that of external regulation.

Many of the strategies used in the external regulation of understanding could be used in self-regulation. For instance, *Think Trix* comprises a collection of cues to guide thinking (Adger et al., 1995; see Chapter 5). The teacher uses symbols on flash cards to indicate what is required. Eventually, he or she withdraws the prompts. This occurs in conjunction with aids for structuring and representing thought visually through graphic organizers such as web and block diagrams. Co-operative learning is a part of the process. This combined strategy is not meant to be a one-off event, but should occur regularly so that it becomes an automatic, unprompted routine. In effect, what begins as an externally regulated strategy becomes a self-regulated strategy.

There are a number of relatively simple strategies which some discover for themselves. These include re-reading what has not been understood, identifying and marking key points, note-taking, summarizing, consulting other sources of information and drawing maps which show the relationships between elements of information. Of course, this does not mean that these strategies are used to their best advantage. Note-taking, for instance, might be little more than verbatim transcripts when reformulation or translation could be more effective. Other strategies which may have to be taught include the construction of summative headings which capture the essence of a section of text and the generation of analogies (Newton, 1990).

Some strategies generally have to be taught and practised. The SQ4R approach to learning from text is an example (Thomas and Robinson, 1972). The acronym stands for *Survey, Question, Read, Reflect, Recite and Review. Survey* refers to acquiring an overview of what the topic is about; *Question* reminds the reader to ask themselves who, where, what, why questions about the topic; *Read* prompts them to seek answers to the questions; *Reflect* tells the reader to look for overall structure, deliberately relate the new knowledge to prior knowledge and elaborate on it; *Recite* amounts to recalling the new subject; and *Review* is the appraisal stage. Another procedure describes how to solve problems. It uses the acronym IDEAL where *I* prompts the learner to identify the problem, *D* is the definition of it as a representation, *E* reminds the student to explore potential solutions, *A* refers to the action that should now take place, and *L* prompts the learner to look back over the event and evaluate the outcome (Bransford and Stein, 1984).

A number of such ordered plans of action have been found to be effective when used under supervision. Some, however, are often so complex that it is hard to imagine that they would continue to be used unprompted. In self-questioning, for instance, learners may be taught to use a sequence of questions which they ask themselves when learning something new. The sequence relates to:

- the topic in hand (What is the information about? What is the topic? What do I know about it? What does it relate to?);

- the details (What are the most important points? How do the parts relate to one another? Does the information make sense? What do I have to remember?);
- the task (What is the task? What will I have to do to complete it?);
- the approach (How will I approach the task? Is there another way of doing it? What use will I make of the result?);
- change in knowledge (How does the new knowledge compare with what I used to have? Does this new knowledge affect other things I know?);
- an increase in understanding (What if...? How does...? Why does...? How could...? What about...?);
- progress (How am I doing? Where will this approach lead me? Is it the best way of proceeding?);
- completion (Have I answered the question/completed the task? Is there anything else I should do?);
- satisfaction (Do I understand? Do I understand enough to justify stopping? What do I need to do to achieve more understanding?);
- the future use of the knowledge (How can I make sure I remember this new knowledge? What use will I make of it?).

(Baird, 1986)

Such a system may work well under external regulation but, unless the student maintained a physical record of the steps, it may not lend itself well to self-regulation.

Osman and Hannafin (1992) classify regulation strategies according to whether they are embedded (integrated with the material to be learned) or detached (separate from the material to be learned). At the same time, they classified strategies as being content-dependent (its range of application being limited to the topic under study) or content-independent (having a relatively wide range of application). A question to stimulate the recall of relevant knowledge may be embedded in the text while a detached block of questions for practice may appear at the end of a chapter. A learner may deal with numbers by thinking of them as their domino equivalents, a strategy that is likely to be useful only for certain numerical operations and so is content-dependent. The SQ4R strategy, on the other hand, is largely content-independent in that it might be used in different domains of learning.

The Practice of Self-Regulation

It seems reasonable to expect that knowing when understanding has failed and what you can do about it is potentially useful. Encouraging and enabling learners to take responsibility for their learning can be productive and the use of self-regulatory strategies tends to be associated with higher achievement (Wolters, 1998). Marine and Escribe (1994), in connection with learning the subject of statistics, found that those who used metacognitive capabilities tend also to be more successful than those who do not. Mason (1994), in testing the contribution of an analogy (a mail delivery system) in teaching about the human circulatory system to Italian fifth graders, found there to be a high correlation between a learner's awareness of the meaning and instructional purpose of the analogy and understanding the target. In short, metacognitive knowledge and understanding of the target topic went hand in hand. Correlational studies, of course, do not establish a causal connection. In teaching reading, however, Jacobs and Paris (1987) found that instruction in metacognition produced readers with a higher degree of comprehension. Redding (1990) also finds that 'considerable evidence has accumulated that suggests an emphasis on metacognition during training can result in significant improvements in problem solving for the task, as well as in transfer of skills across tasks'. Carr et al. (1994) come to a similar conclusion regarding the teaching of mathematics. Nevertheless, Ablard and Lipschultz (1998), in a study of self-reported strategies for dealing with homework amongst 12-year-old students in the USA, remind us that that the conscious use of self-regulatory strategies is not essential for success. Some students seem able to win through without conscious self-regulation.

Reviewing research on metacognition, Garner and Alexander (1989: 145) found that neither children nor adults generally monitored their cognition. It seems that some metacognitive 'strategies are difficult to learn and easy to abandon'. They concluded that although metacognition develops with age, motivation and belief in the value of metacognition also matter when it comes to thinking about your own learning.

The Development of Metacognition

In terms of survival, the possession of self-regulatory strategies or, at least, a tendency to develop them will benefit an organism with limited and fallible processing capabilities (Flavell, 1987). Very young children are not aware of their thinking and do not use strategies intentionally or consciously. They can use self-regulatory strategies after about 4 years of age, but are unlikely to notice that these help. When shown two strategies for learning vocabulary, for instance, they generally do not notice that one is more effective than the other unless it is drawn to their attention. It seems that, while some young learners can regulate their learning, they need support in doing it (Pressley and Ghatala, 1990; Marton et al., 1993; Keenan et al., 1994).

Children may respond to the question, 'Do you understand?' at any age, but that does not mean that their answer is necessarily well-founded. Barnett and Hixon (1997) had second, fourth and sixth graders (7, 9 and 11 years old) predict their success in mathematics, social studies and spelling tests. All made fairly accurate predictions in the social studies tests, and fourth and sixth graders also made accurate predictions in the mathematics tests, while sixth graders had difficulty in predicting the spelling success. The tests were compiled by the class teachers and related to the topics in hand in each class. The researchers say these tests were neither testing the same kinds of knowledge nor were they focusing on one kind of knowledge in a given area. Nevertheless, their data merited the view that metacognitive skills can often be weak in real learning contexts. However, 10-year-old children do seem to have a fairly shrewd idea of what might indicate an understanding in other learners. For instance, when asked to select someone who is likely to understand, they are more likely to select someone who says that the lesson outcome 'hangs together' than they are someone who says it was 'enjoyable' (Newton and Newton, 1998). As was described previously, even when they know in general terms what counts as understanding, they may still be unsure of what counts in a particular context and may not have a sound basis for judging the quality of understanding.

Even 15-year-olds can have difficulty conceptualizing their metacognition and in giving clear, personal statements about it (Berry and Sahlberg, 1996). This does not, however, mean that there is no self-regulation of learning. Regulation of learning can be unconscious. For instance, a learner may not be aware of what it is that makes her say she does not understand. She may not be able to point to the place where understanding broke down and she may not know that the feeling of mental unease is an indicator of understanding failure. Equally, losing the thread of the argument when reading some difficult account may prompt someone to re-read the page, but the process may be automatic. Self-regulation may also be conscious but the learner may lack the language to describe it. Language is thought to help people control and monitor learning behaviour so it has a role to play in self-regulation. Young children often talk through their mental processes, revealing self-regulation in action. Later, this talk is internalized (Vygotsky, 1962).

Learning to Learn

Teachers sometimes overestimate learners' self-regulation skills and so fail to support them (Carr and Kurtz, 1990). Biggs and Moore (1993) have described ways in which students' metacognition may be developed: through experience, implicitly through teaching, and explicitly through teaching. Experience generally teaches students some self-regulatory strategies. They may be used automatically and the student may not be able to describe them clearly, but if they result in understanding then we can have little to complain about. In practice, these strategies could be fragmented and inefficient and something more is needed. Implicit opportunities for developing self-regulation may also be embedded in a learning task. The teacher scaffolds progress towards the double end of learning the subject and acquiring new learning skills. Discussion can help clarify expectations, the plan of action, the need for monitoring progress and the checking of the outcome. Explicit instruction in self-regulation is a more detached approach in which strategies are taught directly.

In general, the teaching of strategies divorced from their areas of application is less likely to encourage their continued use than if they are taught and practised in context. This does, however, risk tying them to a limited number of contexts when they could have a wider use. To reduce this risk, the area of application of strategies needs to be discussed and opportunities provided for their more general use (Pressley et al., 1985). The ultimate goal is their independent use in self-regulation.

What is achieved and how it is achieved must depend on the age and experience of the learner. For instance, teachers may model a self-regulation strategy by talk as they complete a task for younger schoolchildren. The children may first shadow the process and then use it independently. Comparing the effects of using and not using the strategy may highlight its value. Strategies need to be simple, easy to recall, and productive. Plan–Do–Review is one that will be familiar to many primary school teachers. Its purpose is to cue and order the course of events as a child engages in a task. Prompt the children to organize their thoughts in this way and, when they are successful because of it, attribute their success to it. Like effort, the use of a self-regulation strategy is in the control of the learner so that a difficult task is not always an impossible task.

Older learners have often developed strategies of their own, and it could be useful for others to hear about them. A natural selection process will have eliminated weak and cumbersome strategies, but those that remain may be somewhat idiosyncratic. By itself, this natural process may not be enough and refinement could make such strategies more effective. Discussion about the various kinds of learning approaches (for example, shallow versus deep approaches), learning goals (for example, meaning versus performance) and self-regulation strategies could support the process. This would include instruction and practice on identifying what is to be learned and what the outcome is to be, distinguishing between what is and is not known about the topic, constructing a plan of action, monitoring and adjusting the plan as necessary, and evaluating the outcome (Glaser, 1984; Clark, 1997). Paradoxically, facility in self-regulation can develop from external regulation. Success is when external support is removed and self-regulation stands alone.

Some students do not regulate their learning when they should because they do not know their learning is going in the wrong direction. Others do not know what will count as success so produce, on that occasion, unwanted outcomes. Some fail to transfer a strategy from one context to another. Still others lack the motivation or the will to engage in a task they neither value nor find interesting.

Self-Regulation and Motivation

Self-regulation is tied to motivation in a number of ways. As already mentioned, if successful learning is felt to be due to self-regulation, this places success in the control of the learner. With an attribution of this kind, learners are less likely to feel helpless and to be demotivated. At the same time, self-regulated learning places some aspects of a task in the hands of the learner. That is, the self-regulated learner is likely to feel a greater degree of autonomy than the externally regulated learner. As a result, an attitude of self-determination may be stronger and motivation more positive. Self-regulation can also allow a significant degree of personal goal setting. Given strategies that can achieve these goals, self-efficacy is likely to be greater.

There is, however, another connection with motivation. Self-regulation can also be applied to motivation itself. Wolters (1998), studying a group of North American students (about 19 years of age), found they used a variety of strategies for regulating their motivation. For example, some reminded themselves that they wanted a good grade (a performance goal), some planned to watch television or talk with a friend when they finished a task (rewards), and others found ways of relating the topic to their own lives (increasing task interest, relevance and value). He found that these students 'actively monitored and regulated their willingness to provide effort and persistence for academic tasks'. Self-regulation highlights the role of volition. Volition is the wilful engagement with the learning task to achieve a goal. It does not provide an additional reason for completing the task, such as a self-produced reward, or highlight a reason for completing the task. Once motivation has brought someone to begin a task, it might be that it is will that sustains engagement.

Conceptions of learning, motivation and self-regulation are aspects of the total learning environment and illustrate its complexity. The learning environment also includes other things which shape learning behaviour and one of these, the assessment of learning, is the subject of the next chapter.

Summary

Learners may regulate, control and sustain their learning by drawing on learning knowledge and regulatory strategies. Although not essential for success in learning, self-regulation can help. Younger learners are unlikely to have a conscious awareness of their self-regulatory strategies and may neither recognize them for what they are nor use them consistently. Even adults may not monitor their learning and act on the information that it provides. Self-regulation may be taught and developed through practice, allowing for the age and level of development of the learner. Self-regulation strategies may also be used to enhance motivation itself.

References

Ablard, K.E. and Lipschultz, R.A. (1998) 'Self-Regulated Learning in Higher-Achieving Students', *Journal of Educational Psychology* 90: 94–101.

Adger, C.T., Kalynapur, M., Blount Peterson, D. and Bridger, T.L. (1995) *Engaging Students: Thinking, Talking, Cooperating*, Los Angeles, CA and London: Corwin/Sage.

Baird, J.R. (1986) 'Improving Learning Through Enhanced Metacognition', *European Journal of Science Education* 8: 263–82.

Barnett, J.E. and Hixon, J.E. (1997) 'The Effects of Grade Level and Subject on Student Test Score Predictions', *Journal of Educational Research* 90: 170–4.

Berry, J. and Sahlberg, P. (1996) 'Investigating Pupils' Ideas of Learning', *Learning and Instruction* 6: 19–36.

Biggs, J.B. and Moore, P.J. (1993) *The Process of Learning*, New York: Prentice Hall, 3rd edn.

Bransford, J.D. and Steen, B. (1984) *The IDEAL Problem Solver*, New York: Freeman.

Brown, A.L. (1987) 'Metacognition, Executive Control, Self Regulation and Other Mysterious Mechanisms', in F.E. Weinert and R.H. Kluwe (eds), *Metacognition, Motivation and Understanding*, Hillsdale, NJ: Erlbaum, 65–116.

Carr, M., Alexander, J. and Folds-Bennett, T. (1994) 'Metacognition and Mathematics Strategy Use', *Applied Cognitive Psychology*, 8: 583–95.

Carr, M. and Kurtz, B.E. (1990) 'Teachers' Perceptions of Their Students' Metacognition, Attributions, and Self-Concept', *British Journal of Educational Pscyhology* 61: 197–206.

Cheng, P. (1993) 'Metacognition and Giftedness: The State of the Relationship', *Gifted Child Quarterly* 37: 105–12.

Clark, R.C. (1997) 'Metacognition and Human Performance Improvement', *Performance Improvement Quarterly* 10: 20–33.

Flavell, J.H. (1979) 'Metacognition and Cognitive Monitoring', *American Psychologist* 34: 906–11.

—— (1987) 'Speculations about the Nature and Development of Metacognition', in F.E. Weinert and R.H. Kluwe, *Metacognition, Motivation, and Understanding*, Hillsdale, NJ: Lawrence Erlbaum, 21–30.

Garner, R. and Alexander, P.A. (1989) 'Metacognition: Answered and Unanswered Questions', *Educational Psychologist* 24: 143–58.

Glaser, R. (1984) 'Education and Thinking', *American Psychologist* 39: 93–104.

Jacobs, J.E. and Paris, S.G. (1987) 'Children's Metacognition About Reading: Issues in Definition, Measurement, and Instruction', *Educational Psychologist* 22: 255–78.

Keenan, T., Ruffman, T. and Olson, D.R. (1994) 'When do Children Begin to Understand Logical Inference as a Source of Knowledge?', *Cognitive Development* 9: 331–53.

Marine, C. and Escribe, C. (1994) 'Metacognition and Competence on Statistical Problems', *Psychological Reports* 75: 1403–8.

Marton, F., Dall'Alba, G. and Beaty, E. (1993) 'Conceptions of Learning', *International Journal of Educational Research* 19: 277–300.

Mason, L. (1994) 'Cognitive and Metacognitive Aspects in Conceptual Change by Analogy', *Educational Studies* 22: 157–87.

Newton, D.P. (1990) *Teaching with Text*, London: Kogan Page.

Newton, D.P. and Newton, L.D. (1998) 'Some Conceptions of Understanding Amongst Ten-Year-Olds', *Educational Studies* 3: 339–63.

Osman, M.E. and Hannafin, M.J. (1992) 'Metacognitive Research and Theory', *Educational Technology* 40: 83–99.

Pressley, M., Borkowski, J.G., and O'Sullivan, J.T. (1985) 'Children's Metamemory and the Teaching of Memory Strategies', in D.L. Forrest-Pressley, G.E. Mac-Kinnon and T.G. Waller (eds), *Metacognition, Cognition, and Human Performance*, New York: Academic Press, 111–53.

Pressley, M. and Ghatala, E.S. (1990) 'Self-Regulated Learning: Monitoring Learning From Text', *Educational Psychologist* 25: 19–34.

Redding, R.E. (1990) 'Metacognitive Instruction: Trainers Teaching Thinking Skills', *Performance Improvement Quarterly* 3: 27–41.

Schunk, D.H. (1994) 'Self-Regulation of Self-Efficacy and Attributions in Academic Settings', in D.H. Schunk and B.J. Zimmerman, *Self-Regulation of Learning and Performance*, Hillsdale, NJ: Lawrence Erlbaum, 75–100.

Thomas, E.L. and Robinson, H.A. (1972) *Improving Reading in Every Class*, Needham, MA: Allyn & Bacon.

Vygotsky, L.S. (1962) *Thinking and Speech*, New York: Plenum.

Wolters, C.A. (1998) 'Self-Regulated Learning and College Students' Regulation of Motivation', *Journal of Educational Psychology* 90: 224–35.

Zimmerman, B.J. (1989) 'A Social Cognitive View of Self-Regulated Academic Learning', *Journal of Educational Psychology* 81: 329–39.

13 Evaluating Understanding

Overview

A problem with evaluating understanding is the difficulty in accessing someone's mental constructions. The need for clarity about various features of an assessment is emphasized. Some ways of assessing understanding are illustrated and the place of assessment in the learning environment is described.

An Inescapable Condition

An understanding is not directly accessible to others, and we cannot rely completely on someone's opinions about it. Instead, we usually have to rely on what can be inferred from various behaviours. What counts as understanding depends on the context so the assessor needs to be clear about what is to be evaluated. A starting point would be to seek evidence of a relevant, coherent mental structure. This structure can often vary in richness according to the degree of integration of its elements and their relationships with other knowledge. We may want evidence of the degree of richness. Beyond that is what understanding may enable. It may produce an explanation, make a prediction, justify or criticize an argument, evaluate a situation or position, or solve a problem. Each of these applications of understanding could be in areas close to or remote from one the student knows. This generative capacity is often the reason for understanding in the first place so testing for capability in application could be a central feature of assessment (Perkins, 1994).

The differences described above are largely of a qualitative kind, and could be arranged hierarchically. The popular Bloom taxonomy offers one hierarchy in which knowledge and comprehension underpin 'higher level' thinking processes like application, analysis and evaluation (Bloom et al., 1956). Such a hierarchy, however, tends to obscure the possibility of a bootstrapping effect between levels. In attempting to apply a partially developed understanding, the coherence and structure of that understanding may be enhanced as a consequence. This process may be seen in a novice's developing grasp of a subject. As engagement continues, more or less isolated and relatively small mental structures are integrated so that a greater coherence develops. Principles, rather than the surface features of situations, begin to govern the novice's responses. The conditions which determine the legitimate application of knowledge are learned and, as experience accumulates, it plays an increasing part in achieving goals (Glaser, 1990). Collis and Biggs (1989) devised the SOLO taxonomy, which captures something of this by classifying a response according to the evidence it gives about the nature of the mental structure. The taxonomy ranges from *no relevant response*, through *simple structures*, to *relationships* and *wider connections of the relationship*.

Conceptions of this kind are useful in that they suggest what we should consider to be a high quality of understanding. Evidence of higher degrees of integration and widening capabilities in application are generally taken to indicate quality of understanding. This means that assessment should provide opportunities for a student to show different degrees of integration of knowledge and different breadths of capability. Simply increasing the number of questions is not enough if they only assess one level of quality.

Some Mechanics of Assessment

Teachers are often advised to consider the what, why, how, when, and where of assessment, and so each will be considered here in turn in connection with evaluating understanding.

What is Being Assessed?

It is one thing to say that understanding will be assessed but what will count as understanding? Students should know this early in a course because this can shape how they approach their learning. If a richly integrated structure is expected, the teacher should be able to exemplify what counts as rich. If application is to be assessed, will in be in near or remote contexts, or in both? Will application mean using understanding to explain a novel event, to evaluate critically, to justify, or to solve a practical problem? What counts as a good explanation, justification or solution needs to be known.

Why is it Being Assessed?

Assessment often takes time that could be used for teaching, so there has to be a good reason for it. Reasons tend to come under three heads: formative, diagnostic and summative.

Formative assessment allows the teacher to monitor the quality of learning so that action can be taken if it is inadequate. It might also show that students have reached what Graham and Perry (1993) have called transitional knowledge. This is when explanations are vague and imprecise, glossing over some features and omitting others. In SOLO terms, simple structures may be present but there is no overall coherence in the response. This could be an indication that the student would benefit from support in moving to a fuller coherence.

Assessment may also be used to diagnose the cause of failure in order to take remedial action. Diagnostic assessment could be relatively brief and may be written, oral or practical. A teacher may suspect the cause of the failure and set a task to test the hypothesis. For instance, a child who produces $627 \div 3 = 29$ may have forgotten to include the 0, may not know how to deal with that 2 since it is less than 3, and so on. If the teacher suspects it is the last of these, he or she may ask the child to try $696 \div 3$ and $618 \div 3$. The answers may lead the teacher to review what division means, scaffold the child's learning of how to deal with the problem and show the child how to check the answer.

Summative assessment is used to obtain evidence of a student's level of learning at some point. In this context, it is particularly important to provide tasks which either provide evidence of understanding at different levels or cover a range of levels of understanding.

When is the Assessment to Occur?

Assessment can occur during a course on more than one occasion, and it can occur at the end of a course. The former tends to be continuous assessment, while the latter is terminal assessment. Terminal assessment tends to be summative and is, for the student, a big event. A lot can hang on it, and it often amounts to a judgement of personal worth. Continuous assessment, on the other hand, spreads the risk. It may be summative and formative at the same time, since there may be an opportunity for the student and teacher to do something about poor-quality learning.

An assessment is, in essence, another task to do with the topic to be understood. The additional mental engagement in preparing for and doing the assessment may itself enhance understanding. Usually, this is a good thing. The more learning there is, from whatever source, the better it is for the student. However, when testing the effect of some new teaching and learning strategy, this has to be taken into account. Is it the strategy that produced the gain in understanding or was it the test of understanding itself? Care has to be taken to use the same test across all strategies and groups of learners. Even so, at the end of the day, all that can often be claimed is that it is a particular strategy and test together that produced better results than some other strategy and the test.

How is Understanding to be Assessed?

There is a variety of ways of assessing learning. Since the focus here is on assessing understanding, tasks that could easily be completed using memorization alone are likely to be inadequate: they will not discriminate between those who understand and those who do not. Even with a task with the potential to test understanding, when we hear words and see actions we associate with understanding, it does not necessarily mean that understanding exists. For example, if a child is shown a jelly and asked to indicate whether it is a solid, a liquid or a gas, the child might say it is a solid. This could be a guess, it could be that the child sees the jelly hold its shape, and it could be that the child actually sees the jelly's properties as nearer those of a liquid but does not discriminate between liquids and solids. Nor does the wrong word necessarily indicate the absence of understanding. Another child may have said that the jelly is 'sort of liquidy' because they see the jelly's tendency to take on the shape of the container. This, however, may be nothing more than a qualification of an underlying understanding that says, on balance, jelly is a solid. In other words, initial responses, right or wrong, may have to be probed further.

Language is often a rather rough and ready way of explaining what we feel, believe, understand and see, and the same word can mean slightly different things to different people. Children, in particular, feel the limitations of their vocabulary and often indicate approximation in their responses ('It's sort of like...'). The absence of the correct words may not mean an absence of understanding. Equally, using the right words does not always indicate an understanding. Non-verbal responses, such as pictures and actions, can also show understanding (for example, Ernst, 1997). Most of us are also sensitive to non-verbal behaviour. Non-verbal cues such as prolonged response time, reduced eye contact, body shifting, hand movement and restlessness can indicate a lack of understanding. Gesture and speech also normally co-operate in conveying meaning and a mismatch between words and hand gestures can indicate a misunderstanding, even though the words are correct (Jecker et al., 1965; Goldin-Meadow et al.,1992).

However, like other indicators of understanding, none of these is infallible and the absence of evidence does not necessarily indicate the absence of understanding. This makes it wiser to use a range of approaches rather than to rely on only one.

Where is the Assessment to Take Place?

Where an assessment takes place also merits a few words. Learning in a subject is commonly located in a particular place with a particular person. This place is a part of the total learning environment and may put students into an appropriate frame of mind for responding to questions in that subject. Moving students to a different place for testing and using strangers as examiners can have adverse effects on test scores (Garcia and DeHaven, 1974; Jacoby and Brooks, 1984).

Windows on Understanding

A teacher needs to monitor understanding during a lesson as well as at its end in order to tune teaching to suit the students. Responses to tasks and questions can help but so can body language. Here are some examples of windows on understanding although none gives a perfect view, given the inaccessibility of another's mind.

Closed Questions

These are usually intended to elucidate a particular response. If common misconceptions associated with a topic are known, they may be offered as bait. For example, it is commonly believed that if a set of numbers is drawn from a hat on one occasion, it is less likely that they will be drawn on the next occasion. A question to check for such a belief could be:

Last week, the winning lottery numbers were 7, 8, 9, 23, 33, 37.
I would stand more chance this week if I chose a completely different set of
   numbers.
I agree/I do not agree.

A request for a justification of the answer would significantly add to its value since, if someone 'does not agree', it does not necessarily mean it is for the right reasons. Similarly, errors in structure might be built into a map of a story, situation or event. The learner is to detect the false links (for example, see Figure 13.1).

Sometimes, the form of the response can show the nature of the mental structure. For example, a child who expects a torch bulb to light when connected to a battery by only one wire may view electricity as a substance that flows from a battery and is consumed in the bulb. The detective work of error analysis is an interesting source of information on causes of understanding failure.

More Open Questions

These questions are structured to some extent but allow a wider range of responses than closed questions. For example, someone might be asked to identify similarities and differences between understanding in maths and in science and record them, as in Figure 5.1. It is, of course, possible that lists appropriate to each column have been memorized. The evidence provided by

Figure 13.1   *A story map with errors (Tolkein's* The Hobbit*). For example, Bilbo Baggins was not a wizard and Gandalf did not trust Smaug.*

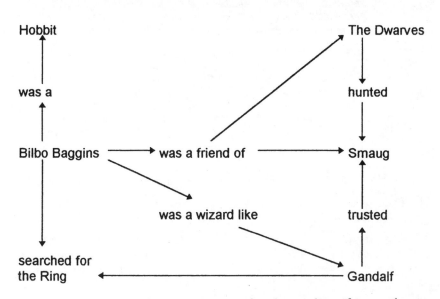

such a task would be a better indicator of understanding if it was known that the task was new to the student and had required them to reorganize or translate existing mental structures into another form.

Free Response Questions

These allow an even wider range of responses. Free writing about, say, Guy Fawkes's plot, could be used to provide insights into a child's understanding of that event. Here is the response of a 6-year-old.

> There was a king. There was a man who wanted to blow up. There was a plot. They got barrels of gunpowder. They went under the Houses of Parliament. They let a man Guy Fawkes hide in between it. He didn't want them to do it. His brother worked in the Houses of Parliament. A man grabbed a horse. He told the police. Some got caught by getting killed. Some didn't. They got caught alive. Then they got killed. They lived happily ever after. *(Corrected only for spelling.)*

This can be cast into the form of a map revealing the extent of the connections the child has made (Figure 13.2).

Open questions can elicit the listing of facts without revealing the presence of significant connections between them. It may be that a student has a multi-structural view of the subject rather than a relational one, but more focused questioning may reveal that. Examples of questions which focus

Figure 13.2 *A map of some features which might reasonably be assumed to be understood based on the child's writing. Question marks indicate some points which could be explored further. As transitional knowledge, such points could be developed to increase the already remarkable degree of integration shown by this young child.*

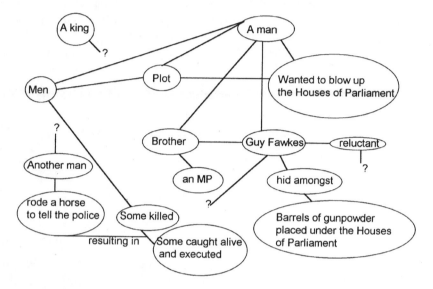

attention on particular relationships are: 'How did Cromwell control Parliament?' and 'What do Pepper Moths show us about the evolutionary advantage of camouflage?'

Concept Mapping

Concept mapping is an open ended way of finding how people relate elements of information about a domain and link it to other information (Howard, 1987; Morine-Dershimer, 1993). In the Guy Fawkes example above, the connections were revealed through continuous writing but, given some experience of concept mapping, the child might have produced a version of Figure 13.2 herself. However, scanty maps may not always mean there is a lack of mental connections. Students may not include all they know in the map, or they may be unpractised in the technique. For this reason, some prefer to ask students to write what they know about a topic. This is then converted into a concept map by the tester but such a conversion can take time (Fellows, 1994).

Discussion and Explanation

Discussing a topic with a student can reveal a lot about his or her mental structures. It requires some skill to avoid cueing or leading the respondent to particular answers and to let them feel they can answer honestly, without giving the answers they believe you want. An advantage of such interviews is that responses can be pursued immediately.

The use of algorithms in mathematics is a example of where facility in obtaining an answer, although useful, does not necessarily indicate understanding, either of the concepts or the procedures. Niemi (1996a, 1996b) has demonstrated that attaching an explanation task can be effective for showing understanding. His interest was in the understanding of fractions by North American 10-year-olds. The explanation task amounted to written responses to questions such as: 'What is a fraction?', 'Why are there two numbers in a fraction?' and 'How can you tell when two fractions are equal?' The children were encouraged to include pictures and prepare their responses as though they were to give a presentation on the television to peers.

Think-Aloud Protocols

Another 'window on the mind' is to ask someone to think aloud as they reason. Think-aloud protocols are transcribed and analysed to show the direction of thought, inferences, failures and successes. It is not clear to what extent people are able to report completely or correctly on their reasoning processes and they may vary in their ability to do so.

Think-aloud approaches are generally seen as a researcher's tool, but it is not uncommon for a teacher to ask a learner to talk through what they are doing in order to detect a point at which understanding fails. Think-aloud is illustrated in a number game played by an elementary school teacher with children. The game requires the players to add the numbers on the cards. The teacher noticed one child add 26 and 10 by the process: $26+1+1+\ldots+1$. Another child did it as $(2+1)6=36$. This suggests the first had not yet understood place value while the second child had. In a written test, children would simply write the answer. Since both responses are correct, differences in processes would not be noted (Dominick and Clark, 1996).

Observation and Eavesdropping

Understanding may also underpin procedures. Observing a student carry out a procedure does not, in itself, provide evidence of understanding unless the task is unfamiliar or calls for a modification or development of an existing procedure. It is also common for the quality of learners' understandings to be revealed when they discuss activities and tasks in work groups. This makes discrete eavesdropping another source of information about the quality of understanding.

Problem Solving

Understanding can have a generative capacity so another approach is to give a problem to solve. Success is taken as evidence that there is understanding behind it. A difficulty is that many problems can also be solved by a rote-learned procedure or algorithm, or by a combination of partial understanding and learned procedure. Nevertheless, this is a popular approach in some areas. If the difficulties can be overcome, checking responses can be relatively easy and there is the opportunity to show a greater degree of understanding than some other forms of assessment allow. Authentic assessment is related to authentic learning and is used when understanding is assessed in a situation where it would normally have to be used. Assessing student teachers on teaching practice is a form of authentic assessment. However, once a situation becomes authentic, control over the opportunities it allows is often limited. This means that assessment will probably have to be frequent if it is to give some confidence in a student's ability to cope with the range of problems such a situation might provide. On the other hand, more controlled situations may allow this to be assessed more quickly but it leaves a doubt that performance will be adequate in authentic situations. A compromise would be a mix of both forms of assessment.

Understanding as a Part of the Learning Environment

Knowing when understanding is sound or weak, rich or poor is information that a student might act on. Some of this information may be produced by the students for themselves. Self-assessment by attempting the exercises provided in a book or a past examination paper is only one source. Another would be to prepare a sheet with columns having the titles 'What I learned' and 'What I did not understand' (an adaptation of the lesson reaction sheets of Schumm et al., 1997). The first column generally shows the student that some progress has been made so that deficiencies do not loom as large as they might. The second column shows what has to be dealt with, either by self-study, by consultation with a teacher or through peer support. One more approach to self-evaluation includes the learning log. This is a continuous prose version of the reaction sheet that can be more wide-ranging and cover, for instance, motivation and planned actions (Schumm et al., 1997).

However, evaluation is often tinged with judgement. The student who fails and attributes failure to causes beyond his or her control may simply give up. Some students aim to prove themselves in competition with others. Inevitably, this means that after the assessment there will be those who see themselves as inadequate. In a climate where examination success is a measure of people's worth, an approaching evaluation fills them with anxiety, any feeling of self-efficacy is reduced and motivation evaporates or even becomes negative.

An assessment shows students what counts. If it predominantly tests memorization, that can be a significant factor in shaping students' approaches to learning, tending to make them shallow or reproductive learners. Even when memorization is not a dominant factor, if the amount of material to be learned is large and time is short, both students and their teachers are likely to look for short cuts to examination success. In such circumstances, an attempt to thwart students by setting a memorization-proof examination (to the extent that that is possible) could produce more failures. In turn, that risks a helplessness descending on both students and their teachers.

Where understanding is valued and to be encouraged, its quality needs to be evaluated. This needs to occur in the classroom, informally and regularly and also more formally to satisfy society's need for measures of educational outcomes. But, quality and quantity are not easy bedfellows when it comes to learning. Overloaded schemes of work and syllabuses will work against understanding. At the same time, there is worthwhile learning to be done in many subjects which do not involve significant amounts of deep understanding. This may be important for the safe, rapid or efficient execution of some task and so has to be included.

Summary

It is not easy to be certain that someone understands because we have no direct access to their mental structures. Understanding can be viewed in terms of its level of integration and coherence and also in terms of the capabilities it gives. The what, why, when, how and where of evaluation need to be considered and evidence obtained from a variety of sources. Evaluation has an important role in the learning environment because it provides information about the quality of learning for the teacher and the student. It could also have deleterious effects on a student and a teacher if the outcomes it purports to measure are seen to be beyond the student's or teacher's control.

References

Bloom, B.S., Engelhart, M.D., Furst, E.J., Hill, W.H. and Krathwohl, D.R. (1956) *Taxonomy of Educational Objectives, 1: Cognitive Domain*, New York: McKay.

Collis, K.F. and Biggs, J.B. (1989) 'A School-Based Approach to Setting and Evaluating Science Curriculum Objectives: SOLO and School Science', *Australian Journal of Science Teachers* 35: 15–25.

Dominick, A. and Clark, F.B. (1996) 'Using Games to Understand Children's Understanding', *Childhood Education* 72: 286–8.

Ernst, K. (1997) 'What a Picture Can Be', *Teaching PreK-8* 28: 26.

Fellows, N.J. (1994) 'A Window into Thinking: Using Student Writing to Understand Conceptual Changes in Student Learning', *Journal of Research in Science Teaching* 31: 985–1001.

Garcia, E.E. and DeHaven, E.D. (1974) 'Use of Operant Techniques in the Establishment and Generalisation of Language: A Review and Analysis', *American Journal of Mental Deficiency* 79: 169–78.

Glaser, R. (1990) 'Towards New Models for Assessment, *International Journal of Educational Research* 14: 475–83.

Goldin-Meadow, S., Wein, D. and Chang, C. (1992) 'Assessing Knowledge Through Gesture, *Cognition and Instruction* 9: 201–19.

Graham, T. and Perry, M. (1993) 'Indexing Transitional Knowledge', *Developmental Psychology* 29: 770–8.

Howard, R.W. (1987) *Concepts and Schemata: An Introduction*, London: Cassell.

Jacoby, L.L. and Brooks, L.R. (1984) 'Nonanalytic Cognition: Memory, Perception, and Concept Learning', in G.H. Bower (ed.), *The Psychology of Learning and Motivation*, New York: Academic Press, 1–47.

Jecker, J.D., Maccoby, N. and Breitrose, H.S. (1965) 'Improving Accuracy in Interpreting Non-Verbal Cues of Comprehension', *Psychology in the Schools* 2: 239–44.

Morine-Dershimer, G. (1993) 'Tracing Conceptual Change in Pre-Service Teachers', *Teaching and Teacher Education* 9: 5–26.

Newton, L.D. and Newton, D.P. (1998) *The Science Coordinator's Handbook*, London: Falmer.

Niemi, D. (1996a) 'Assessing Conceptual Understanding in Mathematics', *Journal of Educational Research* 89: 351–63.

—— (1996b) 'A Fraction is not a Piece of Pie', *Gifted Children Quarterly* 40: 70–80.

Perkins, D.N. (1994) 'Do Students Understand Understanding?' *Education Digest* 59: 21–5.

Schumm, J.S., Vaughn, S. and Sobol, C. (1997) 'Are They Getting It?' *Intervention in School and Clinic* 32: 168–71.

14 In Conclusion

Overview

Various aspects of support for understanding are brought together and some implications highlighted. Planning to support understanding is described and how teachers might become aware of how to press for understanding is outlined. Some obstacles which impede teaching for understanding are mentioned.

Supporting Understanding

Quantity of knowledge is not synonymous with quality. We can be rich in knowledge but poor in sense. Understanding is what makes sense of otherwise disparate items of information. Understanding is a worthwhile goal in that it can reduce a chaotic mental world to a more predictable and satisfying state. It also facilitates further learning and recall of knowledge and enables responses, particularly in novel situations, to be flexible and appropriate. At a time when information is cheap and access to it is easy, understanding is what makes it meaningful and manageable.

Understanding is often acknowledged to be an aim of learning, but learning serves a variety of ends and increasing understanding is only one of them. For instance, access to higher education and to particular careers are often paramount aims for both students and their teachers. At the same time, syllabuses and teaching schemes that are overloaded allow little time to support a growing understanding. As one student put it, understanding is a luxury. The result, of course, is a student who cannot respond flexibly, cannot think critically or creatively and who has acquired habits of mind that put more weight on the quantity of knowledge acquired than the quality of understanding developed. This is not to say that everything must be understood in depth: some things might legitimately be memorized in many academic and professional courses. There are, however, certain ideas that are worth understanding and relate to the satisfaction of human needs in the broad sense. Is such understanding really a luxury?

Nothing can force an act of understanding, only the learner has control of the mental processes that are needed and probably does not even have a conscious control of all of them. Support for understanding comprises several courses of action, none necessarily sufficient in itself. What support can do is provide favourable conditions and adjust those conditions as the process develops.

A significant part of a favourable condition is provided by support for thinking about the subject in hand. It involves regulating the learning situation to make relevant mental engagement more likely. This can be through activities intended to focus attention and foster relevant inference-making. For instance, instructional load may be controlled so that mental capacities are not overwhelmed and analogies provided to develop understanding through better known parallels. At the same time, learners are different. Some strategies may be used fairly indiscriminately while others depend on the age, experience, preference and habits of the learner. This is recognized, for instance, in the distinction that has been made between pedagogy and androgogy. Pedagogy refers to the form of teaching appropriate to young learners, while androgogy is what is appropriate to mature learners. Of course, such a division cannot be complete or precise; there is inevitably some overlap.

A teacher is not the only one who can regulate the learning situation. Learners often develop metacognitive skills that help them monitor and control their learning. Some of these may be used without conscious thought; others are deployed deliberately. Self-regulation that has developed from experience may be improved by tuning existing strategies and adding others, particularly with older learners who have some awareness of their own thinking processes and can deploy strategies themselves. This is when learning and practising in the contexts where such strategies would naturally be used may increase the likelihood that they will be used repeatedly.

Given effective strategies for supporting cognition, learners must know what counts. Understanding is not the same in all contexts. While conceptions of what counts develop with time and experience, they may be inappropriate, insufficiently differentiated, or not quite the same as the teacher's or lecturer's conceptions. Conceptions of learning and of what counts could affect learning across a whole domain yet may receive little attention.

Neither adequate strategies nor appropriate conceptions will count for anything unless students are willing to learn. Students should see the particular value of understanding, expect to have a worthwhile degree of success, and feel that the emotional price will not be too high to pay. Each of these is complex and often dependent on the others. Experience teaches a student the likelihood of success: a low expectation could be realistic and well-founded. If students also attribute failure to factors beyond their control, they are likely to see little point in even approaching the task. Where success is perceived to be a measure of a person's worth, an expectation of failure has the potential to be emotionally disabling. In such contexts, it is not that some avoid learning that is surprising; rather, it is that some engage in it willingly.

There are many variables in the learning environment that bear on what a student does about the quality of learning. The assessment of learning, which seems an extraneous, even innocuous matter, can have wide-ranging effects. First, it teaches a student what counts, whatever the teacher or anyone else says. Second, it is what measures success and so helps to shape motivation. Third, it is a direct threat to self-esteem and self-worth, and can elicit emotions that make a good performance less likely.

A Positive and Productive Learning Environment

MacAulay (1990) writes that classroom environments should be positive and productive. Few would argue with that, but what is positive and what is productive depends, of course, on your point of view. In this context, it is taken to mean an environment that fosters understanding. What could one look like? I suggest that it would be one where there is a continuous process of monitoring and responding to the various aspects of the learning environment. This is not to say that monitoring must be formal: the teacher needs to appraise the quality of learning as the lesson proceeds, and respond quickly if the lesson is not to be lost.

The sequence of events might begin with scene-setting, eliciting prior knowledge about the value of a topic and about the topic itself, and eliciting beliefs about what is to count as understanding. These initial actions might be followed by clarification of the value of the topic, making what will count clear and raising expectations of success, perhaps by reminding the learners of relevant, past successes. The presentation of the body of the topic in a way that controls instructional load but expects relevant active participation may follow. Support for understanding may appear in the form of questions focused on its particular processes. Motivation may be maintained during this period by drawing attention to successful learning and deflecting the attribution of failure from non-controllable causes. Final acts might include an appraisal of understanding which includes an express attempt to reduce the risk of adverse emotional interference by, for instance, mentioning that the results will not be announced publicly and an opportunity will be available to show an improvement, if the student wishes. The opportunity also introduces an element of autonomy for the student.

This thumbnail sketch of some features of a positive and supportive environment is one of many that could be made. Its purpose is to highlight the way support for understanding is itself embedded in a context and contributes to other aspects of the environment and, in turn, benefits from them. For instance, setting the scene may also stimulate curiosity as well as focus attention. Talk about the value of a subject and setting up learning goals must also touch on subject matters. Similarly, eliciting prior knowledge may also stimulate interest. This does not, of course, occur by accident.

Planning for a Positive and Productive Environment

Teachers need to be clear about what counts as understanding in the subjects they teach and tell their students about it (Brophy, 1991; Carlson, 1991). Although they do not have to become a different kind of teacher to support understanding, they may need an orientation which makes understanding something they actively support. New teaching skills may not be needed. Instead, skills are deployed to maximize and focus support where and when it is needed. However, while supporting the mental processes of understanding, other aspects of the learning environment may need attention.

Even when the will and the strategies are there, understanding can be an early casualty of the overfull syllabus, the heavy workload or, what amounts to the same thing, a shortage of time. More emphasis might be placed on understanding in examinations, thereby redefining what counts for student and teacher. But, by itself, such a squeeze is likely to make students and teachers slip into ways of gaining marks without understanding. If, in spite of that, they fail, the situation is likely to be perceived as beyond their control; they are helpless so may as well give up. Time and how it is used are therefore important.

Experienced Teachers

The complexity of the environment makes planning difficult but essential. Experienced teachers do not appear to plan in detail or stick to a particular course of action (Moallem, 1998; Young and Reiser, 1998) but their behaviour is probably more like the skilled chess player who knows clusters of moves well and can deploy them as needed as a game develops. Experience has taught teachers some effective strategies. Planning for them comprises decisions about the general approach while having well-rehearsed strategies waiting on the sideline. If all goes according to the general plan, the strategies will be used as they are needed. If not, or if a potentially more productive opportunity presents itself, another direction might be taken. This flexibility allows a useful lesson to develop in an essentially underspecified situation. That is more likely if the teacher has knowledge of the variables in the learning environment and has a well-practised repertoire of general and specific strategies for use in it.

Although experience may give the teacher an advantage when it comes to renewing or changing a teaching orientation, critical deliberation before and after a lesson is valuable in establishing new routines. Planning should become more formal as strategies are revised and practised. Evaluation is equally important if the wheat and the chaff in plans are to be separated.

Student Teachers

Some student teachers, seeing the facility with which some practised teachers teach and the apparent absence of preparation, mistakenly conclude that lesson plans are an unnecessary burden. A lesson plan is a pre-arranged sequence of events in which a variety of strategies appear, as needed. A successful sequence that is repeated is soon learned and readily recalled. An experienced teacher has also practised the strategies to the point that they may be adapted and deployed automatically. In short, the lesson plan is there and, in addition, is likely to be flexible. Without that experience, student teachers should plan lessons so that they know what they will do, how they will do it and why they are doing it. Initially, teaching may lack flexibility and a ready response to the unexpected but that will develop as sequences and strategies become familiar.

One way of proceeding for both experienced and inexperienced teachers is suggested below as a series of questions. The answers provide the basis for a plan of action.

- Do I understand this topic myself?
- What is it that should be understood in the topic?
- Why is this of value to the learner?
- What will count as understanding in this context?
- How will I set the scene?
- How will I make the value of the topic explicit?
- How will I elicit knowledge about the topic?
- How will I elicit conceptions of learning?
- What will I do with what I find?
- What will be the sequence of learning events?
- Will there be provision for active mental engagement in all its parts?
- How and to what extent will the instructional load be controlled?
- Where is support for the understanding processes likely to be needed?
- What form will that support have?
- Could there be opportunities for some autonomy in learning?
- How will I increase the likelihood that there will be evidence of successful learning for the learner?
- Should this evidence come early/frequently in the lesson?
- How will any adverse effect of emotions be controlled?
- How will an appraisal of learning be made?
- How will the risk of attribution of failure to uncontrollable causes be reduced?
- What other aspects of the learning environment need to be considered?
- Can any of the above be combined so that goals may be achieved economically or so that there will be mutual reinforcement?

Some learners, of course, have to regulate or prefer to regulate their own learning. This has to be recognized in the preparation of materials.

Only Connect

All this shows that helping someone 'connect' can be a complicated business. A teacher who can do it well has a lot of skill. The skill is not only in responding appropriately to each aspect of understanding in isolation but in handling them together. Nevertheless, I have argued that understanding is worth the effort and, in any case, I suspect that most teachers would prefer to have their learners understand: it can be a very satisfying achievement.

Bringing about change is not always easy. An orientation amongst teachers that presses for understanding does not come from mere exhortation: the situation is too complex. Understandably, some teachers resist and challenge it and feel insecure and confused by it (Hardy and Kirkwood, 1994). Strauss (1993) also pointed out that mental models of teaching and learning are implicit and teachers are often not aware that they hold them. Presenting alternative ideas about teaching and learning may fail because teachers do not see them as alternatives.

In general, teachers do not lack teaching strategies. If nothing else, they evolve from observation of others and direct experience (Cavalcante et al., 1997). But this observation and experience may be in a system where understanding *is* a luxury, where passing examinations and doing well in tests by any means is what matters, and where advancement does not depend on teaching for understanding. Practices which are not the best for supporting understanding are unlikely to be questioned. In fact, they are likely to be perpetuated as student teachers acquire them by apprenticeship.

Instead of exhorting teachers to change, a better start would be to have them examine their beliefs and practices and learn to deploy their strategies better to foster understanding. Some may not fully appreciate the value of understanding. All need to know what counts as learning in the specific context of the subjects that they teach. Since such conceptions may be unconscious, they may need to be made available for reflection. Probing for such beliefs is not always easy as teachers are likely to respond with already conscious, conventional wisdom rather than with the deep conceptions that actually control their practices in the classroom. It may help if teachers can contrast their actual practices with what they believe them to be in a way that does not threaten their self-esteem. Do they ask 'why' questions? Where does the balance of their lessons lie? Is it overly biased towards the reproduction of knowledge? What are appropriate and reasonable learning aims for a particular topic? Teachers need to know when memorization and understanding are appropriate and what the nature of that understanding is.

How might a press for understanding be made? People find it easier to grasp new ideas that relate to what is familiar (Northfield, 1992; Cohen and

Barnes, 1993). If strategies are few and imperfect, at least they will be familiar and will serve as a starting point. These strategies might be examined for their potential to support understanding and lessons planned and tried using them deliberately for that end. If there is a need to develop strategies further, that would now be apparent. Strategies could be extended and supplemented by explanation, exemplification and practice. Developing skill in focused questioning, for instance, could be an instance. Another could be when students in higher education are taught sophisticated concepts without telling them why they are important, what they can do, and what their role is. This risks such concepts being unconnected and seen as irrelevant and can have very adverse consequences for understanding (Sierpinska, 1994). Strategies for tying together areas of study may have to be devised. The aim is to have teachers believe their actions can make a difference and press for understanding, rather than be passive and leave it to chance.

It is one thing to have teachers with the skills and knowledge to press for understanding and another for them to be free to do so. Change is hindered by the embedded nature of education. What goes on in the classroom is embedded in school activity, which lies in an organizational phase of education and within a local community. These schools feed other schools or institutions of further and higher education, which in turn supply the professions. Each level has expectations of those that feed it. If, for instance, they press for large quantities of knowledge, understanding will be squeezed out in an attempt to meet their requirements. Too much content almost inevitably leads to memorization. To compound the difficulty, some policy makers behave as though teaching is telling and learning is receiving (Cohen et al., 1993). A failure to understand understanding makes educational policies more likely to favour memorization and the acquisition of information. An overly instrumental view of education which gauges it by its immediate contribution to employment and the economy can also tip the balance towards training and a quantitative view of knowledge. Bureaucracy can routinize teaching and destroy innovation (Talbert and McLaughlin, 1993). Tightly constrained, teaching becomes dull, unadventurous and unrewarding. A belief that everything needs to be recorded on paper as evidence of compliance with requirements can take away teaching time but time is what understanding needs. Even motivation can suffer (Soodak and Podell, 1996). Aggressive demands for more effective schools and better learning with severe penalties for 'failing schools' could bring about less teaching for understanding and more cramming like that common in Victorian schools. It would be more helpful if it was clear that better does not always mean more.

Effort must be made to remind everyone that understanding is worthwhile, it is a requirement of many programmes of study, and its achievement needs skill, support, effort and time. All should understand that supporting understanding is not an add-on piece of the learning environment. The learning environment is complex and highly integrated. Parts cannot be taken out, tinkered with and replaced without the need to consider the parts they mesh with. Further, mental engagement is not only for the student: teaching for understanding calls for the mental engagement of teacher as well. Successful teaching for understanding, however, brings enormous rewards for both.

References

Brophy, J. (1991) 'Conclusion', in J. Brophy (ed.), *Advances in Research on Teaching, Vol. 2.*, Greenwich, CN: JAC Press.

Cavalcante, P.S., Newton, D.P. and Newton, L.D. (1997) 'The Effect of Different Kinds of Lesson on Conceptual Understanding in Science', *Research in Science and Technology Education* 15: 185–93.

Carlson, W.S. (1991) 'Subject-Matter Knowledge and Science Teaching', in J. Brophy (ed.), *Advances in Research on Teaching, Vol. 2.*, Greenwich, CN: JAC Press.

Cohen, D.K. and Barnes, C.A. (1993) 'Conclusion: A New Pedagogy for Policy', in D.K. Cohen, M.W. McLaughlin and J.E. Talbert, *Teaching for Understanding: Challenges for Policy and Practice*, San-Fransisco: Jossey-Bass, 240–75.

Cohen, D.K., McLaughlin, M.W. and Talbert, J.E. (1993) *Teaching for Understanding: Challenges for Policy and Practice*, San-Fransisco: Jossey-Bass.

Hardy, T. and Kirkwood, V. (1994) 'Towards creating effective learning environments for science teachers', *International Journal of Science Education* 16: 231–51.

MacAuley, D.L. (1990) 'Classroom Environment: A Literature Review', *Educational Psychology* 10: 239–53.

Moallem, M. (1998) 'An Expert Teacher's Thinking and Teaching and Instructional Design Models and Principles: An Ethnographic Study', *Educational Technology Research and Development* 46: 37–64.

Northfield, J. (1992) 'Conceptual Change and Teacher Education', paper presented at the Annual Meeting of the American Educational Research Association, April 20–24.

Sierpinska, A. (1994) *Understanding in Mathematics*, London: Falmer.

Soodak, J. and Podell, H. (1996) 'Teacher Efficacy: Toward the Understanding of a Multi- Faceted Construct', *Teaching and Teacher Education* 12: 401–11.

Strauss, S. (1993) 'Teachers' pedagogical content knowledge about children's minds and learning', *Educational Psychologist* 28: 279–90.

Talbert, J.E. and McLaughlin, M.W. (1993) 'Understanding Teaching in Context', in D.K. Cohen, M.W. McLaughlin and J.E. Talbert, *Teaching for Understanding: Challenges for Policy and Practice*, San Fransisco: Jossey-Bass.

Young, A.C. and Reiser, R.A. (1998) 'Do Superior Teachers Employ Systematic Instructional Planning Procedures?' *Educational Technology Research and Development* 46: 65–78.

Glossary

algorithm a procedure for carrying out a particular task especially in mathematics and commonly referring to ways of carrying out operations such as addition, subtraction, multiplication and division.

authentic learning learning in contexts where that learning is relevant; learning in real-life situations.

capacity referring to the maximum mental resource that someone can make available at a given time.

cognition the mental processing of knowledge involving, amongst other things, giving attention, drawing on prior knowledge, and reasoning; commonly referred to as thinking and its products.

concept commonly, an idea.

concept map usually, a two-dimensional arrangement of ideas particularly for the purpose of showing connections between them.

correlation a real or apparent relationship between variables; it is important to bear in mind that, although variables may change together, one is not necessarily the cause of the other, as the connection could be accidental or brought about by a third variable.

deep approach a commonly used label for an approach to learning that is characterized by attempts to establish meaning; a *meaning-directed approach* is similar.

enculturation a cognitive socialization in which, amongst other things, conceptions of learning and what counts in a subject are acquired; the process can be both formal and informal.

epistemic relating to the nature of knowledge.

higher order thinking thinking involving, for instance, analysis, synthesis and evaluation as opposed to, for instance, memorization.

holistic wholes rather than parts.

hypothesis a more or less tentative explanation or working idea to be tested.

inference a connection or relationship that is made mentally.

instructional load the processing load imposed by the way that the instruction is designed in addition to that inherent in what is to understood.

learning environment the many components of a situation that bear upon learning, learning approaches and their outcomes.

memorization   the acquisition of information for ready recall but without a concern for understanding.

mental engagement   the mental action of attending to and processing information, here having the intention of understanding it.

mental model   a hypothesized mental representation that behaves as though it is a model of some aspect of the real or imagined world; it may be mentally articulated to parallel the behaviour of what it models (for example, a scene in a story may be modelled mentally and that model updated as the story progresses) .

mental representation   a pattern of excitation in the brain which stands for (represents) objects, ideas, relationships, situations, events and other knowledge; the same information may be represented in different ways as, for instance, by a mental model or by a proposition.

metacognition   thinking about the thinking processes; by monitoring the progress and outcomes of thinking, metacognition provides information that may be used to control the thinking processes.

numerosity   an inborn sense of number; it is more precise with small numbers.

proposition   a sentence-like structure that connects concepts and says something true or false about the world (for example, 'some gardens have trees'), hypothesized to feature in cognition.

scaffold   a structure or procedure used to support learning; it is withdrawn as the learner acquires independent facility in what is being scaffolded.

schema   a mental structure that represents an organized body of knowledge; large or small, it sets up expectations about some aspect of the world (plural, variously schemata and schemas).

script   the mental representation of a pattern of behaviour relevant to a particular range of situations (for example, what to do in restaurants).

self-determination   here, being in control of one's own learning; a feeling of autonomy in connection with learning.

self-efficacy   here, a belief about being able to deal effectively with a particular learning task.

self-worth   beliefs about one's own value.

self-regulation   a learner's control of his or her learning processes.

surface approach   a commonly used label for an approach to learning that is characterized by attempts to acquire knowledge without a particular regard for understanding and commonly associated with memorization; a *reproduction-directed approach* is similar.

surrogate teacher   something that has the role of a teacher (for example, textbooks, certain videotapes, certain computer software).

syllogism   two given statements from which a third follows or may be inferred.

volition   controlled by the will; intentional.

working memory   a mental peculiarity that, in effect, serves the purpose of holding, relating and reflecting upon information; a hypothesized mental system for the processing of information but with limited capacity.

Name Index

Subject index